THE PUFFIN CA

Hope Rogers (2000)

Ken Weber is professor emeritus at the Institute of Child Study at the University of Toronto. Among his many achievements, Ken was the founder and first chair of the academic special education program at the Faculty of Education at the University of Toronto. He is the author of *Special Education in Ontario Schools* (Highland Press). He is the former chair of the Ontario Provincial Tribunal in Special Education. He is the author of a range of academic materials still in use in over sixty countries. He is the editor or co-editor of three dictionaries for student use. At the Institute of Child Study, he developed programs in the pedagogy of reading. He was elected to the Academy of Canadian Writers in 1979.

In his non-academic life, Ken Weber is the author of the best-selling Five Minute Mysteries series, which has won a number of awards and is currently published in sixteen languages. His most recent series is called *The Armchair Detective*. He lives in Caledon, Ontario.

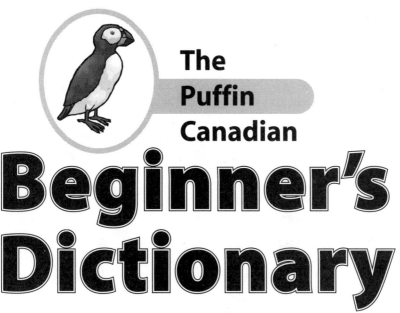

The Puffin Canadian Beginner's Dictionary

2nd edition

Editor Ken Weber, Professor Emeritus
Institute of Child Study/Faculty of Education
University of Toronto

Editorial Consultants Beverly Caswell, Instructor
Institute of Child Study, OISE/University of Toronto

Cecile Hennigar, Reading Consultant (ret.)
Metropolitan Toronto Separate School Board

MaryPat Weber-Poulin
International Baccalaureate Instructor
International School Systems

Puffin Books

PUFFIN

Published by the Penguin Group

Penguin Books Canada Ltd, 10 Alcorn Avenue, Toronto, Ontario, Canada M4V 3B2

Penguin Books Ltd, 27 Wrights Lane, London W8 5TZ, England

Penguin Putnam Inc., 375 Hudson Street, New York, New York 10014, U.S.A.

Penguin Books Australia Ltd, Ringwood, Victoria, Australia

Penguin Books (NZ) Ltd, cnr Rosedale and Airborne Roads, Albany, Auckland 1310, New Zealand

Penguin Books Ltd, Registered Offices: Harmondsworth, Middlesex, England

First published 2001

10 9 8 7 6 5 4 3 2

Manufactured in Canada

NATIONAL LIBRARY OF CANADA CATALOGUING IN PUBLICATION DATA

The Puffin Canadian beginner's dictionary

2nd ed.

Previous ed. compiled by Rosemary Sansome

ISBN 0-14-130966-0

1. English language—Dictionaries, Juvenile.   I. Weber, K. J. (Kenneth Jerome), 1940–   II. Sansome, Rosemary. Puffin Canadian beginner's dictionary.

PE1628.5.P84   2001 j423   C2001-900985-2

Visit Penguin Canada's web site at **www.penguin.ca**

The
Puffin
Canadian
Beginner's
Dictionary

aardvark (also called **anteater**) an animal with large ears and a long nose

abandon to leave forever: *The bear **abandoned** its den.*

abbey a place where monks or nuns live and work

abbreviation a short way of writing a word or phrase: *MP is an **abbreviation** for Member of Parliament.*

abdomen 1 in people and animals, the part of the body below the chest **2** in insects, the third, usually largest, part of the body

abduct to take away a person

ability the power to do something

able having the power to do something: *Franco is **able** to run fast.*

aboard on a ship, bus, train or airplane: *Let's get **aboard** the bus now!*

aboriginal any of the first persons to live in a country

about 1 just before or just after **2** having to do with: *This is a book **about** trees.*

above 1 overhead: *the sky **above*** **2** higher than

abrupt sudden, very quick and short: *an **abrupt** ending*

absent not here

abuse ① (a-BEWZ) to mistreat someone or something

abuse ② (a-BEWSE) harmful use of something or mistreatment of someone

academic 1 having to do with education and learning **2** an idea that is not important right now

accelerate to move or cause to move faster: *Jean accelerated in order to get past the other car.*

accelerator a pedal that is pressed by the foot to make a car go faster

accent the way people say words: *You can hear many different accents in Canada.*

accept to take what is offered

access 1 the way in or the approach: *The only access to the island is by boat.*
2 the opportunity to see someone or experience something: *We have access to the library every day.*
3 to call up information on a computer

accident 1 an unexpected, unfortunate event
2 by chance: *We met by accident.*

accompany 1 to go with: *I will accompany Ram to the store.*
2 to play an instrument while someone sings or dances

accomplish to finish a task successfully

accomplished skilled: *Terry is an accomplished violinist.*

accordion a musical instrument

account 1 a report of something that has happened: *Let's hear Mario's account of the accident.*
2 a list showing money spent, owed or taken in (see **bank account**)

accumulate (a-KEWM-u-late) to gather or pile up

accurate correct and exact

accuse to say that someone has done something wrong

ache to have a pain that keeps on hurting: *My foot is aching now!*

achievement something special that is done

acorn the nut of an oak tree

acquire to get or obtain

acrobat someone who entertains with balancing and jumping acts

across from one side to the other

act 1 to do something
2 to take part in a drama

action 1 a movement
2 something that is done: *Laura's quick action saved the kitten.*

activate to start or make happen: *This button will activate the alarm.*

active busy or working

activist someone who urges others to think in a certain way

activity a pastime or occupation

actor a person, usually male, who acts in a play, movie or on television

actress a female person who acts in a play, movie or on television

actual real

adapt to alter or change: *You can adapt the system so that it will run on batteries.*

add 1 to find the sum of two or more numbers
2 to put together with something else: *Todd added sugar to his cereal.*

adder a small snake

addition 1 adding numbers
2 something added: *We put an addition on our house.*

additional extra

address 1 the number, street, community and province where someone lives
2 a formal speech: *The prime minister addressed the House of Commons.*

adjective any word that tells what someone or something is like: *Beautiful, small, hard and green are adjectives.*

adjust to change the shape, form or position of something so that it fits

adjustable able to be changed to fit better

ad lib to speak or act freely without a plan: *Reesa lost her speech and had to ad lib.*

admiral a very important officer in the navy

admiration the belief that someone or something is very good

admire to believe someone or something is very good: *I admire you for trying so hard.*

Aa 3

admission an entrance fee

admit 1 to let someone enter
2 to say you were the one
who did something: *Jade*
admitted *that she ate the*
candy.

adopt 1 to take someone into
your family
2 to start using a practice or
custom

adore to like very much

adult a fully grown person

advance to move forward

advantage a better situation,
or a quality that helps more:
Amon is tall and therefore has
an ***advantage*** *in basketball.*

adventure an exciting
experience

adverb any word that tells
you how, when or where
something happens: *Often,*
somewhere, now and slowly
are ***adverbs.***

advertisement
(ad-VER-tis-ment) words
and pictures that try to
make you buy something

advice something said to help
a person decide what to do

advise to tell someone what
you think is best to do

affect to make a difference:
Good news! The storm did
not ***affect*** *the crops!*

affection the feeling you have
for someone or something
you like

affluence having a lot of
expensive things

afford to have enough money
to pay for something

afraid in fear of

after 1 later than: *Marv came*
in ***after*** *Tabitha.*
2 past the time of: *Mom*
went to sleep ***after*** *dinner.*

afternoon the time from
noon until evening

afterwards, afterward later

again once more

against 1 on the opposite
side to: *I am* ***against*** *the*
whole idea!
2 on or next to: *The stick was*
leaning ***against*** *the wall.*

age how old someone or
something is

agent a person who arranges
things: *a travel* ***agent***

agenda a list of things to be
done

Aa

agile able to move quickly and easily

ago in the past

agree to think the same as others

aground trapped on sand or rocks in shallow water: *Ships often run **aground** at Sable Island, Nova Scotia.*

ahead in front

aid 1 something that helps: *a hearing **aid***
2 to help: *Soldiers **aided** the flood victims.*

AIDS a disease in which the body loses the ability to fight off infection

aim 1 to try to do something: *The class **aimed** to finish by noon.*
2 to point: ***Aim** your finger at the light.*

air what everyone breathes

air bag a safety balloon in a car that fills with air if the car is hit hard

air conditioner a machine that cools or heats air

aircraft any vehicle that flies

air force a group of people trained to use aircraft in war

airplane a flying vehicle with fixed wings and a motor

airport a place where people get on and off airplanes

airtight not letting air in or out: *an **airtight** jar*

aisle (rhymes with tile) a path between groups of seats

alarm 1 a warning sound or sign
2 a sudden feeling of fear: *Jannie felt **alarm** when she saw the dog.*

alas a word showing sadness: ***Alas**, recess is over.*

alert wide awake and ready

alias 1 a made-up name: *The spy's **alias** was B.B. Berson.*
2 under the name of: *This is B.B. Berson, **alias** Grace Bean.*

alibi what someone says to show he was in a different place when a crime happened

alien 1 a person or thing that seems very strange and unfamiliar
2 a being that is believed to be from outer space: *E.T. is a famous **alien** from the movies.*

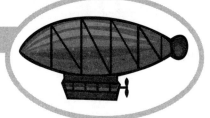

align (a-LINE) to arrange in a line: *The chairs must be **aligned** correctly.*

alike much the same

alive living

all the whole of something

Allah in Islam, the one who is worshipped as the maker and ruler of the world

allergic having an allergy (see **allergy**)

allergy an unusual sensitivity in your body to something: *Kitty's **allergy** to cats makes her sneeze.*

alley a very narrow street, usually between or behind houses

alliance an agreement between two or more people, countries or organizations to work together to do something

Alliance 1 in Canada, an abbreviation for **Canadian Conservative Alliance Party**
2 in Canada, a member of the Alliance political party

alligator a reptile with short legs, long snout, very tough skin and sharp teeth

allow to let something happen

all right 1 safe and well
2 I agree or I accept: ***All right,*** *you may stay up.*

all-star a player who is believed to be more talented than most

ally a person or country that supports another: *Norway is Canada's **ally**.*

almond a flat nut with a hard shell

almost very nearly

alone by yourself or by itself

along 1 from one end to the other: *Kyle ran **along** the ledge.*
2 to go together with: *Come **along** with us!*

aloud in a voice that can be heard

alphabet the letters, in order, that are used to write a language

already before now: *Keesha was **already** here when we came.*

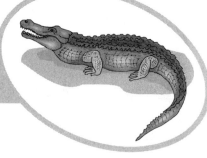

also as well, in addition

altar a kind of table used during worship

alter to change: *A tailor can alter those sleeves.*

alteration a change in something

alternative another choice: *Are there other alternatives?*

although even though: *Although it was hot, she wore a coat.*

altogether entirely

aluminum a light, silver-coloured metal

always at all times

am see **be**

a.m. (also **A.M.**) an abbreviation for **ante meridiem,** the time between midnight and noon

amateur someone who does something for fun and is not paid

amaze to surprise greatly

ambassador an official acting for a government: *Lester Pearson was Canada's ambassador to the United Nations.*

ambition (am-BI-shun) a strong wish to do something: *Leah's ambition is to be an astronaut.*

ambitious to have a lot of ambition

ambulance a van for carrying ill or injured people

ambush to attack by surprise

ammunition the bullets shot from guns

amnesia (am-NEE-zhya) loss of memory

among mixed in with: *Somewhere among the piles of books is your pen.*

amount the total of something: *a large amount of money*

amphibian an animal that can live in water or on land: *Toads and frogs are amphibians.*

amuse 1 to make someone laugh or smile **2** to make time pass pleasantly: *The baby amused herself with a toy.*

amusement something that pleases

an (used in place of **a** before words beginning with a vowel) **1** one: *Please have an apple.* **2** one kind of: *A wolf is an animal.*

Aa 7

anaconda a very large snake that squeezes its prey

analysis (an-AL-is-is) a careful look at all parts of an idea, thing or pattern. When people do an analysis, they are said to be **analyzing**. *The class **analyzed** the clues they found.*

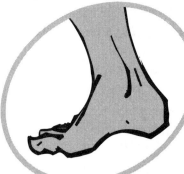

anatomy (a-NAT-o-mee) the internal makeup of living things: *We studied the **anatomy** of toads.*

ancestor (AN-ses-tor) a member of the family who lived long ago

anchor (ANK-er) a heavy metal hook at the end of a chain, used to hold a ship in place in the water: *A ship in port is said to be **at anchor**.*

ancient (AYN-shent) very old

anger a strong feeling you may get when you are not pleased

angle the corner made when two lines meet

angry the feeling of anger (see **anger**)

animal any living thing that can move about (compare with **plant**)

animation (a-ni-MAY-shun) the making of a movie from drawings or models

ankle the thin part of the leg where it joins the foot

anniversary a day when you remember something special that happened on the same day in another year: *It is my parents' **anniversary**. They've been married twenty years!*

announce to say something in front of people

annoy to make someone upset

annual happening once every year: *Our school has an **annual** festival.*

anonymous (a-NON-ee-mus) unknown

another 1 one more: *Have **another** cookie!* **2** a different one: *Try **another** key!*

answer 1 a solution to a problem **2** what you do when asked a question

Aa

ant a tiny insect

antelope a kind of deer

antenna a set of wires or rods for picking up or sending radio and television waves

antennae a pair of wire-like organs on the heads of some creatures: *Ants and lobsters have* **antennae**.

antibiotic (an-ti-by-AW-tik) medicine used to kill bacteria

anticipate (an-TI-si-pate) to expect something to happen

antidote (AN-ti-dote) something taken to work against poison or disease: *Our guide carries an* **antidote** *for poison ivy.*

antique (an-TEEK) something old that is valuable

antler horns on the head of deer, moose and elk

anxious worried

any 1 one or some: *Have you* **any** *wool?*
2 every: **Any** *child can do this!*
3 at all: *Are you feeling* **any** *better?*

anybody, anyone any person

anything any thing: *It's too dark to see* **anything**.

anywhere in any place

apart at a distance: *Halifax and Vancouver are far* **apart**.

apartment 1 a rented room or rooms to live in **2 apartment building** a building with many apartments for rent

ape a large, human-like animal with no tail (compare with **monkey**)

apologize (a-PAWL-o-jize) to say you are sorry

apostrophe (a-PAW-stro-fee) a punctuation mark (') to show ownership or to stand for a missing letter: *Where's Mark's book?*

apparatus special equipment used for doing something: *The magician set up her* **apparatus** *to do a trick.*

appeal to ask for something

appear 1 to show up and be seen: *The dog suddenly* **appeared** *at the door.*
2 to seem: *Wally* **appears** *sad today.*

Aa 9

appearance 1 what someone or something looks like **2** to show up in public: *The mayor made an **appearance** at the game.*

appendix 1 anything added at the end of a book, such as a list (see page 303 for example) **2** a small tube in the body that sometimes becomes diseased and must be removed

appetite the desire for food

applaud to clap your hands to show approval or pleasure

applause the sound of hands clapping

apple a round, juicy fruit that is white inside with skin that is red, green or yellow

appliance (a-PLY-ans) a tool or instrument, usually electric, used for a special purpose like cooking, cleaning or making things

application (a-pli-KAY-shun) **1** a request: *To get the job you must fill out an **application** first.* **2** a computer program that does a certain task

apply 1 to put on or use: ***Apply** a little glue to both sides.*

2 to ask for or request: *Ten people **applied** for the job.*

appoint to choose someone to do something

appointment a time you arrange to see someone: *an **appointment** with the dentist*

appreciate (a-PREE-she-ate) to value something highly: *I really **appreciate** your help with spelling.*

approach to come near to

approval agreement or support

approve to agree to and think highly of

approximate (a-PROK-si-met) nearly correct

aquarium a large glass container where fish are kept (see **terrarium**)

aquatic (a-KWOT-ik) living or growing in or near water: *Seaweed is an **aquatic** plant.*

arc part of the curved line of a circle

arch a curved part over an opening in a building: *An arch can make a wall stronger.*

archeology (are-key-AWL-o-jee) the study of the everyday life of people long ago

architect (ARK-i-tekt) someone whose job is to design and draw plans for buildings

architecture a particular kind of style or design for buildings: *modern architecture. The style of architecture in that city is modern.*

are see **be**

area 1 part of a country or place: *a no smoking area* **2** an amount of surface: *Football requires a bigger playing area than tennis.*

arena a large, covered building with a flat surface inside for having shows or playing games, often on a sheet of ice

aren't are not

argue to talk about something with others who do not agree

argument an excited talk among people who do not agree on something (see **quarrel**)

arise 1 to appear as a result of something happening: *Problems will arise if you disturb a sleeping bear!* **2** to move upward: *I can see smoke arising from that building. It arose yesterday too.*

arithmetic the study of numbers and how they work

arm the part of the body between the shoulder and the hand

armchair a chair with raised parts at the sides to rest your arms on

Aa

armour, armor 1 metal clothes worn in battles long ago
2 sheets of metal on vehicles, like tanks, to protect them

armpit the part of the body underneath the shoulder

arms 1 more than one arm (see **arm**)
2 weapons

army a group of people trained to fight on land

aroma the smell something makes

around 1 on all sides of: *There was a fence **around** the yard.*
2 here and there: *Look **around** for your book.*

arouse to wake someone

arrange to put in order

arrangement the way something has been set up

arrest to take someone into a place like a jail or a police station because she has broken the law

arrive to come to the end of a journey

arrow 1 a sign pointing in a direction
2 a pointed stick shot from a bow

arrowhead the tip of an arrow

art 1 drawings or paintings (see **arts**): *an **art** show*
2 a special skill or ability: *There's an **art** to making dogs obey.*

arthritis (are-THRI-tis) painful swelling in joints such as knees and elbows

article a particular thing

artificial not natural; something made by people or machines: ***artificial** flowers*

artist someone who draws or paints pictures

arts (usually **the arts**) painting, drawing, music, dance, etc.

as 1 equally: *Can you sing **as** well as Tony?*
2 in the same way: *Watch Nadia and do **as** she does.*
3 at the same time: *Zach stared **as** the pony came near.*

4 because: *Work faster as it's going to rain!*
5 though: *Tall as Jill is, she still can't reach the shelf.*

ascend (a-SEND) to go up

ash 1 grey powder left after something burns
2 a kind of large tree with many oval leaves on each stem

ashamed feeling very sorry and guilty for having done something

ashore on land, usually near the sea

aside to one side

ask to present a question or a request

asleep sleeping

asparagus a green, stick-like vegetable

assemble to meet together in a group: *The students assembled in the gym.*

assent to agree to

assignment a task someone gives you to do

assist to help

assistance help

assistant someone whose job is to help

assorted several different types put together: *There are assorted candies in the dish.*

asteroid a small piece of matter in space that moves in an orbit around a larger piece

asthma a breathing disorder caused by the tubes to the lungs becoming narrow

astonish to surprise greatly

astonishment great surprise

astounding very surprising

astronaut a person whose job is to travel in space

astronomer someone who studies the stars and planets. This kind of study is called **astronomy**.

at 1 where: *We were at school yesterday.*
2 when: *We sleep at night.*
3 how: *Marnie ran at high speed.*
4 in what direction: *Hong pointed at the fence.*

ate see **eat**

Aa

atheist a person who believes there is no divine power like God or Allah

athlete someone who trains to be good at sports

athletic good at sports

atlas a book of maps

atmosphere the air around the Earth

atom the smallest unit (see **ion**)

attach to join or fasten

attack to start fighting

attempt to try

attend 1 to be somewhere in order to do something: *attend a meeting* **2** to listen carefully

attendance being at a place to do something: *attendance at school*

attention 1 careful listening, thinking or reading **2 pay attention** to take notice

attic a room or rooms just under the roof of a house

attorney (also **attorney-at-law**) a lawyer

attract to cause interest

attractive very pleasant

auction (AWK-shun) a sale at which items are sold to the highest bidder present

audience people who have come to see a performance, such as a play

audio tape a long, thin tape for recording or playing back sound

audiovisual having to do with recording or playing back sound and images

audition (aw-DI-shun) to try out for a part in something, such as a play

aunt the sister of one of your parents, or your uncle's wife

author a writer of books, stories and information

authority 1 the power to make others do as you say **2** an expert on something

autobiography (AW-to-by-AWG-ra-fee) your life story that you write yourself

autograph the signature of a person who is famous or special for some reason

Aa

automatic able to work on its own and control itself

automobile a car

autumn (also called **fall**) the season when leaves fall from trees and it turns colder

available ready to use

avalanche a large amount of snow, ice or rock sliding suddenly down a mountain

avenue a road, often with trees on both sides

average ordinary or usual: *of average height for her age*

avoid to keep away from

await to wait for

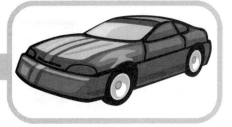

awake not sleeping

award 1 a prize
  2 to give a prize

aware knowing about something

away 1 not here
  2 to another place: *Our cat, Rasta, ran away.*

awesome inspiring respect, fear or admiration

awful very bad

awkward 1 clumsy
  2 not convenient: *an awkward time to visit*

axis the centre point around which something turns: *Earth rotates on its axis once every 24 hours.*

axle the centre shaft on which a wheel turns

Aa 15

Aa **Bb** CcDd

baboon a large monkey with a dog-like face

baby a very young child or animal

babysitter someone who looks after a child when the parents are away

back 1 opposite the front **2** a part of the body between the neck and the waist

backfire 1 an explosion in a gasoline engine **2** to go wrong: *Our plan backfired on us.*

backpack a bag you use for carrying things such as books. It hangs on your back from shoulder straps.

backward, backwards 1 with the front part at the back **2** slow in learning

bacon a kind of meat from a pig

bacteria very tiny living things that can cause changes in larger organisms. Bacteria can cause disease, decay, etc. A single one is a **bacterium**. (see **germ**)

bad 1 wicked or evil: *To steal is bad.* **2** harmful: *Too much rain is bad for crops.* **3** in poor condition: *a bad back* **4** serious: *a bad accident*

badge a small sign worn on your clothes or carried to show that you are a member of an organization

bag a container like a purse or suitcase, or a sack made of paper or plastic

baggage luggage

bagpipe, bagpipes a wind musical instrument

bail 1 to put water out of a boat
2 money promised to get a person out of jail until his trial is held

bail out 1 to jump out of an airplane wearing a parachute
2 (informal) to help someone out of a difficult situation

bait food on a hook or in a trap to catch fish or animals

bake to cook in an oven

baker someone whose job is making things like bread and pastry

balance 1 what is left over when you subtract: *Two from six leaves a* **balance** *of four.*
2 to keep something steady: *The robin* **balanced** *a twig in its beak.*

balcony 1 a platform with a rail around it, along the outside wall of upper floors in a building (see **deck**)
2 the seats in the upper platform in a theatre

bald without any hair or covering

bale a large bundle or package: *a* **bale** *of hay*

ball a round object, solid or hollow, used in games

ballerina a female dancer in a ballet

ballet a story told in music and dance

balloon 1 a small, rubber, coloured bag you can blow up
2 a large bag, filled with hot air or gas so that it floats in the sky

bamboo a plant with tall, hard, hollow stems. Bamboo grows in tropical countries.

banana a long fruit with a thick, yellow skin

band 1 any group of people: *an outlaw* **band**
2 a group of people playing musical instruments
3 a strip of material around something to hold it together: *a rubber* **band**

Bb 17

bandage a strip of material wrapped around a part of the body that is hurt

bandit a robber

bang 1 a sudden, loud noise **2** to bump, or to cause something to close with a loud noise: *Don't bang the door!*

banish to punish someone by sending him away

banjo a stringed musical instrument

bank 1 an organization that deals with money, such as looking after it for people (see **bank account**) **2** one of the buildings where the organization described in **1** runs its business **3** the ground at the edge of a river or canal **4** a large amount of anything that you can get if you need it

bank account an agreement you make with a bank so that it will look after the money you put in

bankrupt not having enough money to pay debts

banner a kind of flag

banquet (BAN-kwet) a fancy, special dinner

baptism a religious ceremony

bar 1 a long, straight piece of metal **2** a block of something like soap or chocolate **3** a place that serves drinks and food on a counter

barbarian a person who is rough and crude

barbecue 1 to cook food outdoors **2** a device on which food is cooked **3** an event held outdoors at which people gather to eat

barber a person whose job is to cut hair

bar code a set of numbers and lines that record information about an item for sale in a store

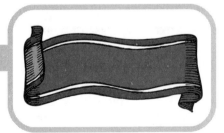

bare uncovered

bark 1 the noise a dog makes **2** the skin of trees and shrubs

barley a type of grain grown for food

bar mitzvah a Jewish religious ceremony for boys at age thirteen. For girls, it is **bat mitzvah** at age twelve.

barn a large building on a farm where things are kept

barren empty, without any plants or trees

barrier something that stands in the way: *There is a **barrier** of trees between the playground and the road.*

base the bottom part of something

baseball a game played with a bat and a ball. The ball in this game is called a **baseball**.

basement the rooms in a building that are below the ground

bashful shy

basic most important

basin a bowl

basket a container made of straw or cane

basketball a game in which players try to put a ball through a hoop. The ball in this game is called a **basketball**.

bat 1 a winged animal much like a mouse

2 a wooden club used in baseball games to hit the ball

batch a number of things together

bath 1 a large tub that holds water for washing the body **2** (also **bathe**) to wash the body

bathroom a room where you can wash and look after the needs of your body

batter 1 a mixture of eggs, milk and flour that is baked into cakes and pastry **2** to damage something by hitting it often: *The wind **battered** down our fence.*

battery a cell used to produce an electric current

battle fighting between groups of people

Bb 19

bay a place at the edge of a lake or ocean where the shore bends inward

be 1 to exist or occur: *How can that be?*
2 to show a certain quality: *Will Lana be upset?*
(**be** has many forms such as **am, are, is, was, were, been, being**) *I am ten years old. They are here. Millie is absent. Nola was absent yesterday. Ramesh and Lee were absent too.*

beach land by the edge of the sea usually covered with sand or stones

beacon a light that is a guide for safety

bead a small, round object

beak the hard part around a bird's mouth

beam 1 a long wooden log that has straight sides
2 a line of light
3 to smile very happily: *Jana's face was beaming when she got the prize.*

bean a long, thin, green or yellow vegetable that grows on vines

beanbag a bag filled with dried beans

bear 1 a large animal with thick fur

2 to put up with: *He can't bear any more pain. He has already borne too much.*
3 to give birth: *The baby was born on Monday.*

beard hair growing on a person's face

beast any big animal

beat 1 to do better than: *You beat me last time.*
2 to hit often: *Beat the rug until the dust is gone.*
3 to stir very hard: *Beat the batter until it is fluffy.*

beautiful 1 very attractive: *a beautiful face*
2 very pleasant: *a beautiful day*

beauty anything pleasing and beautiful

beaver a North American animal with thick fur and a flat tail

became see **become**

because for the reason that: *I got wet **because** it was raining.*

beckon to move your hand to tell someone to come closer

become to come to be: *It **became** very cold last night.*

bed 1 a piece of furniture to sleep on
2 a piece of ground where plants are grown

bee an insect that makes honey and sometimes stings

beech a kind of tree

beef meat from cattle

beehive a home for bees

beet a vegetable that grows a round, red root

beetle an insect with hard covers over its wings

before 1 earlier than: *I was here **before** you.*
2 in front of: *It vanished **before** my eyes!*

began see **begin**

beggar someone who lives by asking for food and money

begin to start: *The game will **begin** right away. I'm **beginning** to get sick. He **began** taking piano lessons. I have **begun** to play the flute.*

beginner someone who has just started something

beginning the start of something

begun see **begin**

behave to show good or bad manners in front of others

behind at the back of

beige a light brown colour

belief what someone thinks is true

believe to feel sure something is true: *I **believe** they took our bikes!*

bell a hollow piece of metal that rings when it is hit

belong 1 to be someone's: *Those skates **belong** to me.*
2 to be a part of something: *I **belong** to the skating club.*
3 to be in the proper place: *Your skates **belong** in the closet.*

below underneath

belt a band worn around the waist

bench a seat for more than one person

bend 1 to curve something: *Try to **bend** the wire around a peg.*
2 to lean over: *He **bent** over to watch the ants.*

beneath underneath

benefit anything helpful: *A dictionary will be a **benefit** to you.*

bent see **bend**

berry any small, round fruit with a seed or seeds in it

beside at the side of

besides as well as: *ten people **besides** me*

best better than any other: *my **best** drawing*

bet 1 to say that a certain thing will happen and that if it does, other people will pay you money. If it does not happen, you will pay money to them: *Klaus **bet** Irene a dollar that the Canucks would win.*

2 the money that is agreed upon in **1**: *Klaus and Irene made a **bet** on the Canucks game.*

better superior, but not the best: *Gaynor can swim **better** than I can.*

between 1 in the middle of two things: *jam **between** two biscuits*
2 something that is shared: *Lou and Bett have seven disks **between** them.*

beware be careful

bewildered very puzzled

bewitched under a spell

beyond farther than: *Don't wander **beyond** that tree.*

Bible (usually **The Bible**) a sacred book in some religions, especially Christianity and Judaism

bicycle, bike a vehicle with one wheel in front of another, moved by pressing the feet on pedals

bid to make an offer to buy something

big large in size or amount

bike see **bicycle**

bill 1 a piece of paper that tells how much money you owe
2 a piece of paper money: *a ten dollar **bill***
3 a bird's beak

bind 1 to tie together (Past tense is **bound**.): *The papers were bound together with ribbons.*
2 (informal) to have an annoying problem: *in a bind*

binding what holds a book together

binoculars special glasses that look like two tubes side by side. When you look through them, faraway things seem closer.

biodegradable (BY-o-de-GRAYD-a-bel) able to decay into its basic elements: *Some soaps are biodegradable.*

biography the life story of someone written by another person

biology (by-AWL-o-gee) the study of living things

biosphere (BY-os-feer) the area on Earth where living things are found

birch a kind of tree with white or grey bark

bird any animal with feathers, wings and a beak

birdseed grains and nuts put together for birds to eat

birth the time when a baby leaves its mother's body and begins to breathe on its own

birthday the date of the year you were born

birthmark a mark on someone's body that has been there since birth

biscuit 1 a small, hard cake made with flour, yeast, baking soda and powder **2** a cracker (see **cracker**)

bishop 1 an important member of the clergy in some religions **2** a piece in the game of chess

bison a large, wild animal found in North America, somewhat like a cow. It is often wrongly called a buffalo. (see **buffalo**)

Bb

bit 1 a very small amount
2 a very small amount of computer information (see **byte**)
3 the part of a bridle that goes in a horse's mouth

bite to use the teeth to cut into something: *Biting your nails can be unhealthy. Your gerbil has **bitten** me!: Lena **bit** into a peach.*

bitter an unpleasant taste

black the colour of darkest night

blackbird a medium-sized bird with black feathers

blackboard a black surface for writing on with chalk

blackfly a black, biting insect very common in Canada

blade 1 the flat, sharp part of a knife or sword
2 something with a flat, pointed shape: *a **blade** of grass*

blame to find fault with, or to say someone did something wrong

blank an empty space

blanket a cover, usually used on a bed

blast 1 a sudden rush of wind or air
2 an explosion

blaze 1 to burn brightly: *The fire is **blazing**.*
2 to show the way: *The Bruce Trail is **blazed** with white markers.*

bleach to make something whiter

bleak bare and unpleasant: *a **bleak** landscape*

bleed to lose blood: *Wally's nose **bled** for an hour.*

blend to mix together

blessing 1 a prayer of thanks or approval
2 a happy thing that has happened

blew see **blow**

blind 1 not able to see
2 (often **window blind**) something you pull down to cover a window

blink to close and open your eyes quickly

blister a sore, reddish spot on your skin with liquid in it

blizzard a very windy snow storm

block a thick chunk of something like wood or stone

Bloc Québécois 1 a political party in Canada
2 in Canada, a member of this party

blond, blonde 1 a light yellow colour
2 a person with light yellow hair

blood a red liquid that moves around in your body

bloom 1 a blossom
2 to have flowers: *Roses bloom in summer.*

blossom on a plant, the coloured part that is usually the prettiest

blot a spot or stain

blouse a shirt

blow 1 to make air come out of your mouth: *Nadia blew out the candles on her cake.*

2 to move in the wind: *Trees were blown over in the storm.*

blue the colour of the sky on a clear summer day

blueberry a small, dark blue fruit

blue box a container for material that will be recycled

blue jay a large, blue, white and grey bird with a crest on its head

blunt 1 not sharp: *a blunt knife*
2 abrupt in manner: *Mia bluntly told Ed to sit down.*

blur to make something look unclear

blush to get red in the face when you feel sensitive or excited

boa constrictor a very large snake that squeezes its prey

board 1 a long, thin piece of wood with straight sides
2 to get on a bus, train or airplane (see **aboard**)

boast to talk in a way that shows you are very proud of yourself (same as **brag**)

boat a vehicle used in water

bobcat a small, North American lynx

Bb 25

body 1 all of a person or animal that can be seen or touched: *Keep your body healthy.*
2 the main part of a thing: *the body of a car*

bodyguard a person whose job it is to protect someone

bog a place that stays wet all year (see **swamp** and **marsh**)

boil 1 a very sore pimple on the skin
2 to heat liquid until it bubbles
3 to cook something in hot, bubbling water

boiler a large container to heat liquid

bold not afraid

bolt 1 a thick, metal pin used for fastening
2 (also called **deadbolt**) a sliding lock on doors
3 to rush off

bomb a weapon that explodes and often does great damage

bone any of the parts of a skeleton

bonfire a large fire outdoors

book 1 sheets of paper bound together inside a cover
2 to reserve a place for yourself somewhere at a later date

bookcase a piece of furniture for holding books

bookmark 1 something you put in a book to show where to start reading
2 to mark the address of an Internet site

boom a loud noise

boot a kind of shoe that covers the leg to above the ankle

boot up to start a computer

border 1 the narrow part along the edge of something: *The sidewalk had a border of flowers.*
2 the line where two countries meet

bore 1 to make others tired by being uninteresting
2 to make a hole with a tool

born, borne see **bear**

borrow to arrange for the use of something for a time: *Mattie borrowed my pen yesterday.*

both the two of something: *Mimi ate **both** tarts!*

bother to worry or annoy someone

bottom the lowest part of something

bough (rhymes with wow) the branch of a tree

bought see **buy**

boulder a very large rock

bounce to spring back after hitting something

bound see **bind**

boundary a line marking the edge of some land

bouquet (bo-KAY) a bunch of flowers

bow ① (rhymes with go)
1 a long, bent stick with a string joining the ends, used to shoot arrows
2 a wooden rod with softer material stretched along it, used for playing violins, etc.
3 a knot with loops, in a rope or lace

bow ② (rhymes with cow) to bend forward to show respect: *Everyone **bowed** to the Governor General.*

bowl (bole) a round, open container for food or liquid

bowling a game in which you roll balls at large wooden pins to knock them down

box **1** a container that usually can be closed
2 to fight with the fists

boxcar a railroad car that can be closed on all sides and the top: ***Boxcars** filled with wheat crossed Alberta.*

boy a male child

BQ see **Bloc Québécois 1** and **2**

bracket **1** a piece of metal fixed to a wall to support something
2 one of a pair of marks like these **( )**

brag see **boast**

brainwave a new, exciting idea

brake the part of a vehicle that can be used to make it slow down or stop

branch **1** a part that sticks out from the trunk of a tree
2 a smaller part or section: *a **branch** of my Mom's company*

Bb 27

brand 1 a mark to show the maker or owner
2 a certain kind of product: *Canada Dry is a brand of soft drink.*

brass 1 a yellowish metal
2 (informal) the most important leaders in an organization

brave ready and able to face danger

bravery the act of being brave

bread a food made by baking dough in loaves

break 1 a short rest from work or play
2 to harm or destroy: *break a window*
3 to fail to obey a rule or keep a promise

breakfast usually the first meal of the day

breath the air a person breathes (see **breathe**)

breathe to take air in and out of the lungs through the nose and mouth

breed a certain kind of animal: *Spaniels are a breed of dog.*

breeze a gentle wind

brick a small block used in building

bride a woman on the day she gets married

bridegroom a man on the day he gets married (see **groom**)

bridesmaid a friend who helps a bride

bridge something built over a river, road or railway

brief short

bright 1 shining: *a bright star*
2 intelligent: *a bright student*
3 cheerful: *a bright smile*

brilliant very bright

bring 1 to carry here: *Please bring the chalk now.*
2 to lead here: *Yesterday he brought his bike to school.*

brink at the edge of something, often dangerous

brisk quick and lively

brittle likely to break or snap

broad very wide from one side to the other: *a broad valley*

Bb

broadcast to send out radio or television waves

broke, broken see **break**

bronchitis (brawn-KITE-is) a disease in the lungs that makes breathing difficult

brook a small stream

broom a long-handled brush

brother 1 a man or boy who has the same parents as another person
2 a term people sometimes use to say they are working together or think alike: *We are all* **brothers** *in this task.*

brought see **bring**

brow 1 the forehead
2 the top of a hill

brown a colour formed by mixing red, yellow and black

browse to look through something casually

browser see **web browser**

bruise a mark that shows up on your skin if you are hit hard

brush a tool with short, stiff hairs or pins. A brush is used for cleaning, painting, pulling through hair, etc.

bubble a small ball of air in liquid. When there are many bubbles moving up and down, the liquid is said to be **bubbling**.

buck 1 a male deer or rabbit
2 to leap like a horse trying to throw off a rider

bucket see **pail**

bud a flower or leaf before it opens

Buddhism a religion based on the teaching of Buddha

budge to move slightly: *I can't even* **budge** *this door.*

buffalo a large animal, somewhat like a cow, found in Asia and Africa (see **bison**)

buffet (buf-AY) **1** a piece of furniture used for storing dishes
2 buffet dinner a dinner where food is set out and you serve yourself

bug 1 any insect or creature like an insect
2 something wrong in a computer program
3 (informal) to bother someone

Bb

bugle a small brass musical instrument

build to make something by putting materials together: *We built a tree house with boards and rope.*

building something that has been built, like a house, school or factory

built see **build**

bulb 1 a glass electric lamp **2** a large seed that is planted in the soil: *Daffodils grow from bulbs.*

bulge to swell out

bulk 1 of large size or amount: *The blue box is bulkier than the red one.* **2** not in packages: *We buy birdseed in bulk.*

bull a male animal such as a moose or elephant

bulldozer a heavy machine, used for clearing land

bullet a small lump of metal made to be fired from a gun

bullfrog a type of large frog

bully someone who attacks or threatens a weaker person

bulrush a tall plant that grows near water

bumblebee a large type of bee that usually makes its home in the ground

bump 1 a swelling on your body **2** to knock against something, usually by accident

bumper a bar at the front and back of vehicles

bumpy not smooth

bunch a group of things joined together: *a bunch of bananas*

bundle a group of things tied together by someone: *a bundle of sticks*

bungalow a house that does not have a second storey

bunk 1 a narrow bed with another narrow bed above it **2** (informal) something someone says that is not correct or true

bunny a rabbit

buoy (boy) a thing that floats on water to warn boats to stay away

burden 1 something that has to be carried in your arms or on your back: *All those groceries are a heavy burden!*

2 a sad feeling that you have in your mind: *Losing the game was a burden to Joe.*

burglar someone who breaks into a building to steal things

burial (BEAR-i-al) the burying of someone who has died (see **bury**)

burn 1 a wound on your body from heat
2 to set on fire

burrow a hole in the ground where an animal lives

bury to put someone or something in the ground and cover it

bus a vehicle with many seats for people to travel in

bush 1 a plant that looks like a small tree
2 an area of wilderness

business (BIS-nes) any situation where people make or offer things for others to buy

bustle to hurry in a busy way

busy 1 doing things all the time
2 full of activity: *a busy street*

but 1 except: *Every province but one agreed to the idea.*
2 on the other hand: *Julie is young but she's fast.*
3 only: *I have but one thing to say.*

butcher someone whose job is to cut and sell meat

butter a food made from cream, which can be spread on bread

buttercup a wildflower with shiny, yellow petals

butterfly an insect with large, coloured wings

button a fastener sewn on clothes; it fits into a hole or loop

buy to get something by giving money: *I bought a CD for my brother. I will buy one for myself too.*

buzz the sound a bee makes

by 1 next to: *by the sea*
2 by means of: *His family came by train.*
3 not later than: *Be here by three o'clock.*
4 during: *An owl sleeps by day.*

byte see **bit 2**

Bb

ca. (also **c.**) an abbreviation for **circa**, which means **about,** used before dates and times: *ca.* 1953

cab 1 the part of a truck where the driver sits **2** (informal) taxi

cabin 1 a small house, often made of logs: *Many early pioneers lived in* **cabins.**

2 a room on a ship

cabinet a kind of cupboard with drawers

cable 1 a thick kind of wire **2** (informal) an abbreviation for **cable TV**

cable TV a system in which television signals are brought into your home through wires rather than through the air to an antenna

café (kaf-AY) a type of restaurant, usually small

cafeteria (ca-fa-TEER-ee-ah) a restaurant where you pick up your food at a counter

cage a box with wires or bars to keep an animal or person from escaping

cake a sweet food made from batter, sugar and other things: *fruit* **cake***; chocolate* **cake**

calamity (ka-LAM-i-tee) something bad that happens suddenly

calculate to figure out by doing arithmetic, or by thinking and planning

calculator a machine that can do arithmetic

calendar a chart showing days, weeks and months

calf 1 the young of cows, moose and elephants. The plural is **calves.**

2 the back part of the leg between the knee and the ankle

call 1 to yell or speak loudly: *Call to him and ask him to come here.*
2 to give a name to someone or something: *We call our cat Muffin.*
3 a conversation using a telephone: *telephone call*

calm 1 not excited or upset: *Frances remained calm during the storm.*
2 still: *a calm sea*

calves see **calf**

camcorder a video camera and recorder that has no wires and can be carried easily

came see **come**

camel a big animal with one or two large humps on its back. Camels are found in desert countries and are used in the same way as horses.

camera a device for taking photographs

camouflage (KAM-o-flaj) to hide something by making it look like the environment around it

camp 1 a place where people take vacations outdoors
2 (often **camp out**) to stay at a place for a while:

The protesters camped out in front of City Hall.

can 1 a round metal container
2 to be able to do something (Past tense is **could**.): *Dorothy can sing loudly, but Vern can't. Deedee couldn't sing at all yesterday*

Canada the largest and most northern country in North America

Canada goose a large water bird with a long neck, black head, and a white patch at the throat

Canadian 1 a person who is a citizen of Canada
2 about Canada or the people, places and things there

Canadian Conservative Alliance 1 a political party in Canada
2 in Canada, a member of this party

canal a kind of river dug by humans between two other bodies of water

canary a small, yellow bird

Cc 33

candle a stick of wax with a string through the centre that is set afire to give light

candlestick something that holds a candle upright

candy a sweet food made mostly of sugar

cane a long, thin stick

cannon a big gun that fires metal balls

canoe (ca-NOO) a light, narrow boat that you move by paddling

Canuck (informal) a friendly name for someone who is Canadian

canvas strong cloth for making things like tents

cap 1 a small hat
2 a top or covering

capable able to do something: *Bart is a very capable babysitter.*

capacity (ka-PA-si-tee) the amount a container can hold: *The pail has a capacity of 100 litres.*

capital 1 the place where people in government meet: *Ottawa is the capital of Canada.*
2 a special letter, like A, B, C, used at the beginning of sentences, names, etc.

capsule 1 a very small container, often used for medicine
2 a separate part on a spacecraft that can be taken off

captain 1 an officer in the armed forces
2 someone in charge of a team

captive a person or animal that has been captured

capture 1 to make someone or something a prisoner
2 to get something by fighting for it

car 1 an automobile
2 the part of a train where passengers sit

carbohydrate (kar-bo-HY-drate) a natural substance in food necessary for health

card 1 a piece of paper, usually folded in half, with a message on it: *Dad sent a birthday card to Aunt Bea.*
2 one of a set made of thin cardboard, with designs and numbers on it. Plural is

often **playing cards.**
(see **deck**)

cardboard very strong, thick paper, often used to make boxes

care 1 worry or trouble
2 to take care of to look after
3 to care for to like very much
4 to care for to look after
5 to care about to be interested in

careful making sure you do things safely and well: *a **careful** driver*

careless not careful

caretaker someone whose job is to look after a building

cargo things taken by ship, plane or truck from one place to another

caribou an animal like a deer that is found only in the far north

carnival a fair or festival, often with a parade

carol a happy song, usually sung at Christmas

carpenter someone who makes things out of wood

carpet a floor covering, usually woven

carrot an orange vegetable shaped like a cone

carry to take things from one place to another

cart a kind of box on wheels

carton a container, usually made of plastic or cardboard

cartoon 1 a drawing that tells a joke
2 a film that uses animation instead of actors

carve 1 to cut something hard into a shape
2 to slice meat

cascade a waterfall

case 1 a container, usually with soft sides: *pencil **case***
2 a suitcase or briefcase

cash coins and paper money

casserole food baked in a large, deep dish: *Chris made a tuna **casserole**.*

Cc 35

cassette a small, hard container with a reel of plastic tape inside for recording or playing sounds or images

cast 1 all the actors in a play, movie or TV show
2 to throw: *He cast a net into the sea to catch fish.*

castaway someone who has been left behind, usually by a ship

castle a large, strong building built of stone

casual careless, not paying much attention: *Zach dressed casually for the party.*

cat a small, furry animal often kept as a pet

catalogue (KA-ta-log) a collection of pictures of things for sale

catch 1 to grab or get hold of something (Past tense is **caught**.): *Oh no! Puffy caught a little bird!*

2 to get an illness: *catch a cold*

caterpillar the furry larva of a butterfly or moth

cathedral a big, important church

cattle cows and bulls kept by a farmer or rancher

caught see **catch**

cauliflower a vegetable with a thick stalk and white flowers for eating

cause to make something happen

cautious (KAW-shus) careful, doing only what is safe: *a cautious person*

cave a big hole in a mountain or under the ground

cavern a cave

CCAP see **Canadian Conservative Alliance 1** and **2**

CD compact disc, a round, flat object on which information is stored that can be retrieved on a computer or **CD player**

CD-ROM an abbreviation meaning **compact disc read-only memory**

cease (sees) to stop doing something

cedar a tree shaped something like a triangle. It stays green all year.

ceiling the flat part at the top of a room

celebrate to do special things to show you are happy: *Our team **celebrated** after winning the game.*

celebration a party you have when something special happens

celery a vegetable with green and white stalks that you eat

cell (sell) **1** a small room where a prisoner is kept **2** the tiny building blocks that make up living things **3** a space in a computer file where data is entered

cellar a room underneath a building where things are stored

cellphone a telephone that works without wires

celsius, Celsius a way of measuring temperature by degrees. In Celsius, water freezes at 0 degrees and boils at 100 degrees. (see **centigrade**)

cement a mixture of clay, lime, sand and gravel that turns hard when water is added

cemetery a place where dead people are buried in graves

cent money: *A penny is worth one **cent**.*

centigrade divided into 100 degrees (see **celsius**)

centimetre, centimeter a measure of length

centipede a long, creeping worm with many legs

centre, center the middle point of something

century a hundred years

cereal food made from grains like corn and wheat

ceremony (SAIR-i-mo-nee) an important and serious event held in front of other people who witness it: *a marriage **ceremony***

certain 1 sure: *Are you **certain** that Jeff is here?* **2** one in particular: *a **certain** person*

certificate (ser-TI-fi-kat) a piece of paper that says you have done something

chain 1 a line of metal loops fastened together
2 a group of stores that have the same name but are in different places

chair 1 a seat for one person
2 (often called **the chair**) the leader of a meeting

chalet (sha-LAY) a small wooden house, often found in areas where people ski

chalk a soft, white stick used for writing

chalkboard see **blackboard**

challenge 1 a difficult task
2 to ask someone to try to do something better than you do

champion a person or a team that is the best at something, usually a sport

championship a competition to decide on a champion

chance 1 a time when you can do something you cannot do other times: *This is your last* **chance** *to buy apples.*
2 an event that is not expected or planned for: *By* **chance** *I saw him on the bus.*

change 1 to make or become different

2 money that you get back when you give more than an item costs (see **exchange**)

channel 1 one of many different sizes of television signals
2 any passage for things to move along, especially water

chapel 1 a kind of small church
2 a special place inside a large church

chapter a section of a book

character 1 a person in a story
2 the sort of person you are

characteristic a quality in someone or something that sets them apart

charge 1 to ask a certain price for something
2 to buy something now and agree to pay for it later

3 to rush at something to attack it
4 in charge to have the job of telling others what to do

charity gifts of money or other help to people who need it

charm 1 to show an ability to make others feel good: *Mandy charmed everyone at the meeting.*
2 a small ornament
3 a magic spell

chart 1 a sheet of paper with information organized so that you can find it fast
2 a map
3 to make a map: *The coast of Nova Scotia was the first to be charted.*

chase to run after someone or something to catch it

chat to talk with someone in a friendly way

chatline a computer and Internet system people can use to have instant conversations in writing

chatter 1 a lot of idle talk
2 a rattling noise, often made by your teeth when you are very cold

chauffeur (show-FER) someone whose job is to drive another person's car

cheap costing a small amount

cheat to do something dishonest

check 1 to go over something to make sure it is correct: *Emily checked the spelling in her story.*
2 a mark that says something has been taken care of, or that it is correct: *There is a check beside every word I wrote!*
3 (also **cheque**) a piece of paper used instead of cash
4 the bill you get in a restaurant

checkout (informal) an abbreviation for **checkout counter**

checkout counter a desk where you pay for things that you have chosen in a store

cheek the part of the face below the eye and above the jaw

cheer 1 to shout loudly to show you are pleased about something: *The children cheered when they heard about the holiday.*
2 to support: *cheer for your team*

cheerful looking or sounding happy

cheese a solid food made from milk

Cc

chemical any substance that is part of chemistry

chemistry the study of how substances affect one another

cheque see **check 3**

cherry a small, red, round fruit with a pit in the centre

chess a board game for two players

chest 1 the part of the body between the neck and the stomach
2 a strong box

chestnut 1 a hardwood tree with large leaves
2 the shiny, brown nut that grows on a chestnut tree

chew to grind food with your teeth

chicken a large bird raised for its meat and eggs

chicken pox an illness that gives you a fever and itchy, red spots

chief 1 most important: *Our chief complaint is that it is too cold.*
2 the person in charge

child a young boy or girl. The plural is **children**.

chili a food made with beans, meat and spices

chill 1 a bad cold that makes you feel hot and dizzy: *catch a chill*
2 to make something cold: *Chill the pudding for an hour.*

chime a sound that bells make

chimney the tall pipe where smoke goes up from a fire

chimpanzee an African animal like a large monkey

chin the part of the face under the mouth

china dishes that are delicate

chip 1 a small piece that has broken off a larger one
2 a piece of deep-fried potato
3 a wafer on which a computer's circuits are stored

chipmunk a small, furry animal with black and white stripes on its back

chisel a tool with a sharp edge for cutting wood, stone, etc.

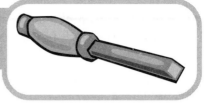

chocolate candy made with cocoa and sugar

choice something you have picked (see **choose**): *made a choice*

choir (kwire) a group of people who sing together

choke 1 to find it hard to breathe because of something in your throat: *The smoke made him choke.* **2** to block up: *The pond was choked with weeds.*

choose to pick out: *Which car did you choose? Oh, you chose the red one. Betty has chosen the blue car.*

chop 1 to cut something with a knife or axe **2** a small, thick slice of pork or lamb

chopsticks a pair of thin wooden sticks used to eat with

chorus (KOR-us) **1** the words repeated after each verse in a song **2** another word for choir (see **choir**)

chose, chosen see **choose**

Christian a member of the religion called Christianity (see **Christianity**)

Christianity a religion based on the teachings of Jesus Christ

chrome (krome) (also **chromium**) (KROM-ee-um) a bright, shiny metal

chrysalis (KRIS-a-lis) the cover a caterpillar makes around itself before it changes into a butterfly or moth

chuckle to laugh quietly to yourself

chunk a thick piece of something

circle the shape of a wheel or round coin

circa (see **ca.**)

circuit 1 the pathway that energy follows to do something: *Our lights are out because the circuit is broken.* **2** any pathway that ends at the same point where it begins

circular shaped like a circle

circus a show that has animals, clowns and acrobats

citizen a person who belongs to a country

Cc 41

claim to ask for something that you say belongs to you: *Brian **claimed** the lost umbrella.*

clap to make a noise by hitting your hands together

clarification (KLAIR-i-fi-KAY-shun) an explanation that makes something clear and easy to understand

clarify to make clear: *Our teacher **clarified** the directions by drawing a map.*

clash 1 to disagree with: *Cindy **clashed** with Hong Lee at dinner.*
2 the sound that cymbals make when they are hit together

clasp to hold very tightly

class 1 a group of pupils who learn together
2 a type or sort: *This store has a different **class** of customer.*

claw 1 the foot of an animal with sharp nails
2 to scratch

clay grey or red earth that sticks together

clean 1 free of dirt
2 to make free of dirt

clear 1 easy to understand: *It's **clear** to me!*
2 to take things away: *Please **clear** the table of dishes.*
3 away from something: *We're **clear** of the storm now.*

clench to close your teeth or fist tightly

clergy men and women who are in charge of churches

clever able to learn and do things quickly and easily

cliff a steep rock or ice face

climate weather at different times of the year

climb to go up or down something high

cling to hold on very tight (Past tense is **clung**.): *Mattie **clung** to her mother's skirt.*

clinic a kind of small hospital

clip 1 to cut something with scissors or other tools like scissors
2 a fastener: *paper **clip***

clock a device to show the time of day

Cc

clockwise the direction in which a clock's hands move

clog a kind of shoe with a thick sole

clone 1 in living things, an organism that is made from another organism and is exactly the same in every way
2 a computer program that is a cheaper version of another program, but does the same work
3 to produce a clone

close ① (rhymes with dose)
1 very near: *close to the fire*
2 careful: *a close examination*

close ② (rhymes with doze)
1 to shut: *Are the stores closing early today?*
2 to end: *The speaker closed with a joke.*

cloth 1 a piece of material for making things such as shirts and curtains
2 a piece of material for wiping things

clothe to dress: *Hope clothed her baby in blue silk.*

clothes, clothing things worn on the body

cloud 1 water vapour floating in the sky
2 dust or smoke hanging in the air
3 to make things hard to understand: *Ed's comment only clouds the point!*

clover a green plant with white, red or yellow flowers. It is a type of grass.

clown someone who makes others laugh by dressing up and acting funny

club 1 a group of people who are interested in the same thing: *a hiking club*
2 a stick used as a weapon
3 one of the four suits in a deck of playing cards

clue a fact that helps you solve a puzzle or mystery

clump a group of plants growing close together: *clump of trees*

clumsy likely to knock things over

clung see **cling**

clutch to grab at something and try to hold on

coach 1 a person who helps others to get better at something
2 a bus that takes people on long trips
3 a kind of box with wheels in which people ride: *The train had three* **coaches** *for passengers.*

coal a fuel that comes in hard, black lumps

coarse not delicate or smooth

coast the edge of land next to the ocean

coat 1 a piece of clothing that you wear over other clothes
2 a covering: **coat** *of paint*

cocoa powder made from the nuts of a tree. It is used to make chocolate and other foods.

coconut a big, round, hard fruit that grows on palm trees

cod a fish found in the ocean

code 1 a set of signs and letters for sending messages
2 a set of rules

coffee a drink made from the seeds of the coffee tree, which are ground up and added to hot water

coffin a long box in which a dead person lies

coin a piece of round metal money

cold 1 without any warmth
2 an illness that makes you sneeze and blow your nose a lot

collage (co-LAHJ) a picture made from pieces of material mixed together in a special way

collapse 1 to fall down in pieces
2 to fall down because you are ill

collar 1 the part around the neck of shirts and coats
2 a band that is placed around the neck of pets like dogs and cats

collect 1 to bring together things from different places: *Manny* **collects** *hockey cards.*
2 to ask for money or gifts for something: *Someone has come to* **collect** *for the United Appeal.*

Cc

collection things that have been collected: *a stamp collection*

collector someone who collects things as a hobby

college a school you may go to after high school

collide to run into someone or something

collision a crash between two moving things

colon a punctuation mark like this **:** used before you write a list

colour, color 1 red, yellow and green are examples of colours
2 to paint or use crayon on something: *colour a picture*

colt a young male horse (see **filly** and **foal**)

column 1 a list of numbers or words, one below the other
2 a special part in a newspaper
3 a tall, thick post used to decorate a building

columnist a person who writes a column (see **column 2**)

.com an abbreviation for **company** used in email

comb 1 a strip of plastic or metal with a row of thin parts like teeth
2 to pull a comb through hair
3 to search very carefully: *The police combed the park for a missing child.*

combine ① (com-BINE) to mix together

combine ② (COM-bine) a machine used to cut and thresh grain

come 1 to move here: *I came as fast as possible.*
2 to arrive: *When will the letter come? It will be coming tomorrow.*

comedian someone who entertains people by making them laugh

comedy a funny play, movie or TV show

comfortable 1 pleasant to wear, to sit on or be in: *What a comfortable chair!*
2 free from pain or worry

comic a paper with stories told in pictures

comical funny

comma a punctuation mark like this **,** used to divide parts of a sentence

command 1 to tell someone to do something: *I command you to stop!*
2 to be in charge: *in command*

commercial an advertisement on radio or television

common not unusual, happening often: *the common cold*

Commons, The see **House of Commons**

commotion (ku-MO-shun) a lot of fuss and noise

communal shared by everyone

commune a place where people live together and try to share everything equally

communicate (ku-MEW-ni-kate) to talk to or send a message to

communication
1 a message: *We received a communication from the boss.*

2 a way or ways of sending a message: *Communication was difficult for the pioneers.*

community a town, city or region and the people who live there

companion someone who is with you

companionship friendly company

company 1 one or more other people or things with you: *The cat kept Alf company.*
2 a business

compare to see how like each other some things are

comparison the act of comparing

compass an device that can show you which way is north

compasses a device for drawing circles

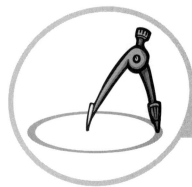

compatible 1 able to work with: *That software is not compatible with my PC.*

2 able to be together in a pleasant way: *Good friends are always* **compatible**.

compete to take part in a competition

competition a kind of test or game for two or more people with a reward for the one who does best

complain to say that you are bothered about something

complaint a statement that says you are bothered

complete 1 whole
2 to come to the end of something: *We have all* **completed** *the test now.*

complex 1 very hard to figure out (see **complicated**)
2 a group of buildings

complicate (KOM-pli-kate) to make very confusing and difficult

complicated difficult because there are a lot of different parts to think about: *a* **complicated** *problem*

compliment praise for a person, idea or thing

composer a person who writes music

composition a story or piece of music

compound 1 something made of two or more things: *Concrete is a*

compound *of cement, sand and gravel.*
2 a word made up of two or more words: *"Someone" is a* **compound** *word.*

compress to squeeze together

computer a device that can be programmed to deal with data very fast

computer graphics a variety of images produced by computer software

computer program the instructions that tell a computer what to do

computer science the study of how mathematics and machinery make computers work

conceal to hide

conceited too proud

concentrate to think very hard about something

concept (CON-sept) an idea

concern 1 to be involved with: *That problem does not* **concern** *you.*
2 to worry: *Meighen is late; I'm* **concerned** *about her.*

concert a show with music

concrete a mixture of cement, sand, water and gravel that becomes very hard

Cc

condense to make smaller: *I wish you would condense your story to 200 words.*

condition the state something is in

condominium (kon-doh-MIN-ee-um) (often called **condo**) an apartment you own rather than rent

conductor 1 the person who leads a choir or orchestra

2 someone who looks after passengers on a train

cone a shape that is round at one end and pointed at the other, such as an ice cream cone

confess to say you have done something wrong

confident brave and sure about something: *I'm confident I'll win the high jump.*

confuse to mix up

congratulate (kon-GRAT-yew-late) to tell someone how pleased you are about something that has happened to her

connect to join together

conquer (KON-ker) **1** to beat the other side in a battle or war

2 to overcome a fear that you have: *Sashi conquered his fear of swimming in deep water.*

conscious (KON-shuss) awake and knowing what is going on around you

conservation the protection of things, especially in nature

conservative a person who prefers things to change very carefully and only bit by bit

Conservative in Canada, a member of the Progressive Conservative political party (see **PC** and **Progressive Conservative**)

conserve to save: *to conserve energy*

consider to think carefully about something

considerable large, a lot: *a considerable amount of money*

considerate kind and thoughtful toward others

console ① (kon-SOLE) to try to make a sad person feel better

console ② (KON-sole) **1** a cabinet to hold a television or a music system **2** (also called **control panel**) a desk, table or keyboard where there are switches to run something

consonant any letter of the alphabet except a, e, i, o, u, and sometimes y

constable a police officer

constellation a group of stars: *The Big Dipper is a constellation.*

construct to build

consultant a person who gives advice

contain to have something inside: *The bag contains mostly candy.*

container anything you can put things into. Jars, boxes, bags, etc. are all containers.

contented satisfied and happy

contents what is inside a container, a book or a message

contest a competition

continent one of the seven very large land areas of the planet Earth

continual something going on and on over a period of time with only short breaks (see **continuous**): *These continual phone calls are getting to be annoying!*

continue to keep on doing something: *Continue with your work until recess.*

continuous something going on and on without a break over a period of time (see **continual**): *That continuous ringing sound is driving me crazy!*

contract an agreement between two people or companies

contraction (kun-TRAK-shun) an abbreviation for writing or saying something: *"Can't" is the contraction of "cannot."*

contradict to say that what someone else is saying is not true

control to be in charge and make something or someone do what you want

control panel see **console** ②

convenient 1 the right time for something
2 easy to get at or use

conversation an informal talk with someone

convert ① (KON-vert) a person who has changed her belief about something and now believes in something different

convert ② (kon-VERT) to change into something completely different

convict ① (KON-vict) a person who is in prison

convict ② (kon-VICT) to find someone guilty of a crime

convince to make someone believe something

cook 1 to get food ready to eat
2 someone whose job it is to cook

cookie a small, thin, hard, sweet biscuit

cool 1 to lower the temperature
2 a temperature that is not warm, but not quite cold
3 (informal) something that is very appealing

co-operate, cooperate to get along so that something can be done: *Our group co-operated on a science project.*

copper a shiny, brown metal, used for making pennies and pipe

copy 1 to write down or draw something that is already written or drawn: *Verna copied the poem in her best writing.*
2 to imitate

copyright an author's or artist's ownership

cord string or thin rope

core the very centre of something: *core of an apple*

cork a piece of bark from a special kind of tree. The piece is made round to fit into the top of a bottle.

corkscrew a tool for pulling corks out of bottles

corn 1 a tall, green plant grown by farmers **2** the yellow kernels from this plant

corner the point where two streets or straight edges meet

coronation the ceremony when a king or queen is crowned

corpse a dead body

correct 1 without any mistakes: *My spelling test was all **correct**!* **2** to make something right that was wrong before: *I have **corrected** my errors in arithmetic.*

corridor a long, narrow passage. A hall is a corridor.

cosmetic any material used to clean or improve the appearance of a part of a person's body, usually the face

cosmonaut the Russian word for astronaut (see **astronaut**)

cost 1 to have a certain price: *My bike **cost** a lot!* **2** the price something is sold for: *The **cost** of that bike is $400.*

costume clothing put on for a special purpose. Actors in plays often wear costumes.

cottage 1 a house by a lake where you go for vacations **2** a small house in the country

cotton a light cloth made from the cotton plant

couch a type of sofa

cougar a large wildcat that is brownish-yellow with a very long tail. It is sometimes called a **mountain lion,** but is smaller than an African lion.

cough (koff) to make a sudden, loud noise to get rid of something in your throat

could see **can**

council a group of people who plan and decide what should be done in a specific place: *a city **council***

count 1 to say numbers in order **2** to use numbers to find out how many people or things there are

Cc 51

counter 1 the long table where you are served in a store, cafeteria or bank **2** the flat surface in kitchens where food is prepared

counter-clockwise in the opposite direction to the movement of a clock's hands

country 1 a land with its own people and government. Canada, China and Peru are countries. **2** the part of a region that is outside towns and cities

countryside a spread of land with farms and villages

couple two: *a couple of birds*

coupon a kind of ticket that you can use to get a free gift or a discount

courage bravery, lack of fear

coureur de bois in early Canada, a man who travelled into the country to trade for furs with the native peoples (see **voyageur**)

course 1 the direction something takes: *a ship's course* **2** a series of lessons in a school

court 1 a place where people decide if someone is breaking the law **2** a special area marked out for games like tennis **3** the place where the king and queen and others live

cousin the child of your aunt or uncle

cover 1 something put over another thing **2** to put something over or around another thing

cow a female animal in the cattle family or among wild animals such as moose

coward someone who cannot face up to a situation

coyote (ky-O-tee) a small wolf

cozy warm and comfortable

CPU an abbreviation for **central processing unit**. It is the part of a computer that controls all its operations.

crab a water animal with a shell, claws and ten or more legs

crack 1 a line on the surface of something that is beginning to break
2 to make a sudden, sharp sound by breaking something

cracker a thin, hard, dry type of bread (see **biscuit**)

crackle the sound that burning wood makes: *a crackling fire*

crafty clever at planning things so that you get your way

crane 1 a machine on wheels with a long arm for lifting heavy things

2 a large bird with long legs and a long beak

cranky very hard to please

crash 1 the loud noise something makes when it is dropped and smashed
2 to hit something with a loud noise: *The dishes crashed to the floor.*

crate a container for carrying things that break easily

crawl to move slowly on your hands and knees

crayon a stick of coloured wax

crazy likely to do strange and silly things

creak to make a squeaky noise

cream 1 the part of milk that has fat in it
2 a colour that is white with a bit of yellow
3 something that looks like cream and is put on your skin: *hand cream*

crease to make a line in something by folding it

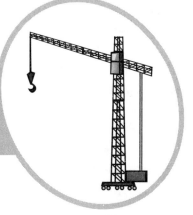

create to make something no one else has made or can make. The one who does this is called a **creator**.

creature any animal

credit a promise to pay later: *The farmer bought a tractor on credit.*

credit card a small, plastic card that says you will pay for something later

creek a small stream

creep to move along quietly or secretly: *The fox crept toward the mouse.*

Cc 53

cremate (KREE-mate) to burn a body after death instead of burying it in the ground

cremation the act of cremating

crest 1 a badge or special sign **2** the very top of something: *Finally we reached the crest of the hill.*

crescent a street shaped like a loop or curve

crew a group of people who work together: *a ship's crew*

crib a baby's bed, usually with bars around it to keep the baby from falling out

cricket an insect that makes a shrill sound, usually at night

cried see **cry**

crime a bad deed that is against the law

criminal someone who has broken the law

crimson the colour of deep red

crisp firm and fresh: *crisp lettuce*

croak to make a hoarse sound like a frog

crocodile a reptile found in tropical climates. It has a long body, short legs and a long mouth with many teeth.

crocus a small yellow, white or purple spring flower

crook a person who cheats people

crooked bent

crop plants grown in large quantity for food: *Wheat is an important crop in Canada.*

cross 1 to move from one side to the other: *cross the street* **2** angry: *Be careful! Dad's really cross with us!*

crouch to lean forward and bend your knees so that you are almost touching the ground

crow a large, black bird whose beak is also black

crowd 1 a large number of people

Cc

2 to push into a place that is already quite full: *Ashlyn* **crowded** *onto our bench.*

crown an ornament that a king or queen wears on the head

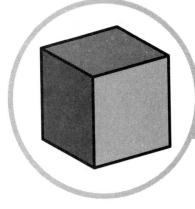

crude put together in a very rough way: *a* **crude** *piece of furniture*

cruel very unkind

cruise to move along without hurrying, especially on a boat

crumb a tiny piece that has fallen off bread or pastry

crumble to break into pieces

crumple to make something full of creases: **crumpled** *clothes*

crush to damage something by pressing on it so that it breaks

crust the hard part around the outside of a piece of bread

crutch a device that can help a disabled person to walk more easily

cry 1 to let tears fall from your eyes: *He was so upset that he* **cried.**
2 to shout very loud

crystal a hard, clear material like glass

cub a young bear, lion, wolf or tiger

cube a shape with six square sides

cucumber a long, green vegetable eaten raw

cuddle to put your arms around a person or animal that you are fond of

cuff on clothing, the part at the end of a sleeve

culprit a person who has done something, usually bad

culture 1 all the arts like music, painting and writing. These are usually called **cultural activities.**
2 the beliefs and way of living that a group of people share: *The* **culture** *of people in India is often different than that in Canada.*

cunning crafty

cup a container for drinking or measuring

cupboard a piece of furniture that stands against a wall. It has doors and shelves for storing things.

cure to make well again

curiosity a wish to find out about things

curious 1 wanting to know about something
2 unusual: *a curious smell*

curl 1 a piece of hair twisted into a tube shape
2 to sit or lie comfortably with your body bent around itself

currant a small, dried fruit like a raisin or grape

current water, air or electricity moving in one direction

curtain a piece of cloth hanging over something, often a window

curve a line that is bent

cushion a soft pillow

custom something that is usually done. Giving someone a present at a birthday party is a custom.

customer a person in a store who is buying something

customize to make something look special or work in a special way just for you: *You can customize the operations of your computer.*

cut 1 to use scissors or a knife to open, divide or shape something: *Is Ellie cutting up the paper now?*
2 an opening in your skin made by something sharp

cute pretty and gentle

cutlery knives, forks and spoons

cycle a series of events that are repeated in order: *Spring, then summer, fall, and winter make up a cycle.*

cylinder the shape of a soup can

cymbals a musical instrument made of two round pieces of metal that you bang together

Cc

dad, Dad an informal word for father

daffodil a plant with yellow flowers that blooms in spring

daily every day

dairy a place where milk is put into containers: *Some **dairies** make butter and cheese.*

dam a wall built across a river to control the flow of water

damage 1 the harm done to something
2 to harm something

damp a little wet: ***damp** clothes*

dance 1 an event where people gather to have fun
2 to move about in time to music

dandelion a weed with a bright yellow flower

danger a kind of risk that may cause harm: *In a dry summer, there is a **danger** of forest fires.*

dangerous likely to cause harm: *it is **dangerous** to play on the street.*

dangle to hang loosely

dare 1 to be brave or sometimes foolish enough to do something: *Sheila **dared** to climb the big tree.*
2 to ask someone to do something risky: *Sheila, I **dare** you to climb that tree!*

daring very brave or very foolish

dark 1 without any light: *It's **dark** in this cave.*
2 not light in shade or colour: *a **dark** green coat*

dart 1 a short arrow
2 to move suddenly and quickly

dash 1 a punctuation mark like this —
2 to run very quickly for a short distance

data many facts and figures or pieces of information that can be put in a report or stored in a computer (For one piece of information, use **datum**.): *The* **data** *are ready to be entered now.*

data bank a large store of information

database a store of data that are arranged so that people can make comparisons with new data once they collect it

data processing entering and working with the data in a computer

date 1 the day, month and year something happens
2 a fruit that grows on a palm tree
3 an agreement to go out with someone: *We made a* **date** *to visit the fair.*

daughter a girl or woman who is someone's child

dawdle to walk very slowly

dawn the time of day when the sun rises, also called **daybreak**

day 1 the twenty-four hours from one midnight to the next
2 the part of the day when it is light, also called **daytime** and **daylight**

daycare supervised care of people, usually children, during the day

daydream to let your mind wander while you are awake

dazed not able to think properly. People are often dazed after an accident.

dazzle so bright it hurts your eyes to look

dead without life

deadline the time by which something must be finished

deaf unable to hear

deafening so loud that nothing else can be heard

deal 1 an agreement: *We made a* **deal** *to finish by tomorrow.*
3 to manage something: *First, I have to* **deal** *with this broken window.*
4 to give out: *You* **deal** *the cards. I* **dealt** *(delt) last time*

dear 1 loved
2 costing a lot: *a very* **dear** *piece of software*
3 the word that begins letters, as in "Dear Winnie"

death at the end of life, and after

debate a discussion in which people give different opinions about a topic

debt (det) something that you owe someone

decay to rot and then break down and lose strength: *Too much candy causes tooth decay.*

deceive (de-SEEV) changing or hiding the truth to mislead someone

December the twelfth month of the year

decide to make up your mind

deck 1 a floor on a ship
2 a pack of cards
3 a platform where people can sit, often attached to a house (see **balcony**)

declare to say something important that you want everyone to know

decode to change a message from secret language into language anyone can read

decorate to make something look dressed up

decrease to make smaller or fewer

dedicated set aside for a special purpose: **dedicated port**

deduct to take away: *I'll deduct three dollars from the price of the book.*

deed 1 something that someone has done: *a good deed*
2 a paper that tells who owns a piece of land

deep a long way down from the top

deer a fast, graceful, brown animal. The males have antlers. *One deer is in the field. Two deer are over there.*

default 1 a failure to do something
2 an operation a computer will do unless the user tells it to do something else

defeat to beat someone in a game or in a battle

defend to keep safe from harm

definite fixed or certain: *a definite date for the trip*

definition a very precise explanation

Dd 59

defy to say or show you will not obey

degree 1 a step or a level that tells an amount: *It is one degree warmer today.*
2 a certificate that confirms you have finished a level of school: *She has a university degree.*

dehydrate to become dried out

delay 1 to make someone or something late
2 to put off doing something until later

delete to erase or take out something

deliberate on purpose

delicate soft, fine and fragile

delicatessen (abbreviation is **deli**) a store selling special foods, especially meats and cheese

delicious tasting or smelling very good

delight to please very much

deliver to take things to a place

demand to ask for in a way that shows you feel strongly

democracy a method of government where people are free to choose those who run things: *In a democratic country, everyone is free and equal.*

demolish to tear something down

demonstrate to show: *Lena is demonstrating how a mixer works.*

demonstration 1 an event where people see how something works
2 a lot of people marching down the streets to show what they think of something

den 1 the home of an animal
2 a room in a house, usually for one person

denim very sturdy cotton cloth, usually blue

dense thick

dent to make a hollow in something by hitting it: *That car has a dented fender.*

dentist someone whose job is to look after your teeth

deny to say something is not true

60

depart to go away

depend to trust someone: *Bob depends on Reenie to feed his dog.*

deposit to put into: *The trash should be deposited in the basket.*

depress 1 to make someone feel sad: *We were depressed for a while after our team lost.*
2 to push down on

depth how deep something is

derive to get from: *Grandma derives pleasure from birdwatching.*

descend (dee-SEND) to go down

describe to say what someone or something is like

description the words that tell about someone or something

deselect to remove an option from a computer menu

desert (DEZ-ert) a very dry area of land where few plants grow

deserted (di-ZER-ted) left by everyone: *a deserted house*

deserve to have a right to something: *I deserve to be thanked!*

design 1 a plan or pattern for something
2 to make a plan or pattern for something

desire to want very much

desk a kind of table where you write and study

desktop the surface of a desk

desktop publishing using a personal computer to write, design and print

despair to give up hope

desperate ready to do foolish or even dangerous things

despise to dislike very much

dessert (di-ZERT) sweet food eaten after the main part of a meal

destination (des-tin-A-shun) the place you are going to

destroy to ruin something

destruction when something is destroyed

detached not attached: *a detached house*

Dd

detail a piece of information about a topic

detective someone whose job is to find out who did a crime

detergent a kind of soap

determined with your mind made up

detest (dee-TEST) to hate

develop 1 to become bigger or more mature: *The calf began to develop horns.*
2 to put together: *Our class developed a plan to raise funds.*
3 to build houses on a piece of land

device a tool or instrument that helps you do things

devise (dee-VIZ) to think up and then make a plan or a tool: *Dottie has devised a way of fixing the sink.*

dew tiny drops of water that settle on things outside during the night

diabetes (die-a-BEE-teez) a disease caused by the wrong levels of sugar in the blood

diagonal 1 a slanting line
2 the opposite corner

diagram a picture or graph that explains something

dial a design, usually round, showing numbers or letters

dialect the special way some people speak

dialogue box, dialog box a message on your computer screen

dial-up to use a modem and telephone line to connect with another computer or network

diameter a straight line drawn across the centre of a circle

diamond 1 a very hard, jewel-like, clear glass
2 one of the four suits in a deck of playing cards
3 the field where a baseball game is played

diary a book in which you write your feelings each day

dictionary a book where you find the meaning of a word, and how to say and spell it

did see **do**

die to stop living: *The king has died. I'm sorry to say the cat is dying.*

diesel (rhymes with weasel) a type of engine

diet 1 special meals that some people eat
2 to eat in a way that will help you to lose weight

differ to have an opposing opinion

difference how one thing, idea or person is unlike another

different not like someone or something else

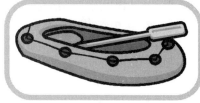

difficult not easy

difficulty 1 not easily: *He opened the window with difficulty*.
2 something unable to be done or worked out: *The difficulty with your idea is that it's too costly*.

dig to move soil to make a hole in the ground: *Wally dug a hole for the tree*.

digest what your stomach does to food so that your body can use it

digital any electronic system that converts data to a system of numbers for broadcasting and receiving, such as in digital television or digital audio recording and playback

dignified looking serious and formal

dignity a way of looking and behaving that brings out respect in others

dilemma a difficult decision, usually with two or more different choices to make

dim not bright

dime a coin worth ten cents

dimple a small hollow in the chin or cheek

dinghy (DING-ee) a small boat

dingy (DIN-jee) looking dirty and messy

dining room a room where meals are eaten

dinner an important meal during the day

dinosaur a large animal that lived on Earth millions of years ago

diploma a formal paper that says you have learned to do something

direct 1 to show someone the way
2 as straight and quick as possible: *the direct route*

direction the way you go to get somewhere

Dd

directory 1 a list of names, numbers or other items **2** a list of computer files

dirt any unclean substance, like mud or dust

dirty marked with dirt or stains

disable to make something unable to perform as it usually does

disabled a word used to describe someone who cannot perform all the tasks of daily life without some kind of special help

disagree to have a different opinion or idea

disappear to go away and not be seen again

disappoint to make others sad by not doing what was hoped for: *I am disappointed in Tom's work today.*

disaster something bad that happens very suddenly

disciple (di-SY-pul) a believer and follower

discomfort a lack of comfort and good feeling

discount an amount taken from the price of something for sale

discourage to try to keep someone from doing something

discover to find out about something

discovery what is found out about something

discuss to talk with people who have different ideas

disease illness

disgraceful something bad enough to cause shame: *That was very disgraceful behaviour!*

disguise to make yourself or something look different to deceive others: *I plan to disguise myself with a wig.*

disgust a feeling that something is very unpleasant

dish 1 a shallow, flat-bottomed bowl **2** a special preparation of food: *My favourite dish is spaghetti.*

dishonest not honest

disk 1 (also **disc**) any round, flat object like a plate **2** (also **diskette**) a plate for storing computer information (see **floppy disk** and **hard disk**)

disk drive a device a computer uses to read and write data

dislike to have no liking for someone or something

dismal looking or feeling gloomy

dismay a feeling of lost hope, and sometimes fear too

dismiss to send someone away

disorder a lack of order or careful arrangement

display 1 a show: *What a display of dancing!*
2 to show: *Cal displayed his Lego collection.*

displeasure the feeling when you are annoyed

disrespect any action that shows you do not respect someone or something

dissolve to melt

distance the space between two places

distant far away

distinct easy to see or hear: *The tree is distinct on the horizon.*

distinctive standing out in a special way: *Moira has a distinctive way of speaking.*

distress great sorrow or worry

district an area in a town or country

disturb 1 to bother someone at rest
2 to move something out of place

disturbance an event that upsets everyone around it

ditch a long, narrow hole in the ground

dive to jump headfirst into water

divide 1 to share something among others
2 to split into smaller parts
3 to find out how many times a number will go into another: *Six divided by two is three.*

divorce to end a marriage legally

dizzy a feeling in your head that everything around you is spinning

DJ (informal) the abbreviation for **disc jockey**, a person who hosts a musical show on radio or at a special event such as a dance or a wedding (see **VJ**)

do to carry out an action: *She must do the dishes now. If she doesn't, we can't go. When they're done, we'll go.*

Dd 65

*What is she **doing** now? Please **don't** bother her!*: (Special uses of **do**: 1. in questions: ***Do** you play hockey?* 2. in negatives: *Yes, **don't** play on the street.* 3. to make a stronger sentence: ***Do** stop that noise!*)

dock a place where boats are tied up for loading and unloading

doctor the abbreviation **Dr.** is used with a name: **Dr.** Smith
1 a person whose job is to treat sick people
2 a person who has the highest university degree

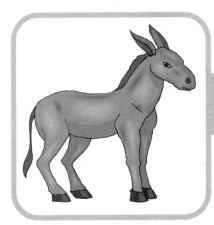

document a written piece of information

documentary (dok-yew-MEN-tree) a non-fiction film or TV show

dodge to move quickly to get out of the way

doe a female deer or female rabbit

does see **do**

dog a four-legged animal usually kept as a pet

doll a toy in the shape of a person

dollar an amount of money

dolphin a marine mammal shaped like a small whale

dome a roof shaped like the top half of a ball

done see **do**

donkey an animal that looks like a small horse with large ears

doodle to scribble on paper while you are thinking of something else

door a slab of wood, metal or glass that fills a doorway and opens or closes

doorway a hole, usually rectangular, that is cut into a wall

dormant like being asleep

dory a rowboat

DOS an abbreviation for **disk operating system**

double twice as many

doubt (rhymes with out) the feeling you have when you are not sure of something

doubtful not sure

dough 1 (rhymes with so) a mixture of flour and water: *Dough is used in making bread and pastry.*
2 (informal) money

doughnut, donut a small cake with a hole in the centre

dove a bird that looks like a pigeon

down 1 somewhere lower: *Run **down** the hill.*
2 very soft feathers

doze to be nearly asleep

dozen a set of twelve

drag to pull something heavy along

dragon an imaginary monster

dragonfly a large, brightly coloured insect

drain 1 a pipe for taking away water
2 to take away water by using pipes, etc.

drama a play

drank see **drink**

draw 1 to make a picture with a pen, pencil, etc. *Sean's picture was **drawn** perfectly.*
2 to end a game with the score tied

drawer a container that slides in and out of furniture, such as a table or desk

drawn see **draw**

dread great fear

dreadful very bad: *That was a **dreadful** mistake.*

dream to imagine things while you are asleep

drench to make someone wet all over

dress 1 a single piece of clothing that covers the whole body
2 to put clothes on

dresser a piece of furniture with drawers for keeping clothes

drew see **draw**

Dd

drift 1 snow or sand blown into a pile by the wind **2** to be carried along slowly on the water or by the wind **3** to pile up because of the wind: Snow **drifted** in to cover the sidewalk.

drill 1 a tool for making holes **2** to practice a lot

drink to swallow liquid: Eddie **drank** all the milk. Have you **drunk** your milk?

drip to let drops of liquid fall

drive to make a machine or animal move: You are **driving** very fast! I **drove** to town twice today! Matt has never **driven** a bus before.

driveway a short road into someone's property

drizzle very light rain

drop 1 a tiny amount of liquid **2** to let something fall

drove see **drive**

drum a hollow musical instrument you bang with a stick or your hand

drunk see **drink**

dry not damp or wet

dryer a machine for drying wet things

duck 1 a water bird with webbed feet and a flat beak

2 to bend down quickly to get out of the way

due 1 expected: The bus is **due** at 10 a.m. **2** caused by: The accident was **due** to thick fog.

dug see **dig**

dull 1 not interesting: a **dull** movie **2** not bright: **dull** colours **3** not sharp: a **dull** knife

dumb 1 not intelligent **2** see **mute**

dump 1 a place to put garbage **2** to leave something that you want to be rid of **3** to put something down carelessly

dungeon (DUN-jeun) a prison underneath a building

duplicate to make an exact copy of something

during while something else is going on: Bernie fell asleep **during** the game.

dusk the time of day just before it gets dark

Dd

dust 1 dry dirt, like fine powder
2 to clear away dust

duty what you ought to do

duvet (doo-VEY) a very thick blanket

dwarf a person who is very small

dwindle to slowly get smaller and smaller

dye to change the colour of something

dying see **die** and **dye**

dynamite something that is used to blow up things: *a stick of* **dynamite**

dyslexia (dyz-LEX-ya) a learning problem in which someone has difficulty recognizing, understanding and writing letters of the alphabet: *A person with* **dyslexia** *is said to be* **dyslexic**.

Dd

CcDd**Ee**FfGg

each every single person or thing in a group

eager filled with a strong wish to do something

eagle a large bird of prey with a hooked beak and strong claws

ear 1 the part of your body that you use to hear with, located on the side of your head
2 the group of seeds on a stalk of grain or corn

early 1 near the beginning: *early in the day*
2 sooner than expected: *Our teacher came back early.*
3 in the near future: *Do this at the earliest opportunity.*

earn to get something by working for it: *Mattie earns $500 a week. Lee certainly earned the praise he got.*

earnest serious and eager: *an earnest student*

earphones see **headphones**

earring an ornament worn on the ear

earth 1 soil in which plants grow
2 (also **Earth**) our planet

earthquake a time when the ground moves

earthworm a long, thin creature with no legs that crawls above, on top of and through the soil

ease freedom from work, difficulty or discomfort

easel a stand for holding a picture, chalkboard, etc.

east 1 a compass point
2 the direction where the sun rises
3 (often **the Far East**) the part of the world that includes Asia

70 **Ee**

Easter a very holy day in the Christian religion

eastern from the east or in the east

easy 1 able to be done or understood without much trouble: *an **easy** question* **2** comfortable: *an **easy** chair*

eat to take food into the body: *Has he **eaten** already? She **ate** the whole thing!*

eavesdrop to secretly listen to someone else's conversation

eccentric (ek-SEN-trik) likely to behave in a strange way

echo a sound you hear again because it bounces back to you

eclipse a time when the sun comes between the moon and the earth, so that the moon cannot be seen. The same word is used when the moon comes between the sun and the earth.

ecology the study of how all living things act on one another

economical (ek-a-NOM-i-kal) avoiding waste and expense

economics the study of how money is used

ecosystem a group of living things acting together in a particular environment

edge the part along the end or side of something

edible able to be eaten safely

edit 1 to correct and improve a piece of writing **2** to take out parts of a movie or a TV or radio show

editor 1 the person who prepares a piece of writing before it is printed **2** (often called **editor-in-chief**) the person in charge of a newspaper or magazine

education the teaching and learning of knowledge and ideas

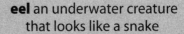

eel an underwater creature that looks like a snake

eerie strange and frightening

effect 1 a direct result: *Note the **effect** of sunlight on this cloth.* **2** working, under way (see **effective**): *The new rules are now in **effect**.* **3** belongings: *Hamish's personal **effects***

Ee

effective 1 working, under way (see **effect**): *The rules will become* **effective** *in May.* **2** producing a result you want to get: *Advertising is an* **effective** *way to improve sales.*

efficient (ee-FISH-ent) producing a result in the best way: *Bob's method of cleaning is more* **efficient** *than Jan's.*

effort a serious attempt to do something

egg an oval object with a shell, produced by birds, insects and reptiles

either one or the other of two people, things or ideas: *It's* **either** *right or wrong.*

eject to force out

elaborate very full of carefully worked-out detail

elastic a strip of material that can stretch in length and then return to its former size

elbow the bony part in the middle of your arm where it bends

election a time when people vote to choose who will be in charge

electric worked by electricity

electricity (ee-lek-TRI-si-tee) energy that moves along wires to produce the light, heat and power that make machines work

electronic activity controlled by devices, such as a computer: *We can now send mail to you* **electronically**.

elegant very special and proper in appearance

element 1 one of many parts that make up a whole thing: *Oxygen is one of the* **elements** *in our atmosphere.* **2** a preferred time and place for someone: *Baljit is in her* **element** *when we go to the library.*

elementary simple and basic

elementary school a school with the first grades that students attend while receiving their education

elephant a large, grey animal with tusks and a long nose called a **trunk**

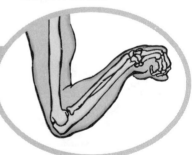

elm a tall hardwood tree, often with a shape like an umbrella

else besides: *Ask someone else.*

elude to escape or avoid in a clever way

email mail that is sent or received electronically

embarrass to make yourself or someone else feel foolish

emblem a thing or a picture that has special meaning: *The beaver and the maple leaf are emblems of Canada.*

emerald a green jewel

emergency something important that happens suddenly

emigrate to go to another country to live (see **immigrate**)

emotion a strong feeling like joy or sorrow

emotional showing that you are easily affected by feelings: *Maggie can be very emotional about dogs.*

emperor a male ruler of an empire

empire a group of countries ruled by one person. Sometimes **empire** is also used to refer to a large business group.

employ to pay someone to work for you: *If you employ someone, you are an employer. People you employ are called employees.*

empress a female ruler of an empire

empty with nothing in it or on it

enable 1 to make possible: *The sunny weather enabled us to finish on time.*
2 to make something ready to work: *The monitor is enabled now.*

enchant to charm or delight

encore the long applause at the end of a show that asks a performer to do more

encounter to meet or be faced with: *We encountered a lot of difficulty with our homework.*

encourage to make someone full of hope and desire so that she will do something

encyclopedia (en-sy-klo-PEE-dee-ah) a set of books or CDs full of information about a variety of topics

end 1 to be finished: *The show will end in thirty minutes.*
2 to finish: *The singer ended his concert.*

endangered at risk of harm or death: *Blue whales are an endangered species.*

Ee 73

endeavour, endeavor
(en-DEV-or) to try very
hard to do something: *I will*
endeavour *to swim forty
laps.*

ending the end of something

endurance the ability or
power to endure

endure 1 to suffer: *Pasha*
endured *a lot of pain when
he broke his back.*
2 to continue for a long
time: *The prime minister's
good work* ***endured*** *for
years.*

enemy one person or many
persons opposed to you so
strongly that they want to
hurt you

energetic full of the strength
and desire to do many
things

energy power or force

enforce to make people obey:
Police officers ***enforce*** *the
laws.*

engine a machine that makes
things move and work

engineer someone whose job
is to design and build
things

enjoy to like watching,
listening or doing
something

enlarge to make something
bigger

enormous very big

enough what is needed

enrol, enroll to enter your
name to become part of
something: *Wynona is*
enrolled *in ballet this fall.*

enrolment, enrollment
the list of people who are
part of something: *The*
enrolment *in grade two is
larger this year.*

enter 1 to come in or go in
2 to decide to take part in
a race or competition
3 to put into or record:
Enter *your name on the
top line.*
4 to tell a computer to go
ahead with something

entertain to make time pass
pleasantly

entertainment anything that
entertains people

enthusiasm
(en-THEW-zee-a-zum)
a very great interest

Ee

enthusiastic so interested in something that you spend much time on it

entire whole

entrance the way into a place

entry 1 a way into a place
2 the act of entering: *Their entry was not seen by the guard.*
3 someone or something in a competition

envelope a paper folder for a letter

environment the area around someone or something: *Fish live in a wet environment.*

envy a feeling of jealousy: *To have envy means you are envious.*

epidemic something, usually a disease, that happens to a lot of people in an area

episode an incident or event

episodic (e-pi-SAW-dic) happening once in a while

equal the same as something else in every way

equator an imaginary line around the centre of the Earth

equipment the things you need to do something

eraser a device used to take out marks or errors

erect standing or sitting upright

erode to wear away

erosion a wearing away because of the action of wind or water or overuse by people

err (air) to make a mistake

errand a short journey you take to do something or get something

escalator a set of stairs that move up or down

escape to get free

especially (es-PESH-a-lee) more than anything else: *I like vegetables, but I especially like carrots.*

essential very necessary

establish to set up or bring about: *The pioneers established a new method for building cabins.*

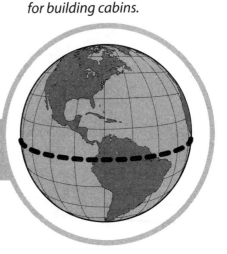

estate 1 an area of land with a lot of houses on it
2 an area of land that belongs to one person
3 a person's possessions left after death

estimate to make a guess about something

etc. an abbreviation for **et cetera,** which means **and others like this**

eternal forever

eternity a period of time with no end to it

ethnic about a group that has the same language and culture

euro, Euro money used by certain countries in Europe

evacuate (ee-VAK-yew-ate) to make a place empty: *The town was **evacuated** because of a flood.*

evaporate to disappear into the air

eve the night before a special day: *Christmas **Eve***

even 1 equal: *The score is **even**, two to two.*
2 level, parallel: *The top of the picture is **even** with the window now.*
3 calm, steady: *Brian has an **even** temper.*
4 still: *This one is **even** bigger!*
5 a number that two will go into: *Six is an **even** number.*

evening the time at the end of the day between sunset and darkness

event something that happens

eventually (ee-VEN-chew-a-lee) in the end

ever at any time: *Have you **ever** read this?*

evergreen any tree that stays green all year

every each, all: ***Every** week has seven days.*

everybody, everyone all persons

everyday ordinary, not special

everything all things

everywhere in all places

evidence something that gives a reason to believe: *The bones are* **evidence** *that bears were here.*

evil wicked and wrong

evolve to grow or develop slowly

ewe (you) an adult, female sheep

exact just right

exaggerate (ex-A-jer-ate) to make something seem more than it is

exam, examination a test

examine to look at something very carefully

example 1 anything that shows how something works or what it is like **2** a person or thing that is worth being imitated: *Percy's behaviour is a good* **example** *for everyone.*

excel to be very good at something

excellent very good

except apart from: *Everyone had cake* **except** *me!*

exceptional (ek-SEP-shun-al) very unusual

exchange to give something and get something in return

excite to arouse interest

excitement the feeling of being excited

exclaim to make a sudden sound because you are surprised or excited

exclamation mark a mark like this **!** at the end of a sentence to show strong feeling

exclude to keep someone or something out: *They were* **excluded** *from the game.*

excursion a special journey, like a field trip

excuse ① (ex-KEWS) an explanation of why something was done wrong: *My* **excuse** *is that I did not hear you!*

excuse ② (ex-KEWZ) to forgive: *We should* **excuse** *her because she is new on the job.*

execute 1 to do or perform something: *Lydia* **executed** *a perfect dive.* **2** to put someone to death

exercise 1 an activity that improves your health
2 work that you do to practice something you are learning
3 to perform this activity or work

exhausted tired out

exhibition a demonstration of something

exile someone who must live away from his or her own country

exist 1 to be real: *Do ghosts really exist?*
2 to live: *These monkeys exist only in west Africa.*

exit 1 the way out
2 to leave a place, an event or a computer program

expand to get bigger

expect to think something is likely to happen

expedition a journey made for a special purpose

expensive with a high price

experience 1 what you learn from things you see and do
2 something that has happened to you: *Losing our dog was a sad experience.*

experiment a test to find out if an idea works

expert someone who knows a lot about a topic

explain to make something clear so that others can understand it

explanation something said or written to help people understand something

explode to blow up with a loud noise

explore to look all around an area for the first time

explosion when something blows up with a loud bang

explosive anything that may explode

export to send goods to another country (see **import**)

expose to uncover or make open to public view and understanding

exposure the amount of light a camera lets in when a photograph is taken

express 1 to send something somewhere fast
2 to describe an idea or feeling with words

expression 1 a way of saying something
2 the look on someone's face

extreme 1 very great: *extreme* cold
2 the farthest away: *the extreme edge*

eye 1 (also called **eyeball**) the part of your body that you see with, between your forehead and your cheek
2 the hole in the end of a needle

extension a part that has been added to make something bigger

extinguish to put out a fire

extra more than needed

extraordinary very unusual

extravagant more than is really necessary

eyebrow the curved line of hair above each eye

eyelash one of the short hairs around the eye

eyelid the piece of skin that moves to cover the front of your eyeball

eyewitness a person who is present for an event and watches it happen

Ee

fable a short story that teaches a lesson

face 1 the front part of your head
2 a surface or side of something: *the face of a cliff*
3 to be turned toward something: *Our classroom faces the street.*
4 to deal with something or someone unpleasant: *You have to face that messy room sooner or later.*

facelift a procedure that changes the surface of something to make it look newer

facsimile (fak-SIM-i-lee)
1 see **fax**
2 an exact copy of something

fact something you know is real or true

factor anything that helps to make something happen: *Rain was a factor in the car accident.*

factory a place where people and machines make things

fad strong but brief excitement about something

fade to slowly become fainter in colour or in volume

fail 1 to try to do something but be unable to
2 to stop working: *Our printer failed in the middle of a job.*

failure someone or something that has failed

faint 1 not bright or clear: *a faint cry*
2 to pass out

fair 1 light in colour
2 right or just: *a fair trial*
3 a type of festival

fairly almost or quite: *I'm fairly sure we will arrive by noon.*

fairy a tiny being with magical powers

faith 1 belief in something
2 a religion: *the Christian faith*

faithful always ready to do what you have promised

fake an imitation of something: *She **faked** an illness to stay home from school.*

fall 1 autumn
2 to move downwards suddenly: *If I **fall**, will you catch me? Oh, oh! Tad has **fallen** off his bike! Marie **fell** yesterday.*

false 1 not real: ***false** teeth*
2 not true: *Rashid made a **false** statement to the police.*

familiar well known to you: *a **familiar** face*

famine a time when there is very little to eat

famous being very well known

fan 1 a device that moves air
2 someone who admires a person, hobby or sport very much: *Gina is a great hockey **fan**.*

fancy not plain or ordinary

fantasy something imagined, not real

far a long way

fare the money you pay for a ticket to travel

farewell goodbye

farm an area of land used to raise crops or animals for food: *The person who keeps a **farm** is a **farmer**.*

farther a greater distance (see **further**): *Pete lives **farther** from the park than Aisha.*

fashion 1 a way of dressing or behaving
2 to make something: *Marni **fashioned** a toy with pieces of paper.*

fast 1 swift or quick: *a **fast** car*
2 ahead of the correct time
3 strong and close: ***fast** friends*
4 to go without food

fasten to close something so it will not open: *Please **fasten** the snaps on my dress.*

fat 1 thick and rounded
2 the white, greasy part of meat

Ff

fatal causing a person or animal to die: *a fatal accident*

fate 1 the final state for a person or thing: *Everyone worried about the fate of the missing sailor.*
2 a power that decides what will happen: *Some people believe that fate rules our lives.*

father 1 a male parent
2 a male who establishes something: *Alexander Graham Bell is the father of telecommunications.*
3 a title for a priest

faucet (FAW-set) a device to control the flow of water (see **tap**)

fault 1 something wrong that spoils a person or thing
2 responsibility for a mistake: *It's my own fault I missed the bus.*

favour, favor something kind you do for someone

favourite, favorite liked the most

fawn a baby deer

fax an abbreviation for **facsimile**, a letter or image sent over telephone lines

fear 1 a worry that something bad will happen

2 to be afraid of someone, or afraid that something will happen

feast a special meal

feat something you do that is brave or difficult

feather one of many light, flat, fluffy parts that cover the skin of a bird

fed see **feed**

federal in government, made up of groups that agree to work together: *In Canada, the federal government meets in Ottawa.*

federation (fed-er-A-shun) groups that have united to do something together: *Canada is a federation of provinces and territories.*

fee a charge or payment

feeble weak

feed 1 to give food to a person or animal: *I fed the cat last night.*
2 to eat: *The pigs are feeding now.*

feel 1 to touch something to find out what it is like **2** to know something inside yourself: *I felt sad yesterday.*

feeler on the head of an insect, a wire-like growth used to sense things

feeling an emotion or sense that you have inside yourself: *a feeling of joy*

fell see **fall**

felt 1 see **feel 2** soft cloth made from wool or fur

female any living thing that can become a mother

feminine belonging to the female gender

feminist someone who strongly supports the rights of women

fence a kind of wall around a field or garden

fender metal covering over a wheel

fern a plant with feather-like leaves

ferry a boat that takes people across a body of water, such as a river or channel

fertile 1 able to grow a lot of healthy plants **2** able to have babies

festival a time when people gather to celebrate something

fetch to go get and bring back

fever a high body temperature that makes you feel ill

fibre, fiber long, narrow material similar to a thread

fibreglass material made from fine glass fibres woven together

fibre optics the means of sending and receiving information through thin, flexible wires

fiction a story that is made up: *Most novels are **fictional**.*

fiddle 1 (informal) a violin **2** (informal) to play a violin **3** to play with something in an idle way

fiddlehead a slender, curved fern that is good to eat

fidget to make short, quick movements when you feel unable to be still

Ff 83

field 1 an area where crops are grown
2 an area for playing games like soccer
3 an activity or topic: *Heidi's* **field** *is science.*

field trip a visit by a school class to some place to learn about it

fierce angry or frightening

fight to take part in a struggle, battle or war: *The two armies* **fought** *until dark.*

figure 1 a sign for a number: *1, 2 and 3, are* **figures***.*
2 the form or shape of something

figure skating an elegant and artful form of skating on ice

file 1 a collection of data stored in a computer
2 a folder for storing letters, documents, etc.
3 to put letters, documents, etc. in a folder
4 a long, narrow line of people
5 a tool used to make things smooth

fill to make something full

filly a young, female horse (see **colt** and **foal**)

film 1 a roll of thin plastic, used in cameras to take pictures

2 another word for **movie**
3 a thin covering you can see through: *There is a* **film** *of dust on the shelf.*

filter any device that changes something as it passes through: *First, you* **filter** *the liquid to take out the dirt.*

filthy very dirty

fin one of the thin, flat parts that stick out from a fish's body to help it swim

final the very last

finally at last

find to come across something because you have been looking for it

fine 1 very thin and delicate: **fine** *thread*
2 dry and sunny: **fine** *weather*
3 very good: *a* **fine** *effort*
4 money that is paid as a punishment: *a $5* **fine**

finger one of the five separate parts at the end of the hand

fingernail the hard surface at the end of each of your fingers

fingerprint the mark you make on something with the tip of a finger

finish to complete something

fir a tall tree with cones and short, flat, green needles

fire 1 the flame, heat and light that come from burning something
2 to dismiss from a job

fire alarm a device that makes noise to give warning of a fire

fire escape steps or a ladder to help you get out of a building

firefighter someone whose job it is to help control and put out fires

fireplace an open place at the bottom of a chimney where a fire can be lit

fireproof not able to burn

firewood wood that is made ready for burning

fireworks paper tubes filled with powder that send out loud bangs and coloured sparks and smoke

firm 1 solid or secure: *He climbed out of the water onto* ***firm*** *ground.*
2 a business: *Ramesh's mom works for a clothing* ***firm***.

first before all others

First Nations native peoples whose ancestors were living in Canada when the explorers came from Europe

fish 1 an animal with scales and fins that lives underwater
2 to try to catch fish

fist a hand with all the fingers pressed in toward the palm

fit 1 healthy
2 just right: ***fit*** *for a king*
3 to be the right size and shape: *Those pants should* ***fit*** *you.*

fitness when your body is healthy and strong: *Lois exercises because she believes in* ***fitness***.

fix 1 to mend: *Our car has been* ***fixed*** *now.*
2 to make secure: *The post is firmly* ***fixed*** *in the ground.*
3 a difficult situation: *Are we ever in a* ***fix*** *now!*

Ff

flag a square or rectangular cloth with a design that means something very special to certain groups of people

flair a special ability: *Janet has a flair for public speaking.*

flake a thin, light piece of something: *soap flakes*

flamboyant (flam-BOY-ant) bold and showy

flame fire that is shaped like a tongue

flannel soft cloth made from cotton or wool

flap 1 to move up and down like a bird's wings
2 an attached part that hangs over something: *a flap on an envelope*

flash to shine suddenly and brightly

flashlight a portable light powered by batteries

flat 1 level and smooth
2 in music, a note that is one halftone lower

flatter to praise someone in an exaggerated way

flavour, flavor how something tastes

flaw a weakness

flea a small, wingless insect

flee to run away

flesh the part of the body that covers your bones

flew see **fly**

flex to bend

flexible bends easily

flight 1 a journey through the air
2 an escape
3 a set of stairs

flinch to move back suddenly because you have been startled

fling to throw something very hard

flipper a broad, flat, hand-like limb on certain animals, such as seals

float to be carried on liquid or air

flock a group of birds or animals

flood a large amount of water that spreads across dry land

floor 1 the part of a building on which you walk
2 a storey in a building: *The Lux Building has fourteen floors.*

Ff

flop 1 to fall or sit down suddenly **2** (informal) a failure

floppy disk a small, coated disk a computer can use to store or retrieve information

florist a person whose job is to sell flowers and plants

flour a powder made from grain, used in making bread and pastry

flourish (FLER-ish) to grow or be well: *My plants are flourishing under your care.*

flow to move along like a river

flow chart a step-by-step diagram that shows how something happens

flower 1 a plant grown for its decoration **2** the coloured blossoms on a plant

flown see **fly**

flu see **influenza**

fluent able to express yourself very well: *Jean-Jacques is fluent in French and German.*

fluff soft, light stuff that comes off wool and feathers

fluid any liquid

fluke (informal) a bit of good luck that helps you

flung see **fling**

flute a musical wind instrument

flutter to move a little, like a flag in the wind

fly 1 a small insect with wings: *one fly; two flies* **2** to move through the air: *Have you ever flown to Winnipeg on a plane? I flew there last week.*

flyer a piece of advertising delivered to your home or handed to you in public

foal a young horse, either male or female

foam 1 a mass of bubbles **2** thick, soft rubber or plastic

focus to concentrate on

fog damp air that looks like smoke

foil 1 a very thin metal that bends like paper **2** to keep from being successful: *Edie turned on the lights and foiled the robbers.*

fold to lay part of something on top of another part: *Fold the towel before you put it away.*

Ff

folder a cover, usually made of stiff paper, used for presenting or storing your work

foliage leaves

folk people

follow to go after

font in printing, a design of letters of the alphabet

food anything that you eat to help you grow and have energy

fool someone who is very silly

foolish to be silly

foot the part of the body at the bottom of the leg: *one foot; two feet*

football a game played by two teams who try to move a ball past each other's goal line.

(**Soccer** is known as **football** everywhere except Canada and the United States.)

footprint the mark left by a foot

footsteps the sound your feet make as you walk

for 1 in place of: *I will go for you.*
2 in the amount of: *I have a bill for five dollars.*
3 the distance of: *I can see for a long way.*

4 toward: *Sammy made a move for the blue line.*
5 to find: *Everyone looked for Anna.*
6 in exchange of: *I'll trade you my other stick for that puck.*
7 to be given to: *The juice is for you.*

forbid to say that someone must not do something: *Elise was forbidden to go out.*

force 1 to make someone do something
2 a group of people, often with weapons, who join together to do something
3 power

forecast to say what you think is going to happen

forehead the part of the face above the eyebrows

foreign 1 someone or something from a country other than your own
2 unfamiliar

forest an area with many trees and other plants

forgave see **forgive**

forge 1 to make a copy of something and pretend it is the real one
2 a place where metal is heated and hammered into a shape

forgery a false copy of something

forget to fail to remember: I've **forgotten** my lunch money. Joe **forgot** his lunch.

forgive to pardon someone: I **forgave** you; have you **forgiven** me?

forgot, forgotten see **forget**

fork 1 a tool with thin, pointed parts to stick into something
2 the point where a road splits and goes in two directions

form 1 the shape of something
2 to make something or put something together: We **formed** a committee in our class.
3 a special piece of paper on which you write information

formal accepted by most people as correct and proper

format 1 the shape or design something has
2 to give something a shape or design

former something that existed before now: Matt's **former** home was in Vancouver.

formula a plan or method for doing something

fort a strong building, built for protection. A very large fort is a **fortress**.

fortunate lucky

fortune 1 a lot of money
2 luck

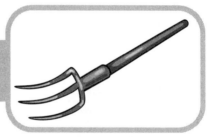

forward in the direction you are facing

fossil any part of a dead plant or animal that has been in the ground for millions of years and has become hard like stone

foster to encourage or promote development

foster child a child who is being raised and cared for by adults who are not his parents

Ff

foster home a family home where a foster child lives

foster parents parents who are raising and caring for a child who is not their own

fought see **fight**

foul dirty and bad

found see **find**

foundation the solid part under something, such as a building

fountain a device that shoots water into the air

fowl a bird

fox a wild animal that looks similar to a small dog, with pointed ears and a long, bushy tail

fraction 1 part of a number. $\frac{1}{2}$ and $\frac{1}{4}$ are fractions.
2 any very small part of something: *We have only found a* **fraction** *of the money.*

fragile easily broken

fragment a small piece that has broken off something

frame 1 the firm edge around a painting or picture
2 a structure made of parts joined together: *the* **frame** *of a bicycle*

free 1 with nothing to stop you: *I am* **free** *to go anywhere I please.*
2 not costing anything

freeze 1 to change from water into ice: *Our pond* **froze** *last night.*
2 to be very cold: *My hands feel* **frozen**!

frequent happening a lot

fresh 1 not tired or old: *The general brought in* **fresh** *troops.*
2 new or renewed: *a* **fresh** *start*
3 not preserved or put in cans or bottles: **fresh** *vegetables*

fret to keep worrying about something

friction the feeling of one thing resisting another when the two are rubbed together

friend someone you like who likes you too

fright sudden fear

frighten to make someone afraid

Ff

Frisbee a plastic toy, shaped like a dinner plate, that glides through the air when thrown properly

frog a small, jumping amphibian, usually green, with rubbery skin

from out of: *Benny took a cookie from the jar.*

front 1 the most important side or surface of something: *The main door is at the front of the building.* **2** a place or position before something: *at the front of the parade* **3** the leading edge of a weather system: *a storm front*

frost ice that looks like powder and covers things in very cold weather

frostbite an injury that can occur if a part of your body gets too cold

froth see **foam**

frown a look on your face that shows lines on the forehead, usually expressing sadness or anger

froze, frozen see **freeze**

fruit the part of a plant that you can eat

fry to cook in hot fat

fudge a type of soft, very sweet candy

fuel anything that is used to produce heat or energy

fugitive a person who is running from something

fulcrum a fixed point on which a lever balances

full no more room

function 1 the special purpose of something: *As captain, your function is to lead the team.* **2** a special ceremony: *The function was held in our dining hall.* **3** an operation stored in a computer's memory

fund money to be used for a special purpose

funeral the ceremony that is held when someone dies

fungi (FUNJ-eye) plural of **fungus**

Ff 91

fungus a very simple plant that can be as small as a grain of yeast or as large as a mushroom (see **fungi**). *Unlike other plants, fungi can live without light.*

funny 1 amusing: *a **funny** joke* **2** odd or strange: *a **funny** smell*

fur the soft covering, like hair, on some animals

furious (FEW-ree-us) very angry

furnace a large device, like a stove, used to heat a whole building

furniture items like beds, chairs and tables

further (also **furthermore**) in addition to (see **farther**): *I have nothing **further** to add.*

fuss to worry or be bothered about something

future the time that is still ahead

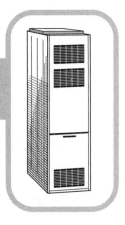

Ff

gadget any small, useful tool

gain to get something you did not have before: *We gain a lot of knowledge from books.*

gala a big party

galaxy a very large group of stars that are held together by gravity

gale a very strong wind: *The ship sank in a gale.*

gallery 1 a place where paintings are shown
2 the upstairs seats in a theatre or church

gallop the way a horse moves when it is running as fast as it can

gamble 1 to take a chance: *Wendy gambled that it would not rain and held a picnic.*
2 see **bet**

game something that you play by rules. Hockey and checkers are games.

gander a male goose

gang a group of people who do things together

gap a space between two things

garage 1 a building where vehicles, such as cars, are kept
2 a place that sells gasoline and fixes cars

garbage leftover things that have no use

garden a piece of ground where vegetables or flowers are grown

gargle to rinse your mouth and throat with liquid

garment a piece of clothing

gas anything, like air, that is neither solid nor liquid

gash a deep cut

Gg 93

gasoline, gas a liquid fuel that vehicles and machines need to run

gasp to breathe in noisily because you are surprised or sick

gate a type of door in a fence

gateway 1 the place where a gate is
2 something that links two computer networks

gather 1 to bring together: *The Smith family **gathered** for a birthday gala.*
2 to pick: ***gather** dandelions*

gave see **give**

gay 1 brightly coloured
2 a man who prefers to share love with another man

gaze to look at something for a long time in a dreamy sort of way

gear 1 the things needed to play a sport or do a job
2 parts of a machine that work together to create movement

geese more than one goose

gem a valuable stone, such as a diamond

gender one of the two groups, male and female, to which all people and animals belong

gene a unit in the cells of your body that you got from your parents and may someday pass to your children

general 1 an important officer in the army
2 belonging to most people or things: *a **general** opinion*

generate to make or cause: *Our team's win on Saturday **generated** a big fuss.*

generous always ready to give or share

Gentile, gentile 1 among Jews, someone who is not Jewish
2 among Mormons, someone who is not Mormon

gentle quiet and kind

gentleman a polite name for a man

genuine real: *Is that a **genuine** Gretzky card?*

geography the study of different parts of the world

geology (jee-AWL-o-jee) the study of the earth, especially rocks

geometry (jee-AWM-e-tree) the study of shapes and figures

gerbil a small animal like a mouse, with light brown fur and long legs

germ 1 another word for bacterium (see **bacteria**)
2 a tiny beginning: *the germ of an idea*

germinate to develop and grow: *When seeds germinate, a plant grows.*

gesture (JES-jer) to communicate with a body movement: *Cecile gestured to Ken to hurry.*

get 1 to become: *I have a fever. I must be getting sick.*
2 to bring something: *Please get me that ruler.*
3 to buy or be given something: *I'm getting a helmet for my birthday.*
4 to make ready: *I'm getting dinner now.*
5 to persuade: *Can you get her to read to us?*

getaway an escape from something

geyser a hot spring under the ground that shoots water and steam into the air

ghetto an area in a city where a minority group lives apart from the rest of the community

ghost the spirit of a dead person that some people believe comes to visit

giant 1 an unusually big person
2 very large

giddy silly

gift 1 a present
2 a special ability: *Lara has a gift for telling stories.*

gigabyte a unit of computer storage space equal to 1024 megabytes (see **megabyte**)

gigantic (jy-GAN-tik) very big

giggle to keep laughing in a silly way because you cannot stop

gill the opening on each side of a fish's head

Gg 95

gimmick a clever idea, usually intended to help sell something

ginger a brownish spice with a unique taste

giraffe a very tall African animal with a long neck

girl a female child

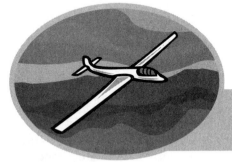

give to let someone have something: *Kaheesha gave me her hat. Lottie was given a prize. I'm giving you one more chance.*

glacier a great river of ice that moves slowly across the ground

glad happy

glamour, glamor unusual charm and interest: *Her glamour always makes people turn and listen.*

glance to look quickly

gland an organ in the body of humans and animals

glare 1 a very strong light
2 to look at someone in an angry way

glass 1 a container like a cup without handles
2 material that is hard, clear and breaks easily
3 anything made of glass, such as a mirror or window

glasses (often called **eyeglasses**) a pair of glass lenses worn in front of the eyes to correct vision

gleam to shine with a soft light

glide to slide very smoothly

glider an aircraft with very long, fixed wings and no engine

glimmer 1 a very weak light: *We can see just a glimmer through the trees.*
2 a small hint: *a glimmer of hope*

glimpse to see something for only a few seconds

glisten to shine with a bright light, especially from something wet, such as snow or water

glitch 1 a small problem
2 an unwanted action or bit of information in a computer program

global all over the world

globe a round ball with a map of Earth on it

gloomy 1 dark: *What a gloomy room!*

Gg

2 sad (see **glum**): *Come on! Don't look so* ***gloomy!***

glory great fame

glossary a list of special words and their meanings

glossy smooth and shiny

glove hand coverings with separate parts for the fingers

glow to shine with the warm light a fire has

glue a thick liquid used to make things stick together

glum not pleased or happy (see **gloomy**)

glutton someone who eats too much and becomes ill or uncomfortable

gnaw (naw) to keep biting at something hard: *See the dog* ***gnaw*** *that bone!*

go to move in any direction: *Stu's boat* ***goes*** *very fast. Shona has* ***gone*** *out to play. Are you* ***going*** *away now? You* ***went*** *yesterday too.*

goal 1 something that you want to do: *Teena's* ***goal*** *is to be a jockey.*
2 a point scored in a game such as hockey: *score a* ***goal***

goalie (also **goalkeeper**) the player who stands at the net in hockey or at the goalposts in soccer

goalpost one of the two posts where the ball must go between to earn a point

gobble 1 to eat very quickly
2 the sound made by a turkey

God in some religions, especially Christianity and Judaism, the being who is worshipped as the maker and ruler of the world

god (male) **goddess** (female)
1 a being that some people think has power over what nature does and what humans do
2 a word to describe someone who is looked upon as very important (see **guru 2**)

godchild in some religions, a child who has godparents who agree to give advice on feelings and beliefs (see **godparent**)

godparent a person who is usually not a child's natural parents but helps with the things that parents do (see **godchild**)

goes see **go**

goggles a special kind of eyeglasses, usually worn for safety

go-kart a small racing car

gold a valuable, shiny, yellow metal

golden coloured like gold

goldenrod a tall, narrow weed with yellow flowers

goldfinch a small, black and yellow bird

goldfish a small fish, usually orange, kept as a pet

golf a game played by using sticks called clubs to hit a ball across the ground

gone see **go**

good 1 something people like and praise: *Good* soup! **2** kind and true: *Good friend!* **3** well-behaved: *Good* dog!

goodbye a word said when you leave someone

goodness the quality of being good

goods things to buy and sell

goose a water bird with a long neck. It may be tame or wild. A well-known kind of goose is the **Canada goose**.

gopher a small, light brown, furry animal that lives in burrows

gorgeous very attractive

gorilla a very large African primate with no tail

gosling a young goose

gossip to talk a lot about other people, often in a mean or unfriendly way

got see **get**

goulash a kind of stew

govern to be in charge and decide what should be done

government the group of people who are in charge of a country: *In Canada, the government is elected by democratic vote.*

Governor General in Canada, the person who does the duties of the British queen or king

gown a very fancy dress, usually one that reaches the floor

GP see **Green Party 1** and **2**

grab to take suddenly without asking

grace 1 beauty in the way someone moves or stands **2** a prayer said at meals

graceful not heavy or clumsy

grade 1 a class in school: *Sarah is in grade two.* **2** a mark or score: *Tom got a high grade for his story.* **3** a short hill: *Walk up the grade to that house.*

gradual happening a little at a time: *a gradual change*

graffiti (gra-FEE-tee) drawings and writings on walls, etc. in public places

grain seeds that grow in plants like wheat. Used for food.

gram a small unit of measure: *1000 grams = 1 kilogram*

grand large, important or wonderful: *That was a grand parade.*

grandchild (also **grandson/ granddaughter**) the child of your son or daughter. Grandsons and granddaughters are **grandchildren**.

grandfather the father of your father or mother

grandmother the mother of your father or mother

granite a very hard kind of rock

granular (gran-YEW-lar) made up of very small grains or parts

grant to agree to give someone what she has asked for

grape a small, soft fruit that has green or purple skin

grapefruit a fruit that looks like a big orange but is yellow

Gg

99

graph a diagram that helps show how numbers and amounts are different from each other

graphics pictures and charts drawn by a person or computer that are used to make something easier to understand or more attractive

grasp to reach out and hold something tightly

grass any green or yellow plant with flat, narrow leaves (see **lawn**)

grasshopper an insect with very powerful hind legs so that it can jump a long way

grate 1 a container made of metal bars, usually used in a fireplace
2 to turn something into tiny pieces by rubbing it against a rough surface (see **graze**)
3 describes the kind of noise your fingernail can make if you scratch it along a blackboard

grateful thankful

grave 1 the burial place of a dead person
2 very serious: *a grave mistake*

gravel a mixture of sand and small stones

graveyard a place where dead persons are buried (see **cemetery**)

gravity the force that holds everyone onto earth

gravy a hot, brown liquid that is made from cooked meat

gray see **grey**

graze to hurt the skin by rubbing against something sharp or rough

grease 1 very thick oil
2 the fat that comes out of meat when it is cooked

great 1 large: *a great deal of money*
2 important: *a great man*
3 very good: *a great idea*

greed a wish for more than you really need

green 1 the colour of leaves and grass in early summer
2 not harmful to the environment

greenhouse a glass building where plants are grown

Green Party 1 a political party in Canada
2 in Canada, a member of this party

greet to welcome someone or say hello

grew see **grow**

grey a colour that is a mix of black and white

grief a feeling of great sadness

grill 1 to cook food on metal bars over heat
2 metal bars on which food is cooked: *You can **grill** hamburgers on a **grill**.*

grim 1 unfriendly and not pleased: *a **grim** look*
2 not pleasant: ***grim** weather*

grin a small smile

grind to crush into tiny bits

grip to hold tightly

grizzly bear (also called a **grizzly**) a large, brown bear, found in parts of North America and Russia

groan a low sound you make when you are in pain or trouble

groceries things, usually food, bought in a store

groom 1 a man on the day he gets married (see **bridegroom**)
2 a person who looks after horses
3 to make something look good by cleaning and brushing it

groove a long, narrow hollow: *The stick made a deep **groove** in the sand.*

grope to try to find something by feeling for it because you cannot see it

gross 1 the total amount: *The **gross** sales at the fair were over $500.*
2 (informal) very unattractive, disgusting

ground 1 the earth
2 a piece of land
3 see **grind**

groundhog a small, brown, furry animal with short legs, about the size of a cat

group a number of people or things

grow 1 to become bigger: *You've **grown** quickly.*
2 to plant something in the ground and care for it: *We **grew** carrots last year.*

growl a deep, angry sound that comes from the back of the throat: *Dogs **growl**.*

grown see **grow**

Gg 101

growth 1 the act of growing: *We studied population growth in grade two.* **2** anything that has grown: *a growth of weeds*

grub a tiny worm that will become an insect

grudge anger against someone that you hold inside yourself

grumble to keep on saying you are not pleased

grunt a sound someone makes as he picks up something heavy

guarantee (GAR-an-TEE) a promise

guard to watch over someone or something

guardian someone whose job it is to look after a child if the parents cannot

guerrilla a soldier who is not part of a country's regular armed force: *Guerrillas are* *known for making surprise attacks.*

guess to say what you think is the answer even if you do not know

guest someone who is visiting

guide 1 to show the way: *Let me guide you out of the parking lot.* **2** a person who takes people to places that are new to them

guilt the feeling you have when you think you have done something wrong

guilty having done wrong: *The cat is guilty of breaking that vase!*

guitar a stringed musical instrument

gulf water that fills a large bend in the land (see **bay**)

gulp to swallow very quickly, usually with noise

gum 1 (also **gums**) the pink part of the mouth where the teeth are attached **2** a candy that you chew but do not swallow

gun a weapon that shoots bullets or pellets

gurdwara in the Sikh religion, a temple or meeting place

gurgle the sound water makes when it runs out of a sink

guru 1 in the Hindu religion, one who teaches how to live wisely
2 a wise and important person

gush 1 to move like water rushing out of a tap
2 (informal) to talk a lot about things that are not important to others

gust a rush of wind

guy (informal) a male person

gymnasium, gym a place for physical exercises and games

gymnastics a sport in which people perform exercises

habit anything you do without thinking about it because you have done it so often

habitat the environment where a particular animal or plant is found

hacker someone who uses computer skills to get into another person's computer system

had see **have**

hail small pieces of ice that fall like rain

hair a soft covering that grows on the head and body of people and animals

haircut a trimming of the hair on someone's head

hairdresser a person whose job is to cut and style hair

half (also $\frac{1}{2}$) one of the two equal parts something can be divided into: *One half and one more half make two halves.*

hall 1 the part of a building that leads from one room to another
2 a very large room: *a school hall*
3 an important public building: *the Town Hall*

halt to stop

halter 1 the straps placed on an animal's head so that it can be controlled
2 a piece of clothing worn on the top half of the body

halve to divide or cut something into two equal parts (see **half**)

ham a kind of meat from a pig

hamburger 1 beef that has been ground into small bits
2 ground beef served on a bun or bread

hammer a tool used for hitting nails

hamper 1 a large basket with a lid: *picnic* **hamper***; laundry* **hamper**
2 to make it difficult for someone to do something: *The workers were* **hampered** *by the cold weather.*

hamster a small animal with smooth, brown fur

hand the body part at the lower end of the arm

handcuffs a pair of metal rings used for locking someone's wrists together

hand-held something that can be worked while held in the hands

handicap anything that makes it more difficult for you to do something

handkerchief a small, square cloth some people carry with them

handle 1 a part added to a tool so you can hold it more easily

2 to touch, feel, hold or use something with your hands

handlebars the bars for steering at the front of a vehicle such as a bicycle

handsome attractive

hang 1 to support something: *to* **hang** *your coat*

2 to grip or hold: **Hang** *on to my arm.*
3 to remain about: *A smell* **hung** *in the air.*
4 (informal) to spend much time: *She* **hangs out** *in the gym.*
5 (informal) to not give up: **Hang on!** *I'll be right there.*

hangar a shed for storing aircraft

happen 1 to take place: *This must not* **happen** *again.*
2 to do something by chance: *I just* **happened** *to see it!*

happily 1 with joy: *MaryPat sang **happily**.*
2 luckily: *The rope broke but, **happily**, no one was hurt.*

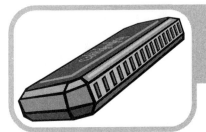

happiness the feeling of being very pleased

happy full of happiness

harbour, harbor a place in the water where boats can stay safely when they are not being used

hard 1 not soft: ***hard** candy*
2 difficult: ***hard** questions*
3 full of energy: *a **hard** worker*
4 not to be argued with: *the **hard** facts*

hard copy computer data that is printed on paper

hard disk (often called **hard drive**) the main disk inside a computer

harden to turn hard or solid

hardly not quite: *There is **hardly** enough water.*

hardware 1 any articles like tools or equipment
2 the equipment that makes up a computer system

hare a kind of rabbit

harm to hurt someone or something: *That sharp nail could be **harmful**.*

harmonica (also called **mouth organ**) a small musical instrument that you play by blowing through it

harmony 1 agreement and friendliness: *to live together in **harmony***
2 in music, the pleasant sound two or more notes can make when they are played at the same time

harness any arrangement of straps to attach things. A harness is put on a horse to attach it to a wagon.

harp a stringed musical instrument

harsh rough and mean

harvest the time when crops are ripe and are gathered

has see **have**

haste hurry

hat a cover for the head

hatch to break out of an egg

hatchet a small axe

hate to have a very strong feeling against someone or something

haul to pull or carry something from one place to another

haunted visited by ghosts: *Some people think that old house is haunted.*

have 1 to own: *She has a computer. We haven't got one yet.*
2 to contain: *The box had candy before, but it hasn't now!*
3 to enjoy or suffer: *We're having a good time. He had an accident.*
4 to make use of: *Please have patience.*
5 to give birth to: *Our cat had kittens.*

hawk a type of bird of prey

hay dried grass, used to feed animals

haze air that is hard to see through

head 1 the part of a person or animal that has the brain and face
2 the person in charge
3 apiece or each: *The tickets are $20 a head.*
4 something that is shaped like a human head: *a head of lettuce*
5 the top of something: *the head of a nail*

headache a pain in your head that goes on hurting

header (also **heading**) the title at the top of a page

headlight a light at the front of a vehicle

headline the large print on newspaper pages

headphones (also called **earphones** and **headset**) a pair of small speakers that can be mounted on the head and placed over the ears

headquarters the main office of an organization

heal to become well again: *The cut on Jason's arm is healed now.*

health the state of someone's body or mind

healthy 1 not ill or injured in any way: *Thank goodness our family is healthy.*
2 helpful to the body or mind: *Vegetables are part of a healthy diet.*

heap an untidy pile

hear to take in sounds through the ears

Hh

hearing impaired to have something wrong with the way you hear things

heart 1 the part of the body that pumps the blood

2 a red, curved symbol that stands for love or friendship

3 courage: *It takes **heart** to keep playing when your team is losing.*

4 one of the four suits in a deck of playing cards

heat 1 the hot feeling from things such as the sun or a flame

2 to make something hot

3 heat wave several days in a row of very hot weather

heaven 1 in some religions, the place where God is thought to be

2 a very happy place

heavy weighing a lot. Heavy things are hard to pick up and carry.

hectare a square piece of land that is one hundred metres long on each side

hedge a kind of wall made of plants or bushes

heel the back part of the foot

height how high something is: *The **height** of that mountain is 4000 metres.*

heir (air) a person, usually male, who will receive money, property or a title such as Sir, when the present holder dies

heiress a person, usually female, who will receive money, property or a title such as Lady, when the present holder dies

helicopter an aircraft with no wings, but blades on top and at the rear

hello what some people say as a greeting

helmet a strong covering that protects the head

help 1 to do something useful for someone else

2 to receive something useful from someone or something

helpless not able to look after yourself: *Most new babies are **helpless**.*

helpline a telephone service people can call to get help

hem the edge of a piece of clothing that is folded under

hemisphere one half of something: *Canada is in the northern **hemisphere** of the planet Earth.*

hen a female bird, such as a chicken

herb 1 a plant used to make a person healthy
2 a plant used in cooking to give the food a stronger taste

herd a group of animals gathered together

here in or to this place: *Would you come **here**, please?*

heritage things from the past that are important to a person, city, country, etc. *Our **heritage** trail passes by a pioneer's home.*

hermit a person who chooses to keep away from other people

hero a person, usually male, who does something very brave

heroine a person, usually female, who does something very brave

herself 1 she and no one else: *Lydia **herself** will be here.*
2 on her own: *Lydia will get here by **herself**.*

hesitate to wait a little because you are not sure

heterosexual a person who prefers to share love with someone from the opposite sex

hexagon a six-sided figure

hibernate to sleep for a long time during cold weather: *Bats, bears and turtles **hibernate**.*

hiccup to make a sudden, sharp sound in the throat

hide 1 to get into a place where you cannot be seen: *I'm **hiding** in the closet now. I **hid** behind a door last time.*
2 to put into a secret place: *The gold is **hidden** in a cave.*
3 skin taken from a dead animal (see **pelt**)

hieroglyphic (hi-row-GLIF-ik) a picture or symbol used instead of writing a letter, word or sentence

high a long way up

Hh

highlight 1 to draw special attention to: *The prime minister's speech will* **highlight** *changes in the law.* **2** the best or most important part: *Taylor's magic trick was the* **highlight** *of the show.*

high-rise a building with many storeys or floors

high-speed in computer systems, something that works very fast

high-strung very tense or nervous

highway an important public road

hijack to take control of something illegally

hilarious very funny

hill an area of ground that is higher than the area around it

himself 1 he and no one else **2** on his own

hind the back or rear: *That horse has a sore* **hind** *leg.*

hinder to make it difficult for someone to do something

Hinduism a religion that is very widespread in India. A believer in this religion is called a **Hindu**.

hinge a piece of metal with a pin in the centre that joins two objects and lets one or both of them swing back and forth

hint 1 a useful idea: *helpful* **hints** *in spelling* **2** to give information without exactly telling what is meant

hip the bony part of the body at the top of the leg

hippopotamus, hippo a very large African animal that lives in water and looks something like a pig

hire to give a job to

hiss to make a long sss sound

history the study of things that have happened in the past

hit 1 to strike something with force: *Mai-Ling* **hit** *the nail with a hammer.* **2** something very popular: *a* **hit** *song*

hitch to tie or fasten: *Let's* **hitch** *your wagon to mine.*

hitchhike to travel on the roads by asking for free rides

hive 1 (also called **nest**) the home of insects such as bees

2 a large, red spot on the skin that is very itchy

hoarse sounding rough and deep

hobby something interesting that people like to do in their spare time

hockey a game played on ice or on a field between two teams that carry sticks to hit a puck or ball into a net

hoe a tool for digging in the ground

hog 1 a large, male pig
2 not to share: *Don't **hog** all the pencils!*

hold 1 to have something in your hands
2 a place inside a ship where cargo is kept

holdup 1 a robbery
2 something that interrupts the flow of things

hole a gap or opening in something

holiday time off from school or work

hollow 1 with an empty space inside: *a **hollow** log*
2 a kind of hole

holly a tree with shiny, prickly leaves and red berries

hologram a laser light image that hangs in the air

holy in religion, something or someone held in special regard (see **sacred**)

home the place where you live

home care when someone who is sick is looked after at home instead of a hospital

homeless without a home

home page the opening page of an Internet web site

home run in baseball, a hit that allows the batter to go around all the bases

homesick the sad feeling you get if you want to be at home when you are somewhere else

homework schoolwork you have to do at home

homosexual a person who prefers to share love with someone of the same sex

honest not stealing, cheating or telling lies: *an **honest** person*

honey the sweet liquid made by bees

honour, honor great respect

hood a covering of material for the head and neck

hoof the hard part around the feet of animals such as horses or cows

hook a piece of wire that is sharp and bent at one end, used to catch something

hoop a large ring

hoot the sound an owl makes

hop a small jump

hope to wish that something specific will happen

hopeless 1 a situation that has no hope
2 to be very poor at doing something

hopscotch a game where players throw stones or discs into squares drawn on the ground and then hop in the empty squares

horizon a line where the sky and the earth or sea seem to meet

horizontal 1 flat and level
2 a straight line across something

horn 1 a kind of pointed bone on the head of some animals

2 a brass wind instrument

hornet a stinging insect, somewhat larger than a bee

horoscope an analysis of the stars that some people believe will tell what is going to happen in the future

horrible very unpleasant and often frightening

horrid very unpleasant and often frightening

horror very great fear

horse a four-footed animal that is often ridden or used to pull things

horsepower a way of measuring power

Hh

hose a long, plastic or rubber tube that carries water

hospital a place where ill or injured people are cared for

host 1 a person, usually male, who entertains guests
2 an entertainer who welcomes people to his or her show
3 a very large amount: *a host of small birds*
4 the main computer in a network of computers

hostage someone who is kidnapped and held for a ransom

hostess a person, usually female, who entertains guests

hotel a place where people pay to have meals or a place to stay for a time

hound 1 a dog used for hunting
2 to bother someone

hour a measure of time lasting sixty minutes

house a building where people, usually families, live

household all the people who live in a single house

House of Commons in Canada, the place where elected members of the government meet to discuss, debate and pass laws

hover to stay in one place in the air

hovercraft an aircraft that can travel on or just above the surface of water

how in what way: *How do you cook that?*

howl a long noise like a cry

hub the centre

huddle to keep close to others in a group

hue colour

huff annoyed

hug to put your arms around someone to show affection

huge very big

hum a low noise that keeps on going

human any child, woman or man

humble not proud

humid very damp and hot

hummingbird a small bird with a long beak and wings that move very rapidly

humorous funny

hunch a feeling you have that something is going to happen

hung see **hang**

hunger a wish for food

hunt 1 to look for something **2** to go after wild animals, usually to kill them

hurl to throw something as far as possible

hurricane a storm with very strong winds

hurry 1 to move or to do something quickly **2 in a hurry** to be impatient

hurt to make a person or animal feel pain

husband a man married to someone

hush when everything suddenly becomes quiet

husky 1 very heavily built and strong: *a husky fellow*

2 a large, strong dog, usually found in northern Canada and often used for pulling sleds

hustle 1 to hurry **2** to cheat someone

hydrant (also **fire hydrant**) an upright pipe where a hose can be attached

hydro electricity

hymn a song of praise

hypertext a system of storing computer files, etc. that allows quick links to other data

hyphen (HY-fen) a mark like this **-** , used in writing to join words or parts of words

GgHh Ii JjKk

I a word you use instead of your own name: *I am tired now.*

ice water in its solid state

Ice Age a time very long ago, when Canada was covered by ice and no people were living here

iceberg a very large chunk of ice floating in the ocean

ice cap a covering of ice over an area

ice cream a sweet, frozen dessert, usually made with cream

ice hockey what some people outside Canada call hockey

ice jam the blocking of a river with ice

icicle a thin piece of ice hanging down from a roof, etc.

icing a sweet mixture on top of cakes, etc.

ID 1 (eye-DEE) an abbreviation for **identification**: *I'll have to show them my ID so they will know who I am.*

2 (informal) to identify someone: *Vlad ID'd the man who stole our car.*

I'd an abbreviation for **I would** and **I had**: *If I could, I'd (I would) help you. I'd (I had) a cold yesterday.*

idea a plan or thought you develop yourself

ideal just what you or someone else wants

identical exactly the same: *identical twins*

identification (eye-DENT-i-fi-KAY-shun) something that shows who someone is

identify to make clear what a person or thing is: *Merika identified the ring as hers.*

idle doing nothing

Ii 115

idol 1 a person greatly admired **2** an object of worship

if 1 in case, in the event that: *If you are going to come, call first.* **2** whether: *We don't know if Jodie is coming.* **3** when: *If you add 2 and 2, you get 4.*

igloo a round house made of snow

ignite to catch or set on fire

ignorant knowing nothing or very little

ignore to take no notice

ill not well, sick

illegal against the law: *To steal is to act illegally.*

illness sickness: *Chicken pox is an illness.*

illuminate (i-LEW-min-ate) to light up

illusion a false belief or a false appearance: *That magician's trick is really an illusion.*

illustrate to make clear by examples or pictures: *If you illustrate the lesson with a film, everybody will come.*

illustration anything that explains or demonstrates

image 1 a picture or other likeness of a person or thing **2** the way you think you look to others

imaginary not real

imagination the ability to make up pictures, stories and ideas in your mind

imagine to develop in your mind a sense of someone or something you cannot see

imaging a way of making pictures of something: *With the new software, we can do imaging of flowers.*

imitate to copy another's behaviour, speech, etc.

imitation a copy, not real: *imitation flowers*

immediately right away

immense very big

immersion completely involved in something: *In French immersion we speak only French.*

immigrate (see **emigrate**)

immune protected or safe, usually from disease

immunize to make someone safe from disease: *I have been **immunized** against measles.*

impact one thing having an effect on another: *The Internet has a big **impact** on how we live.*

impair to lessen the abilities of someone or something

impartial (im-PAR-shal) not favouring one side or another

impatient unable to wait

import to bring in goods from another country (see **export**)

important 1 having great value or meaning: *an **important** part in the play* **2** having great power or influence: *an **important** person*

impossible not able to be done

impress to make people think you are very good at something

impression 1 an idea or thought you have about something: *My **impression** is that everybody likes her.* **2** a mark or shape made by pressing on something: *Lara's heavy boots made deep **impressions** in the rug.*

impressive something so wonderful you remember it for a long time

imprison to put in jail

improve 1 to become better: *David's spelling has really **improved**!* **2** to make something better: *A washing will **improve** the look of your car.*

in 1 into: *Please come **in** here.* **2** at home, indoors: *Trevor stayed **in** because he had a cold.* **3** inside: *All the toys are **in** the box.*

incense ① (IN-sens) something that gives off a sweet smell when it is burned

incense ② (in-SENS) to make very angry: *What her sister said **incensed** Moira.*

include to make something or someone part of a group

income the money a person earns. The money a person must give the government out of income earned is **income tax**.

incorrect wrong

increase 1 to make bigger: *We are going to **increase** the size of the room.* **2** to become bigger: *The rain **increased** the number of puddles on the road.*

indeed really: *very wet **indeed***

independent not needing the help or control of others

index a list at the back of a book that tells on what page to find something

Indian 1 a person from India **2** a name that was once used to describe First Nations people in North America

indigenous (in-DI-jen-us) **1** something that is typical of a region or country: *Beavers and birch trees are **indigenous** to Canada.* **2 indigenous peoples** people who are already living in a region or country when outsiders come in (see **aboriginal**)

indignant to be angry over something you feel is unfair

indoors inside a building

industrious (in-DUS-tree-us) very hard working

industry work done in factories, etc.

inevitable going to happen for sure

infant a baby or very young child

infection (in-FEK-shun) a type of illness caused by bacteria

infectious (in-FEK-shus) likely to spread: *an **infectious** disease*

inflate to blow up to a larger size: ***inflate** a balloon*

inflation a time when the price of things goes up very fast

influence 1 the kind of power that helps to make things happen a certain way: *Our principal used her **influence***

to get the mayor to come here.
2 to use the power described in **1**: *The mayor's decision was **influenced** by our principal.*

influenza (in-flew-EN-zah) (often called **the flu**) an illness that gives you a fever and causes your body to ache

inform to tell about

informal 1 not requiring any special clothing or special behaviour: *The minister held an **informal** gathering.*
2 not official: *an **informal** statement*

information words or images that tell about something

infuriate to make very angry

ingenious clever at thinking up new ways to do things

inhabit to live in a place

inhale to breathe into the lungs

inhaler a device used for taking medicine into the lungs

inherit to receive something from your parents or ancestors

initial (in-I-shal) **1** the first letters of names, titles, etc. *Jennifer Dexel's **initials** are J.D.*
2 the first: *The **initial** step is always the hardest.*

inject to push something into something else. An **injection** of medicine is sometimes pushed into your body through a hollow needle.

injure to cause harm. The harm that is caused is an **injury**.

ink the coloured liquid in a pen

ink jet an abbreviation for **ink jet printer,** a type of printer, run from a computer, that makes letters by pushing ink through tiny holes

inland away from the shore

in-line skates roller skates with three or four wheels in a single line on the bottom of each boot

inn a kind of small hotel

inning in some sports, the time when a team has its turn

Ii

innocent not having done anything wrong   .

input 1 information that is added
2 the act of putting in information

inquiry an examination of something to find out what happened

inquisitive (in-KWIZ-i-tiv) curious

insect a small creature with a body in three sections, three pairs of legs, and sometimes wings

insecticide (in-SEK-ti-side) a poison used to kill insects

insert ① (in-SERT) to put something into something else: *to insert a key into a lock*

insert ② (IN-sert) something added to something else: *an insert in the newspaper*

inside in something

insist to be very firm in saying or doing something: *Calvin insisted the team needed a new coach.*

insolent (IN-so-lent) to be rude

inspect to look very carefully at people or things

inspector 1 a person whose job it is to inspect something
2 an important person on some police forces

inspire to create a feeling that a difficult thing can be done: *The town was inspired by the mayor's speech.*

install to add something that will be used: *Myra installed new software today.*

installation something that is put together for use: *That installation controls our security system.*

instalment 1 an amount of money paid each week or month
2 a part of a story that is told in parts

instalment plan a system that allows you to pay for something over a period of time

instant, instantly very quick, quickly: *Polly was ready in an instant.*

instead in place of someone or something

instinct the sense that makes people or animals do things: *A spider's* **instinct** *tells it to spin webs.*

institute (IN-sti-toot)
1 a special organization: *Bev teaches at the* **Institute** *of Child Study*
2 to set up or start something: *to* **institute** *a new law*

instruction teaching

instructor a teacher

instrument 1 a tool used for doing something. Hammers, computers and shovels are all instruments.
2 something used to play music

insulin medicine used to help control diabetes

insult something rude that hurts a person's feelings

integrate to mix different parts together into one

intelligent able to learn and understand things easily

intend to mean to do something. A person's plan to do something is his or her **intention**.

intense very strong: *intense heat*

interact to work together with someone else

interactive 1 communication or cooperation among people who influence one another
2 a system that allows a computer and a user to work together

intercom a loudspeaker system, used for talking from one room to another

interest 1 the feeling you have that makes you want to know about something
2 extra money paid when paying back money that was borrowed

interface when two or more parts of a computer work together

interfere to become involved in something that has nothing to do with you: *Please do not* **interfere** *in this private conversation!*

intermission in a sports event, concert, play, etc., a period of time when both the audience and the players stop to relax

intern a person who is being supervised while trying out the things he has learned in school. This period of time is an **internship**.

Ii

internal inside. Your stomach and liver are internal organs.

international more than one country

Internet a linking of computer networks all over the world

interrupt to interfere when someone is talking or doing something

interval 1 a period of time between two events 2 in a theatre, a period between two acts of a play

intervene to interfere in an action before what is going on becomes more serious

interview to ask someone several questions about what he thinks

intestines inside your body, the parts below the stomach

introduce to make someone acquainted to other people, or to new ideas or things: We *introduced* Grandpa to the Internet very slowly.

Inuit aboriginal people who live in the far north of Canada and Greenland

Inukshuk a marker made of rocks that Inuit people build

invade to push into another country or place to fight or do harm

invalid ① (IN-va-lid) a person who needs care because of illness or injury

invalid ② (in-VA-lid) not true or correct: an *invalid* entry

invent to think of and make a new machine, device or technique. The person who does this is an **inventor**.

investigate to try to find out as much as possible about something

invisible unable to be seen

invitation a polite request to attend something

invite to ask someone politely to attend something

ion (EYE-on) an atom that has an electric charge

iron 1 a strong, heavy metal 2 a small electric appliance for smoothing out clothing

irritable easily upset: *Francis is* **irritable** *because he has a cold.*

irritate to annoy or anger

Islam the religion of Muslims, based on the teachings of Muhammad and the Koran

island, isle (EYE-land, eyl) a piece of land smaller than a continent in an ocean, lake or other body of water

issue something to be discussed and thought about

it a word used in place of an animal or thing just mentioned: *The moose lay down and soon it was asleep.*

italic a kind of printing like *this*

itch a feeling on your skin that makes you want to scratch

item any one thing in a list or group of things

it's an abbreviation for **it is**

its its own: *The fox cut its paw.*

itself 1 the thing or animal and nothing else: *The radio turns itself off.*
2 a word used to refer to what you are talking about: *The house itself is really pretty small.*
3 normal or usual: *Our cat is not itself today.*

ivory 1 a yellowish-white colour
2 the hard material that makes up an elephant's tusks

ivy a vine with many leaves

Ii

HhIi **Jj** KkLl

jab to poke at something with your finger, fist or the end of a stick

jack 1 a device for lifting things like cars
2 a socket for connecting telephones and computers

jacket a short coat

jagged rough along the edge

jail a prison

jam 1 a sweet, thick food made of fruit, usually spread on bread: *raspberry jam*
2 a lot of people or vehicles crowded together: *a traffic jam*
3 to become stuck: *I can't move the window; it's jammed.*

4 to hurt by being squeezed: *My finger got jammed in the door.*

jar a glass container

jaw the lower part of the face

jaywalk to walk into a street unsafely

jealous unhappy because someone seems to have more or seems to do better. The feeling is called **jealousy**.

jelly similar to jam, but usually thinner (see **jam 1**)

jerk 1 to pull very suddenly
2 (informal) a person you feel is unpleasant

jet 1 a liquid or gas bursting out of a small opening
2 a kind of aircraft

Jew someone whose religion is Judaism

jewel a valuable and beautiful stone, such as a diamond

jewellery, jewelry items like necklaces and rings worn for decoration

jigsaw puzzle a set of small pieces of cardboard, wood or plastic that fit together to make a picture

jingle the sound tiny bells make

jinx a person or thing believed to cause bad luck

job work that you do

jockey a person whose job it is to ride horses in a race

jog to run slowly

join 1 to put two or more things together into a unit: *Join these twenty links and make a chain.*
2 to become part of something: *A new student joined our class.*

joint 1 the place where two parts link together. Your ankles are the joints where your feet are joined to your legs.
2 shared: *That mural was a joint effort by our class.*

joke something said or done to make you laugh

jolly very happy

jolt a sudden bump or surprise

journey the travel you do to get from one place to another

joy great happiness

joystick (also called **paddle**) a hand control on a video game

Judaism the religion of the Jews based on the Bible and the Talmud

judge 1 to decide whether something is good or bad, right or wrong, fair or unfair
2 someone who judges

juggler an entertainer who does throwing and catching tricks

juice the liquid in fruits and vegetables

jump to push your body off the ground with your legs

junction a place where wires, roads or railway lines meet

jungle a forest in a hot and humid country

junior younger

Jj

junk 1 things that people do not want and throw away

2 a kind of boat, usually found in China

junk food food that is not considered very healthy or good for you

junk mail unwanted mail such as flyers, announcements, etc.

just 1 fair: *a just decision*
2 exactly: *It's just what I need.*
3 only: *Don't be afraid! It's just a little snake.*
4 a short while ago: *The accident just happened.*

K an abbreviation for **kilobyte**

kangaroo a jumping, marsupial animal from Australia

karaoke a kind of entertainment in which people from the audience sing along with pre-recorded music

karate a form of unarmed combat from Japan

kayak a small, covered boat that is paddled by one person

keen very interested in something: *a* **keen** *hockey fan*

keep 1 to have something as your own: *He said I could* **keep** *the book.*
2 to make something stay as it is: *Our freezer* **keeps** *the ice cubes from melting.*
3 to continue: *Mara* **kept** *on singing.*

keg a small barrel

kennel a place where dogs are kept

kept see **keep**

kernel 1 the inside of a nut
2 one of the seeds in grain or an ear of corn

kettle a metal container for boiling and then pouring out liquid

key 1 a piece of metal that is shaped so it fits into and opens a lock
2 a small lever you press with your finger to make something happen, as in a piano key

keyboard 1 a set of keys arranged in rows
2 to input data into a computer

keypad a small keyboard, usually with numbers and not letters

keyword a word with a special meaning

khaki (KAR-kee or KAK-ee)
1 a strong, light brown, cotton cloth
2 a light brown colour

kibbutz a communal farm, usually in Israel

kick 1 to hit something with your foot
2 (informal) to enjoy: *I get a kick out of recess!*

kickoff 1 to kick a ball in order to start a football or soccer game
2 the start of anything

kid 1 to tease: *Are you kidding me?*
2 a young goat

kidnap to take someone away by force

kill to make someone or something die

kilobyte a computer term for 1024 bits or bytes of information

kilogram a measure of mass: *1 kilogram = 1000 grams*

kilometre, kilometer (ki-LOW-mee-ter) a measure of distance: *1 kilometre = 1000 metres*

kilowatt a measure of electric power: *1 kilowatt = 1000 watts*

kilt a pleated skirt worn by both men and women

kimono a long, loose gown with a belt or sash, worn when you relax

kin a person's family and relatives

kind 1 sort or type: *a fast-drying kind of paint*
2 ready to help others: *a kind person*

kindergarten in a school, a class for very young children

kindling small pieces of wood, used to start a fire

king the male ruler of a country

kingdom a country or region ruled by a king or queen

kingfisher a brightly coloured bird that lives near water and eats fish

king-size much larger than the usual size

kiss to touch someone with your lips because you care for them

kitchen a room where food is prepared for eating

kite cloth or paper stretched over a light frame and flown in the wind

kitten a young cat

knapsack see **backpack**

knee (NEE) (In English, for words beginning with "kn" the "k" is not pronounced) the joint in the middle of the leg that bends

kneel to rest on your knees

knew see **know**

knife a tool with a handle and a long, sharp edge for cutting. The plural is **knives**.

knit to use needles and yarn to make items of clothing

knob the round handle on a door or drawer

knock 1 to tap on a door **2** to bump into something and push it over

knot the place where two pieces of rope, etc. are tied together

know 1 to have something in your mind that you have learned: *We knew the words, but now we know the music too!* **2** to have met someone before: *I have known Mae-Ling for six months.*

knowledge information that you know and understand

known see **know**

knuckle the joint between your palm and your fingers

Koran a sacred book in the religion of Islam

kosher in Judaism, food, etc. prepared a certain way

krill a tiny ocean creature, somewhat like a shrimp

Kk

label 1 a piece of cloth or sticky paper put on something to give information
2 to give something a name

laboratory (la-BOR-a tor-ee or LA-bra-tor-ee) a room or building where scientific work is done. The abbreviation is **lab**.

labour, labor 1 the work that people do: *You will be paid for your labour.*
2 to work: *The women laboured in the field all day.*

lace 1 thin material, used for decorating
2 string used to tie shoes

lack to be without something

lady a name sometimes used instead of woman

ladybug a small, round, orange insect with black spots

lag to be behind because you are going too slowly

lagoon a large pond, partially separated from other bodies of water

laid see **lay**

lain see **lie**

lake a body of water, much larger than a pond or pool

lamb a very young sheep

lame unable to walk easily because of a sore or injury

laminate to cover with a thin layer of something, usually clear plastic

lamp a device that gives light

LAN an abbreviation for **local area network**, a system in which members of a group are able to communicate through their computers

land 1 all the dry parts of Earth's surface

2 a country: *Canada, our land!*
3 to arrive at a place by ship or airplane: *Our plane landed an hour ago.*

landfill (also **landfill site**) an area where garbage is dumped under supervision

landing a platform in a set of stairs

landlady a woman who rents rooms or apartments in a building she owns. A man who does this is called a **landlord**.

landlord see **landlady**

landmark something well-known and easily seen that guides travellers

land mine a bomb hidden on or under the ground

landscape a wide view of the land around you: *You can see the landscape from that tower.*

lane 1 a narrow road or street
2 a driveway into a farm
3 one of the sections of a road where vehicles can drive

language words spoken or written by people: *English, Urdu and Spanish are different languages.*

lap 1 the part from the waist to the knees when you sit down
2 one time around a racetrack
3 to drink as a dog does, using the tongue

laptop a portable computer that can be held on your lap

large big

larva among insects, the worm-like stage between the egg and the cocoon

laser a system that turns energy into a strong beam of light

lash 1 to tie something down: *We lashed the trunk to the roof of our car.*
2 to hit very hard

lasso (la-SOO) a rope with a loop at the end that can be pulled tightly around something

Ll

last 1 after all the others: *Our team came in **last,** but we had such fun!* **2** to continue: *The movie seemed to **last** forever.*

latch a fastener on a door or gate

late 1 after the expected time: *The subway was ten minutes **late.*** **2** toward the end: *By **late** afternoon it began to rain.* **3** newest: *the **latest** style of dress* **4** no longer alive: *the **late** Mr. X*

later after a time

lather any foam or froth

latitude (LA-ti-tewd) an imaginary line around the Earth. Lines of latitude are above and below the equator. (see **longitude**)

Latter-day Saint(s) see **Mormon**

laugh the sound you make when something is funny

laughter the sound of laughing

launch to send a ship into space or a boat into the water

laundromat a business where you can wash and dry clothes

laundry 1 clothes that need to be washed **2** a business that will wash your clothes for you

law a rule or set of rules in a country or a community that everyone must obey

lawn land that is covered with grass, usually around a house

lawyer a person whose job it is to explain laws

lay 1 to put something down: ***Lay** the book on the desk, please.* **2** to prepare or arrange: *Cal **laid** out all the pens and pencils.* **3** to produce an egg: *The hen **laid** an egg.* **4** see **lie**

layer a single thickness over something: *There is a **layer** of dust on the windowsill.*

lead ① (rhymes with bed) a soft, heavy, grey metal

lead ② (rhymes with seed) **1** to go in front so that others will follow: *Here they come, with Bernie **leading** the way. He **led** the way yesterday too.* **2** a chain or rope for controlling an animal like a dog or horse

leader a person or animal that leads

leadership the ability to make others follow

leading chief or most important: *She is the leading expert in her field.*

leaf one of the flat parts, usually green, that grow on plants

league (leeg) a group of teams that play against one another

leak to have a hole or crack that liquid or gas can get through

lean 1 to bend your body toward something
2 to rest against something
3 not fat: *lean meat*

leap to jump

leap year a year with 366 days. The extra day is February 29. Every fourth year is a leap year.

learn 1 to find out about something: *We learned a lot about pumpkins at the farm.*
2 to find out how to do something: *Learning to read is most important.*

leash a lead, usually for a dog

least 1 less than all others: *least expensive bike*
2 the smallest amount

leather a strong material made from animal skins

leave 1 to go from a person or place: *I have to leave the party now.*
2 to let something stay where it is: *Fran left her books at home.*

leaves more than one leaf

led see **lead** ② 1

ledge a narrow platform, like a shelf

left 1 on the side that is west when you face north
2 see **leave**

left-handed preferring to use your left hand to do things such as write or throw

leg 1 the part of the body between the hip and the foot
2 one of the things that supports a table or chair
3 part of a journey: *The first leg of our trip is from Moose Jaw to Regina.*

legal according to what is allowed by the law

Ll 133

legend a story from long ago that may or may not be true

legislature (LEJ-is-lay-cher)
1 an organization like our parliament that makes laws
2 the building or the room where people in government meet

leisure time when you can do what you want because you do not have to work

lemon 1 a pale yellow, oval fruit with a sour taste
2 a pale yellow colour

lemonade a drink made with lemons, water and sugar

lend to let someone have something of yours (see **loan**): *Sully lent his bike to Hassan.*

length 1 how long something is
2 a piece of rope or chain

lengthen 1 to make something longer
2 to get longer

lens 1 a curved piece of glass or plastic that directs light: *Mae changed the lens in her camera.*
2 the part of your eye that directs light

leopard a large, wild, African or Asian cat with yellow fur and black spots

leotard (LEE-a-tard) a piece of clothing like a tight stocking that goes up to your waist

lesbian a woman who prefers to share love with another woman

less 1 not as much
2 subtract: *Six less four is two.*

lessen to make or become less

lesson 1 the time when someone is teaching you
2 something that you learn

let to allow

lethal able to cause death

let's an abbreviation for **let us**

letter 1 one of the symbols in the alphabet, such as w, x, y
2 a written message sent to someone

lettuce a green-leafed vegetable, usually eaten in salads

level flat and smooth

lever (LEE-ver) a bar that is pulled down or pushed up to move something or to make machinery start working

liable responsible for

liar a person who does not tell the truth

Lib. see **Liberal 1** and **2**

liberal 1 generous or free in giving: *Our teacher is **liberal** with her compliments.*
2 a person who accepts opposite and different ideas easily

Liberal 1 a political party in Canada
2 in Canada, a member of this party

liberate to set free

liberty freedom

library a place where books, computers and other things are kept for people to use for pleasure or to find out information

librarian a person whose job it is to be in charge of a library

lice see **louse**

licence, license (LY-sens) a certificate that says you can do, own or use something: *a driver's **licence***

lick to move your tongue over something

lid the top or cover of a can or pot

lie 1 to rest with the body flat, as it is in bed (past tense is **lay**): *I'll **lie** down now and stay **lying** here for an hour or so. The cat has **lain** here all day.*
2 to say something untrue: *I can't believe she **lied** about that!*
3 something untrue: *He told a **lie**, but he didn't fool me.*

life the time between birth and death. The plural is **lives**.

lifeboat a boat that is used at sea to save lives

life preserver (also called **life jacket**) a device that helps bodies float in water

lift to move something upwards

Ll 135

light 1 the power that makes things able to be seen. Light comes from the sun, fire, lamps, etc.
2 to start something burning: *Dana lit our campfire.*
3 pale: *light blue*
4 having a small mass: *light as a feather*

lighten to make less heavy or less of a problem

lighthouse a tower with a light on top used to warn ships of rocks and other dangers

lightning the bright flashes during a thunderstorm

like 1 to think someone or something is pleasant
2 to be somewhat the same (see **alike**)

likely 1 expected to happen: *We'll likely win because our team is just great.*
2 probably true: *Quite likely Kia took Jean's coat by mistake.*

lilac 1 a shrub with many white, pink or light purple flowers that smell very sweet
2 a pale purple colour

lily a flower with blooms like a long, thin bell

limb 1 a body part like an arm or leg
2 the branch of a tree

lime 1 a white powder, used in making cement
2 a small, green, oval fruit with a very sour taste

limit the farthest point you can get to but not go past

limp 1 to walk with difficulty because there is something wrong with your foot
2 not stiff

line 1 a long, thin mark like this ―――――――
2 a row of people or things

linen strong cloth, used in clothes, sheets, etc.

liner a big ship

linger to be slow to leave

link 1 to join things together: *Everybody link arms and we'll dance!*
2 one of the loops in a chain

lint bits of thread and fluff

lion a large, wild, yellow or light brown cat, found in Africa and Asia

lioness a female lion

lip 1 one of the two edges around the mouth
2 the edge of something: *lip of a milk pitcher*

lipstick a cosmetic for colouring the lips

liquid any element that is like water or oil: *Water is liquid; ice is solid.*

list a number of things written down one after another

listen 1 to pay attention in order to hear something
2 to obey

lit see **light**

literacy enough knowledge about a subject to be able to deal with it: *computer literacy*

literate 1 able to read and write
2 having a good understanding

litre, liter a measure of liquid

litter 1 garbage left lying about, especially on roads and sidewalks
2 a group of young born at the same time to an animal mother: *a litter of pigs*

little 1 not large
2 a small amount

live ① (rhymes with give)
1 to have your life, to be alive
2 to have your home in a place: *Cora lives across the street.*

live ② (rhymes with dive) alive, active

lively full of energy and activity

lives see **life**

lizard a reptile with four legs

llama a South American animal that looks like a small camel without a hump

load 1 something that is carried: *a load of gravel*
2 the amount a person or thing can accept and still work: *That's too much of a load for my machine.*
3 to put things onto something to be carried: *Load the gravel onto the truck.*

Ll

4 to put a program into a computer
5 to put bullets into a gun

loaf in the shape of baked bread. The plural is **loaves**.

loan 1 anything that is lent to someone: *a **loan** of money*
2 to lend something to someone (see **lend**)

loaves see **loaf**

lobster a sea creature with a shell, claws and several pairs of legs

local belonging to one place: *a **local** radio broadcast*

locality (lo-KAL-i-tee) a particular place or district: *There are no buses in this **locality**.*

location a particular spot where something is found or where something is done: ***location** for making a movie*

lock 1 a fastening that keeps people from entering a door or gate, or from opening a box
2 to fasten with a key: ***Lock** the door.*
3 a curl of hair

locomotive the engine that pulls a train

log a piece from the thick part of a tree

logo a symbol that stands for a company or organization

loiter to stand around with nothing to do

lonely 1 sad because there is no one around you know and like
2 far from others: *a **lonely** tree in the middle of the park*

lonesome see **lonely**

long 1 a large distance from one end to the other: *a **long** road*
2 taking a lot of time: *a **long** holiday*
3 to long for to want something very much

longitude an imaginary line from the North to the South Pole (see **latitude**)

look 1 to use your eyes to see something

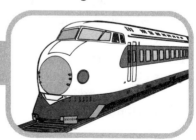

2 to try to find something
3 to seem to be a certain
way: *Elsie looks sad today.*

lookout 1 a person who
watches for danger or for
something that is expected
2 a place where you can
stand to see a long distance

loonie in Canada, a one-dollar
coin

loop a ring made in rope, wire,
thread or ribbon

loose (loos) **1** not tight or
fixed properly: *a loose tooth*
2 not attached or tied to
anything

loosen to make or become
looser

loot (informal) things that
have been stolen

lore knowledge and stories
that have built up about a
subject: *medical lore*

lose (looz) **1** to be without
something you once had
2 to be beaten in a game

loss the losing of something

lot 1 plenty
2 a piece of land, usually big
enough to build a house on

lotion liquid that is put on the
skin

loud 1 very easy to hear
2 noisy

lounge 1 a room for relaxing
2 to relax

louse a tiny wingless insect.
Some kinds of **lice** suck
blood from animals and
people.

love to be deeply fond of

lovely attractive and pleasing

low 1 close to the bottom or
to the ground
2 below the average: *the
lowest rainfall in years*
3 rude or uncomplimentary:
a low blow
4 deep in sound: *a low note*

lowly near the bottom in rank

low-rise a building with only
a few storeys

loyal always true to the things
or people you care for: *a
loyal friend*

luck the way things happen
that are not planned: *There
is good luck and bad luck.*

lucky to have good luck
(see **unlucky**)

Ll 139

luggage suitcases and boxes you take on a journey

lukewarm warm but not hot

lullaby a song that is sung to make a baby go to sleep

lumber wood that is cut to special sizes, used for building

lump 1 a solid piece with no clear shape: *a lump of clay* **2** a swelling on the body

lunar having to do with the moon: *The spaceship returned with lunar rocks.*

lunch a light meal, usually eaten at midday

lung a body part inside your chest, used in breathing

lurk to wait where you cannot be seen

luxury something expensive that you like but do not really need

lying see **lie**

lynx a small to medium-size spotted wildcat found in North America, Northern Europe and Asia

lyrics the words of a song: *Werner can remember the tune but not the lyrics.*

Mach (rhymes with mock) the speed of something compared to the speed at which sound travels. A jet travelling at Mach 2 is moving at two times the speed of sound.

machine a device with different parts that work together to do a job: *a washing machine*

machinery machines or parts of machines

macro a prefix meaning **very large**

mad 1 angry
2 a strong liking for something: *Tanya is mad about motorbikes.*
3 an old-fashioned word for mentally ill

madam a polite word sometimes used when speaking to a woman: *I am sorry, madam, for bumping into you.*

made see **make**

magazine a type of thin book with stories and pictures that is published according to a regular schedule, usually every week or every month

maggot a tiny worm that eats dead flesh

magic the ability to perform clever tricks and things that people can see happening but cannot explain

magician someone who performs magic

magnet a piece of metal that makes other pieces of metal stick to it

magnificent (mag-NI-fi-sent) very special and grand

magnify to make something look bigger: *a magnifying glass*

maid 1 a girl or woman who is a servant
2 an old-fashioned word for girl

mail letters, cards and parcels sent through the post office

main the most important: *a **main** road*

majestic very grand and dignified: *a **majestic** parade*

majesty the word used to speak to a king or queen: *"Your **Majesty**"*

major 1 very important: *a **major** problem*
2 a rank in the army

majority the larger part of a group

make 1 to produce something new by putting things together: *Years ago some native people **made** homes from animal hides.*
2 to cause something to happen: *Kyle is going to **make** me spill this!*

makeup see **cosmetic**

male any living thing that can become a father

mall an area where people can walk and cars are not allowed: *a shopping **mall***

mammal any animal that has a backbone, a warm body, and can feed its babies with its own milk: *People, wolves and whales are all **mammals**.*

mammoth 1 a large, long-haired animal like an elephant that lived in northern parts of the earth before the Ice Age
2 anything very large: *a **mammoth** snowstorm*

man a full-grown male: *two **men***

manage 1 to be in charge of something, such as a store or factory: *A person who **manages** a store is called the **manager**.*
2 to be able to do something even if it is difficult: *Beryl **managed** to make dinner in the dark.*

mane the long hair along a horse's neck or around a lion's head

maniac someone who behaves in a very wild and uncontrolled way

manner the way something happens or is done

manners your behaviour toward other people

mansion a very large house, usually elegant

mantel the shelf above a fireplace

manual 1 a book that tells how to operate or repair something
2 a device you operate with your hands, without electrical power: *manual typewriter*
3 done by hand, not by machine

manufacture (man-yew-FAK-cher)
1 to make large numbers of the same thing
2 to make a new thing from other things: *Karl was able to manufacture a shelter out of branches.*

many a large number

map a diagram showing different parts of the world

maple a type of tall tree whose leaves change from green to red, yellow and orange in autumn and then fall to the ground: *The maple leaf is one of Canada's symbols.*

mar 1 to scratch or damage in some way: *The painting was marred by a water stain.*
2 to add something unpleasant and unwanted: *Her party was marred by a quarrel between two guests.*

marble 1 a kind of shiny stone used in buildings
2 a small, hard, glass-like ball used in games

march to walk like soldiers on parade

mare a female horse

margarine (MAR-jrin) a food that looks like butter but is not made from milk

margin the space around the edge of a page

marine found in the sea. Seals, fish and crabs are marine creatures.

mark 1 a check or a line on a piece of work to show that someone has looked at it: *Verna put a check mark beside every name on the list.*

2 a number or letter on a piece of work to show how good it is
3 a stain or spot on something that spoils the way it looks

marker 1 a type of pen
2 a sign to draw attention to something: *The police put **markers** around the hole in the road.*

market a place where people gather to buy and sell things, usually food

markup the difference between what a store pays for something and the price it is asking for it

marmalade a jam made from oranges or other fruit

maroon 1 a very dark red colour
2 to leave someone behind in a lonely place

marriage a joining together, usually of two people

marry to become someone's spouse

marsh a piece of land that stays wet all year long (see **bog** and **swamp**)

marsupial (mar-SOO-pee-al) an animal that has babies which the mother carries about in a type of pocket in her body until they are older

marvellous wonderful: *a **marvellous** field trip*

mascot an animal, thing or person thought to bring good luck

mash to crush something and make it soft like pudding

mask a covering worn on the face

mass 1 a large amount: *masses of flowers*
2 an important ceremony in the Catholic religion

massage the rubbing of muscles and joints in the body to make them feel better

massive very big

mast a tall pole that holds up a flag or a ship's sails

master 1 a man who is in charge
2 to become very skilled at something: *Lisette has mastered the art of origami.*

masterpiece someone's very best work

match 1 a small, thin stick that gives a flame when rubbed on a rough surface

2 to be the same as or like another: *Bob is a match for Hank in the high jump.*
3 a game played between two players or teams

mate partner; friend

material anything used to make something else

maternal behaving like a mother (see **paternal**)

maternity the state of being a mother

mathematics, math the study of numbers, measurement, shapes and ideas about them

matinee (ma-ti-NAY) an afternoon performance

matter 1 any solid material
2 something you need to think about: *a serious matter*
3 What's the matter? What is wrong?

mattress the soft, thick pad on a bed

mature 1 grown up and like an adult
2 ripe: *mature bananas*

maximum the very most of something

may 1 can: *May I be excused?*
2 will perhaps: *It may rain today, and it might tomorrow too.*

maybe possibly

mayor the person who leads the government of a town or city

maze a confusing set of lines or paths that cross and turn often

me see **I**

meadow a field with grasses and few trees

meal the food eaten at one time, such as dinner

mean 1 unkind and not generous
2 to plan in your mind: *I meant to tell Judy, but I forgot.*
3 to have a meaning: *When I say "Run," I mean "Run"!*

Mm

meaning what someone wants to say with the words she is using

meant (rhymes with tent) see **mean**

meanwhile during the time something else is happening: *Vicki fed the cat; meanwhile, her dog ran away.*

measles an illness that makes red spots show on your skin

measure to find out the size of something

meat the flesh of animals, used as food

mechanical (ma-KAN-i-kal) worked by machinery or like machinery: *a mechanical toy*

medal a piece of metal hanging from a ribbon. It is given to someone to honour them.

medallist someone who has been awarded a medal

meddle to involve yourself in something that has nothing to do with you

media the newspapers, radio and television

medical having to do with medicine and health

medicine liquid or pills a sick person takes

medieval in the period when knights and castles were popular

medium of middle size

meek gentle and timid

meet 1 to come together at a place: *We met in front of the school.*
2 a contest for athletes: *track meet*

meeting an event where people get together to talk about something

mega 1 one million
2 anything very large

megabyte one million bits of computer memory

melt to change from a solid to a liquid: *Let's go skating before the ice melts!*

member someone who belongs to a group

memory 1 the ability to remember
2 something that is remembered

men more than one man

mend to repair something that is damaged

mental in the mind: *We do mental math in our class. No pencils or paper!*

mention to speak of someone or something when you are speaking of other things

menu 1 in a restaurant, the list of food available and how much it costs
2 a list of options a computer has available

merciful showing kindness at a time when punishment is what everyone expects

mercy kindness shown to someone in trouble

merger a joining of two or more things into one

merit good quality or qualities: *Don't you see my plan has merit?*

mess things that are mixed up or dirty

message words that you send because you cannot be present to say them

met see **meet**

metal a substance made from ore, minerals and chemicals, which melts when heated to a very high temperature. Steel and brass are metals.

meteor a small piece of rock that moves through space and burns up when it gets close to Earth

meteorite a lump of rock or metal that has fallen from space and landed on Earth

meter a device that measures how much of something has been used: *The meter showed that Wes bought twenty-two litres of oil.*

method the way in which you do something

metre, meter a measure of length: *100 metres = 1 kilometre*

metric system a system of measurement based on tens, hundreds and thousands

mice see **mouse 1**

micro a prefix meaning **very tiny,** used in front of another word, as in microchip, microcomputer, microfilm, etc., to show that the thing is smaller than usual

Mm

microbe any small organism, such as a virus, that can be seen with a microscope

microchip see **chip 3**

microcosm a small copy or example of something: *Our classroom is a* **microcosm** *of the whole school.*

microfiche (MY-kro-feesh) a type of microfilm on which information is arranged in graphs

microfilm a strip of film with a lot of tiny bits of information on it. The information can be read by using a special machine that magnifies the information on a screen.

microphone a device that changes sound to electricity so that it can come out of speakers

microscope a device that makes it possible to see things too small to see with your eyes alone

microscopic very tiny

microwave an electronic wave used to carry radio or radar information or to heat food

midday at or around twelve o'clock in the day

mid see **middle**

middle a point that is the same distance from all sides or edges, or from both ends of something

midnight twelve o'clock in the night

might see **may**

migrate to move from one area to another

mild see **gentle**

militant very strong and noisy in your belief about something

military anything having to do with a country's armed forces

milk a white liquid that female mammals produce to feed their babies. Many people drink the milk that cows and goats produce.

mill a type of factory

millionaire someone who has a lot of money, a million dollars or more

mime to tell something by means of actions, not words

mimic to copy the actions and speech of someone

mind 1 the part of you that thinks, remembers, etc. *Sheila has an active mind.* **2** to be bothered or concerned: *Do you mind if I go first?* **3** to look after: *Mind your baby sister.*

mine 1 belonging to me: *That book is mine, not Sammy's.* **2** a place where people dig things out of the ground, such as coal **3** see **land mine**

miner someone whose job is to work in a mine

mineral 1 any useful or valuable rock that is dug from the ground. Copper and aluminum are minerals. **2** a substance you need for the health of your body

mingle to mix

miniature very tiny: *a miniature castle*

minimum the very least of something

minister 1 someone who is in charge of a church **2** an important person in the government

minnow a very small fish

minor smaller or less important: *That's a minor problem. Don't worry about it.*

minority the smaller part of a group

mint 1 a place where coins are made: *Canada's mint is in Winnipeg.* **2** a candy with a fresh flavour

minus take away: *Six minus two is four.*

minute ① (MI-nit) a measure of time, sixty seconds

minute ② (my-NEWT) very tiny

Mm

miracle something wonderful that has happened, even though it did not seem possible

mirage (mir-AHJ) a trick of the light that makes people see things that are not there

mirror a piece of glass that reflects images

misbehave to act in a way that is not proper

mischief silly behaviour that often causes trouble

mischievous likely to do mischief

miser someone with a lot of money who tries not to spend it

miserable very unhappy

misery suffering

misfortune something very unlucky that happens

Miss a title that is sometimes used before the name of a woman who is not married (see **Mrs.** and **Ms.**)

miss 1 to fail to hit, catch, hear or find something: *Oops! I missed that question on the test!*
2 to be sad because someone is not with you: *My best friend has moved and I miss her.*

missile an object that is shot or thrown through the air

mission an important job that someone is sent away to do

mist damp air that is hard to see through

mistake something you have done or thought that is wrong: *a spelling mistake*

misunderstand to get the wrong idea about something: *You misunderstood what I said.*

mitt a glove used in playing baseball

mitten a glove with one part for your thumb and one for the rest of your hand

mix to stir or shake a number of things together to make one thing

mixture something made of different things mixed together

moan 1 a low, soft sound that shows you are in pain **2** to grumble

mobile able to move about

moccasin a soft shoe made of leather, with no heel or laces

mock 1 to make fun of something **2** not real: *a mock fight*

model 1 a small copy of something **2** a person whose job is to wear clothes, etc. to advertise them

modern of the kind that is usual now: *a modern house*

moist damp

mold see **mould**

mole a small, grey, furry animal that digs holes under the ground

molecule the smallest unit of something that can exist by itself

mom, Mom an informal word for mother

moment a very small amount of time

monarch a royal person like a king or queen

monastery a house where monks live, work and pray

money the coins and paper that people use when they buy and sell things

monitor 1 an instrument with a screen that displays images from television or from a computer **2** a person who has special jobs to do in a school

monk one of a group of men who live together according to a set of rules because of the religion they believe in (see **monastery**)

monkey a hairy animal with feet, hands it can use like feet, and a long tail (compare with **ape**)

monorail a kind of train that runs on only one track, usually high above the ground

monsoon a season of very heavy rainfall

monster an imaginary creature in stories

month a measure of time. Twelve months make up one year.

Mm

monument a statue or other structure made so that we will remember someone important or something that happened

mood the way you feel: *a good or a bad mood*

moon a natural satellite that goes around a planet

moor to tie up a boat at a dock or at a shore

moose a deer-like animal, but much larger and with huge antlers

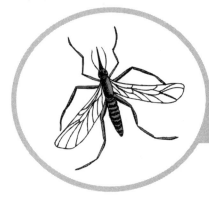

moraine a large amount of earth, gravel and rock formed into a ridge by the movement of a glacier (see **glacier**)

more 1 a larger number or amount
2 again: *I will tell you once more.*

Mormon a follower of the Mormon religion, also called the Church of Jesus Christ of Latter-day Saints, based on the Book of Mormon

morning the time from the beginning of the day until noon

mortal alive and therefore can die: *All humans are mortal.*

mortar a mixture of sand, cement and water, used to hold bricks and stones together in a building

mosaic any picture or piece of artwork made from different pieces of material put together on a flat surface

mosque a house of worship in the Islamic religion

mosquito a small, biting insect found in damp areas, especially in spring

moss a low, green plant that grows in damp places

most 1 more than any other: *Most of the pens are on Paige's desk.*
2 very: *You are most kind, Dean.*

motel a kind of hotel where the rooms open directly to a parking lot

moth an insect with large, pale-coloured wings. Usually, moths fly at night.

mother a female parent

motor the engine that makes a vehicle or machine run

motorbike a bicycle with an engine

motorcycle a large and powerful motorbike

mould 1 furry material that sometimes grows on food that has spoiled
2 a hollow shape that is used to hold liquids like jelly or plaster until they harden

mound a rounded pile of something

mount to get onto a horse or bicycle

mountain a very high hill

mountain lion see **cougar**

mouse 1 a very small, grey or brown animal with a pointed nose and long tail: *three blind mice*
2 a device used with one hand for operating a computer

mouse pad a flat sheet on which a computer mouse is moved about (see **mouse 2**)

moustache (MUS-tash) hair that grows above the upper lip

mouth the part of the face that opens and closes for eating and speaking

move 1 to take from one place to another: *Move the ladder to the other wall.*
2 to go from one place to another: *Cheryl moved from Calgary to St. John.*

movement when something moves

movie a film shown in a theatre

mow to cut grass or hay

Mr. a title used before a man's name whether he is married or not

Mrs. a title used before the name of a married woman

Ms. a title used before a woman's name whether she is married or not

much a lot of something

mud soft, wet ground that sticks to things

muffin a kind of bread that is small and round

mug 1 a kind of cup
2 (informal) a face, usually a funny one: *That's my mug in the middle of the picture!*

mule an animal that is half horse and half donkey

multicultural involving many different cultures equally

multiply to make things bigger: *Four multiplied by two is eight.*

mumble to speak in a way that is not clear

mumps an illness that makes the sides of your face swell

munch to chew very noisily

mural a very large painting on a wall

murder to kill someone on purpose

murmur to speak in a very soft, low voice

muscle one of the parts of the body that become tight or loose to help you move around

museum a place where many interesting things are displayed for people to see. Often the things are old and no longer familiar to people living today.

mushroom a kind of fungus that grows on damp ground and rotted wood

music the sounds made by voices singing or instruments being played

musical 1 having to do with music: *musical instruments*
2 good at music
3 a story told by song and dance as well as by speaking

muskox an animal, similar to a small bison, with long hair and curved horns. It lives in Canada's far north.

Muslim, Moslem a follower of Islam

must have to: *I must leave immediately.*

mustard a yellow powder or liquid used to give food a strong flavour

mute not able to speak

mutiny an attack by sailors or soldiers against their officers

mutter to mumble in an angry way

mutton the meat of a sheep

muzzle 1 an animal's nose and mouth

2 a cover put over an animal's mouth

my belonging to me

myself me and no one else

mysterious (mis-STEE-ree-us) strange and puzzling

mystery a strange and puzzling situation or story

myth a story, not exactly true, used to explain things that have happened in the world

nachos a snack food made of tortilla chips, cheese, salsa, etc.

nag 1 to keep telling someone you want her to do something she is not doing
2 a very old and tired horse

nail 1 a thin, metal pin, with a sharp point at one end and a round, flat head at the other. Nails are used to fasten things together.
2 to attach something with nails: *Mina **nailed** her poster to the door.*
3 (informal) to expose someone who is guilty: *to be **nailed** for cheating on a test*
4 see **fingernail**

naked without any clothes or covering

name what you call someone or something

nanny a person who is paid to look after a family's children

nap a short sleep

napkin a small piece of cloth or paper for wiping your mouth and fingers while you eat

narrate to tell a story

narrative a story

narrator a person who tells or reads a story to others

narrow not wide; with little space between two sides

nasty unpleasant

nation (NAY-shun) a country and the people who live there

national (NA-shun-al) belonging to one country: *Caleb plays on Canada's **national** soccer team.*

native someone born or something grown in a certain place: *Polly is a **native** of Manitoba.*

Native People in Canada, a term used to describe the country's aboriginal people

natural 1 made by nature, not by machines or people **2** normal: *It is **natural** for birds to fly.*

nature 1 plants, animals and everything in the world not made by humans **2** what a person is like: *To be good-**natured** is to be calm and kind.*

navigate to make sure that a ship, airplane or other vehicle is travelling on the right route and going to the right place

navy 1 the part of a country's armed forces that fight at sea **2** dark blue

NB (also **N.B.**) an abbreviation for **nota bene**, Latin for **note well**. NB is used to tell you something is important and that you should pay attention.

NDP see **New Democratic Party** **2** in Canada, a member of the New Democratic Party political party

near (also **nearby**) not far away

nearly not quite: ***nearly** there; **nearly** 3 o'clock; **nearly** $100*

neat tidy

necessary important and needed very much

neck the part of the body that joins the shoulders to the head

necklace a band worn around the neck as a decoration

nectar the sweet liquid that bees gather from flowers

need 1 to require something you don't have: *I **need** some bandages right away!* **2** to have to do something: *I **need** to study for the spelling test.*

needle 1 a very thin, pointed piece of metal, used in making or decorating clothes

2 a thin, pointed leaf on trees such as pine and fir
3 (informal) to tease someone

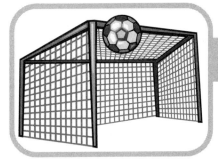

neglect to fail to take care of something

neighbour, neighbor someone who lives close to you

neither not one or the other of two people, things or ideas: *I tried both numbers but **neither** one worked.*

neon a gas often used to make coloured lighting in signs

nephew the son of your brother or sister

nerve 1 one of the channels in the body that carries messages to and from the brain
2 brave or calm behaviour when there is a challenge or danger: *Don't lose your **nerve** when they shout at you!*

nervous 1 afraid and excited because of something you must do
2 easily frightened

nest a cozy place that is safe and protected

net 1 the cage at both ends of a hockey rink or soccer field
2 material like a web for catching and holding small things

network a system of connected things: *a television **network***

networking sharing information and ideas

neutral not taking sides in a disagreement or discussion

never not ever

new 1 just bought or made: *a **new** car*
2 just discovered: *You will be able to see the **new** planet tonight.*
3 different: *a **new** topic to study*

newborn a person or animal that has just been born

New Democratic Party a political party in Canada

news information about what has happened

newspaper a daily or weekly version of the news printed on large sheets of paper

New World an expression used to refer to North and South America

next 1 beside: *Sit next to Bashar, please.*
2 following: *You'll be the next to sing, Marlene.*

nibble to eat something in small bites

nice pleasant

nickel 1 a metal that is mined from nickel ore
2 a coin worth five cents

nickname a name you call someone instead of his real name

niece the daughter of your brother or sister

night the time between dusk and dawn when it is dark

nightmare a frightening dream

nimble able to move quickly and easily

nip to take a small bite or pinch

noble 1 to have excellent qualities
2 to be a member of the ruling class of a country

nobody no person

nocturnal active at night

nod 1 to shake your head up and down to show agreement
2 to let your head fall forward as you go to sleep

noise sound that is loud and usually unpleasant

nomad a person who does not have a permanent home and moves from place to place. Nomads are sometimes called **nomadic peoples**.

nominate (NAW-mi-nate) to suggest someone or something as suitable: *I nominate Libby for class president.*

none not any or not one

non-fiction stories that are true

nonsense anything that has no meaning for you

non-stop never ending

noodle a strip of dough. Noodles are a form of pasta.

noon twelve o'clock in the day

no one no person

normal usual or ordinary

north 1 a compass point **2** the direction to your left when you face the sunrise **3 the North** the part of the world that has the Arctic and parts of countries near the Arctic

northern from the north or in the north

nose the part of the face used to help you breathe and smell

nostril one of the two openings at the end of your nose

notable important

notch a mark like a "V" cut into something

note 1 a short message **2** one sound in music

notebook 1 a book with pages to hold written notes **2** a small, portable computer

nothing not anything

notice 1 to see something and then think about it: *Baljit noticed that you were not in the audience.* **2** an announcement placed on a wall, poster or computer screen

noun any word that tells you what someone or something is called. Air, Ann, chair, joy and Ontario are all nouns.

nourish 1 to feed: *Our old dog was nourished by soft meat.* **2** to develop and improve: *You play the violin well and should nourish that talent.*

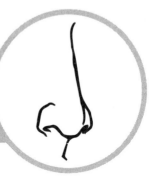

novel 1 a very long story that is published in book form **2** new, different and interesting: *The Clemps have a novel way of celebrating birthdays.*

novelty something new or unusual: *It is hard to believe that email was once a novelty.*

now at this time

nowhere not anywhere

nozzle the part at the end of a pipe where spray comes out

nuclear energy that is produced when atoms split: *a nuclear-powered ship*

nude without any clothes

nudge to push someone gently so that they will notice something

nuisance (NEW-sans) a person, animal or thing that causes trouble

numb not able to feel anything

number the word or figure that tells how many. One, 22, 867 are all numbers.

numerous many

nun one of a group of women who live in a special way because of the religion they believe in

nurse 1 a person whose job it is to look after others when they are ill **2** to look after someone very carefully

nursery 1 a place where very young children are cared for **2** a store where plants and flowers are sold

nut 1 a kind of food found in a hard shell **2** a piece of metal that is screwed on to the end of a bolt to help hold things together **3** (informal) a very silly person

nutrition 1 food **2** the way the body uses food

nylon a strong, thin material, used for making things like clothes and rope

oak a tall tree that produces acorns

oar a long pole with a flat part at one end, used for rowing a boat

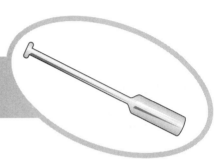

oasis 1 any pleasant spot in the middle of an area that is not so pleasant
2 in the desert, a place with water, grass and trees

oath a very serious promise (see **vow**)

oats a type of grain grown for food

obedient willing to do what you are told to do

obey to do what you are told to do

object ① (OB-jekt) anything that can be seen or touched: *Carly saw a strange green object behind the door.*

object ② (ob-JEKT) to disapprove of something and say that you do: *Andy objected when Frank said that we should bring lunch.*

objection (ob-JEK-shun) an expression of disapproval

objective 1 (ob-JEK-tiv) a goal or purpose: *My objective is to read a book every week.*
2 not influenced by personal feelings or attitude

oblige to have to do something: *You are obliged to finish before leaving for recess.*

oblong oval shaped

observation 1 the act of observing
2 a remark or comment: *Randy's observation about hockey upset everyone.*

observe to watch carefully

obstacle something in the way

obstinate unwilling to change your ideas or opinions

obstruct to be in the way of

obtain to get

obvious very clear and easy to understand

occasion the special time when something happens: *Birthdays are occasions to celebrate.*

occasionally sometimes

occupation any job or hobby

occupy 1 to live in something: *Is this room occupied?*
2 to keep someone interested: *It's sure hard to occupy my baby sister.*

occur 1 to happen
2 to come into your mind: *An idea just occurred to me.*

ocean a very large body of water

o'clock according to the clock

octave in music, a group of eight notes that make up a scale

octopus a sea creature with eight long arms

odd 1 strange and unusual: *an odd odour*
2 not even: *an odd number*
3 not alike: *There are three shoes on the shelf, two that are the same and one odd shoe.*

odour, odor a smell

of 1 source, made from: *a bar of soap*
2 about, concerning: *the story of the king*
3 cause: *The cat died of a disease.*
4 called: *city of North Bay*
5 a distance: *five kilometres west of Moncton*

off 1 not on: *The tap is turned off now.*
2 away from: *The glass fell off the table and broke. Tim will be off school for three weeks.*
3 no longer in place: *Shona took off her coat.*
4 less than: *These were $2 off the regular price.*
5 wrong: *Your answer is off by quite a bit.*

offend to hurt someone's feelings

offensive 1 very annoying: *an offensive smell*
2 to be on the attack

offer 1 to hold out something for someone to take
2 to say that you are willing to do something

office a room where someone conducts business

officer an important person in the armed forces or other organization

official 1 a person who is important at a particular place and time
2 having authority: *an official letter*

offside 1 in hockey, to be ahead of the puck improperly
2 (informal) to be in disagreement with others in a group

often many times

oil a thick, slippery liquid

ointment a healing cream for putting on skin

OK (also **okay**) **1** all right: *OK, you may leave now.*
2 satisfactory: *Jim is feeling OK today because his computer is working OK now.*

old born or made a long time ago

old-fashioned something that was usual a long time ago: *old-fashioned hats*

Old World an expression used to describe Europe, Asia and Northern Africa

olive 1 a small, oval, green or black fruit with a pit inside
2 a brownish-green colour

omelette eggs mixed together with vegetables or cheese and cooked

omit to leave out: *You omitted your address on that form!*

on 1 touching the surface: *The puck is on the ice.*
2 by means of: *We watched the show on TV.*
3 a member of: *Maria is on our team.*
4 near, beside, in the direction of: *on the left; on a ravine*
5 in use: *Is the radio on?*
6 at a point in time: *We saw the game on Monday.*
7 the condition of something: *on fire*
8 be means of: *Ahmed went on the bus.*

once one time: *You can try this only once.*

one 1 a number, written "1" in numerals
2 any thing or person: *If you break **one**, you must pay for it.*
3 the same: *All the horses ran in **one** direction.*

one-way in one direction only

ongoing continuing: *an **ongoing** argument*

onion a round, solid vegetable with a strong taste

on-line to be connected and ready to work: *Is that computer **on-line** yet?*

only 1 no more than: ***only** three chances*
2 one by itself: *There is **only** one cookie left.*

onto on the top of: *Jill jumped **onto** the wagon.*

ooze to come slowly through an opening. Thick liquids, such as oil, are said to ooze.

opaque not letting light come through

open 1 not closed: *The store is **open** until midnight.*
2 to make open: ***Open** the door!*
3 to bring a computer file onto the screen

opening a hole or space in something

opera a play in which everyone sings instead of speaking

operation 1 see **surgery**
2 the working of a machine

opinion what you think of something or someone

opportunity a favourable or suitable time to do something

opposite 1 facing: *on the **opposite** page*
2 as different as possible: *Hot is the **opposite** of cold.*

option (OP-shun) a choice

oral 1 through the mouth: *The medicine must be taken **orally**.*
2 spoken: *Cara didn't need her pen; it was an **oral** exam!*

orange 1 a round, juicy fruit with a thick peel and seeds
2 a colour the same as the fruit in **1**

orbit in space, the path a body takes around another body

Oo

orchard a field where fruit trees grow

orchestra a group of people who play musical instruments together

ordeal a difficult time, often involving pain or trouble

order 1 a command or direction to do something: *Our **orders** say we must leave now.*
2 to tell someone to do something: *Sal was **ordered** to drop the handle.*
3 a request for something that you will pay for: *Here is your **order** of groceries.*
4 to ask for something to be delivered to you: *After the show we'll **order** pizza.*
5 in order arranged in the proper way

ordinary not special in any way

ore rock that contains minerals such as gold and copper

organ 1 a large musical instrument that produces sound with forced air or by means of electronics
2 a part of the body. Eyes, kidneys and muscles are organs.

organic living and growing

organism a living thing: *A drop of seawater is filled with hundreds of **organisms**.*

organization 1 a number of people who come together to do something: *The Rotary Club is a worldwide **organization**.*
2 the act of planning and arranging something: *First, you must complete the **organization** of the event.*

organize to arrange things in a carefully planned way

origami (or-i-GAW-me) the art of folding paper into special shapes, a Japanese tradition

original 1 made first, before any copies or other versions are made
2 new and not taken from another source: *an **original** idea*

orient 1 the Orient the eastern parts of Asia
2 to figure out where you are

Oo

Oriental from the eastern parts of Asia

ornament something added to improve the appearance of something

orphan a child whose parents are not living

ostrich a very large bird with a long neck and legs and very small wings

other not the same as this: *The other road was smoother.*

otherwise or else

otter a furry animal that lives mostly in water

ought (awt) should: *I ought to brush my teeth more often.*

ourselves us and no one else

out 1 not inside: *Is the dog in or out?*
2 not burning or working: *The fire is out. The lights are out.*

outback the most remote part of a country or area

outdoors anywhere that is not in a building

outfit 1 clothes that are for a special purpose: *Mabel wore her hiking outfit on Tuesday.*
2 a set of things needed for doing something

outing a special trip: *an outing on the Bruce Trail*

outlaw a person who has broken the law and is hiding from the police

outline a line around the edge of something to show its shape

outnumber to be more than: *Their fans outnumbered us at least two to one at the game.*

output 1 work produced by people or by a machine
2 information produced by a computer

outside 1 the outer edge or side of something: *The outside of the house needs painting.*
2 unlikely: *There's only an outside chance he will come.*
3 out of doors

outstanding unusually good

oval the shape of an egg

oven the space inside a stove where food is baked or roasted

Oo

over 1 covering from above: *a blanket **over** the bed* 2 finished: *Playtime is **over**.* 3 remaining: *Is there any candy left **over**?* 4 more than: ***Over** 500 people came!*

overall from one end to the other: *The **overall** length makes it too big for us to use.*

overalls a kind of pants, often worn over other pants

overactive with too much energy

overboard over the side of a boat and into the water

overcast covered by cloud

overcharge to ask too high a price for something

overcoat a coat worn over other clothing

overcome to defeat or be too strong for

overdue past the time when something was supposed to happen

overflow the liquid that flows over the sides of a container once it is full

overhead 1 above the heads of people 2 **overhead projector** a machine that projects images onto a screen

overlap to fold or lie over the edge of something else

overpass a section of road that goes above another road

overrate to think something is more valuable than it really is

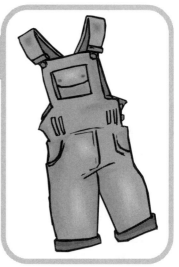

overrule to change the decision made by someone with less authority

overseas across an ocean

overture 1 a proposal or an offer: *We made **overtures** to our teacher for a longer recess.* 2 the beginning part of a long piece of music such as an opera

overturn to push or knock something over

overweight too heavy

owe to have to pay money back to someone

owl a nocturnal bird of prey

own 1 to have something that belongs to you: *I don't* **own** *as many baseball cards as Kirby.*
2 own up to admit that you were the one who did something: *Patti* **owned up** *to breaking the window.*
3 mine: *my* **own**
4 by myself: *on my* **own**

ox a large cow used for pulling heavy loads: *two* **oxen**

oxygen the gas in the air that everyone needs to breathe to stay alive

oyster a sea creature that lives in a shell

Oo 169

NnOo**Pp**QqRr

pace 1 one step
2 the speed at which something or someone moves: *a slow or fast* **pace**

pack 1 a bundle of things put together to be carried
2 a group: *a wolf* **pack**
3 to fill a suitcase or other container
4 to put soft material around something: *glasses* **packed** *in cotton*
5 to crush or crowd together: *Students* **packed** *the gym for the concert.*

package a parcel

pad 1 sheets of writing paper joined at one end
2 a type of cushion
3 to walk very softly and quietly: *The tiger* **padded** *slowly along the path.*

paddle 1 see **oar**
2 to make strokes in water with your arms or an oar

padlock a lock with a metal loop

page 1 a sheet of paper in a book, magazine, etc.

2 one side of a sheet of paper in a book, magazine, etc.
3 to call someone's name out loud or on a pager

pageant a play or show with many people wearing fancy costumes

pager a small electronic device that takes messages and makes a noise when a message is received

paid see **pay**

pail a container with a handle, for carrying liquid

pain the feeling you have when part of your body is injured or ill

paint 1 a coloured liquid that dries when it is put on a surface
2 to use paint to colour something
3 to make a picture with paints

painter a person who paints

painting a picture that has been painted

pair two things together: *a pair of shoes; a pair of ducks*

pajamas loose clothing worn in bed

palace a very large and fancy home where a king, queen or other important person lives

pale 1 without much colour: *a pale face*
2 light: *a pale blue sky*

palm 1 the inside of the hand between the fingers and the wrist
2 a tropical tree with large leaves and no branches

Palmpilot (also **palmtop** and **palmcorder**) a tiny computer that can be held in the hand

pamper to treat a person or animal very well

pan 1 a metal dish used in cooking
2 to wash sand to look for pieces of gold
3 (informal) to say something is not very good: *That movie was panned in our newspaper.*

pancake a flat mixture of flour, milk and eggs that is cooked

panda a large, black and white bear found in China

pandemonium (pan-da-MO-nee-um) a great deal of noise and confusion

pane a piece of glass in a window

panel 1 a long, thin, flat piece of wood, metal or other material used in building
2 a small group of people who sit together to discuss something they know about

panic a strong, sudden fear

panorama a very wide view of something, especially near the horizon

pant to take short, quick breaths after running: *a panting dog*

panther a wildcat much like a cougar found in Asia and Africa

pantomime a play in which actors do not talk but tell a story with movements

pants a piece of clothing worn below the waist that has separate parts for the legs

paper 1 thin sheets made from wood pulp, used for writing on
2 a short version of **newspaper**

paperback a book with covers that bend

paperwork work that someone does on a job to keep track of things and to organize the work that other people do

papier mache (PAY-per ma-SHAY) mashed paper with water and glue added, used to make models of things

parable a story told to teach something

parachute a large cloth in the shape of an umbrella. It has strings attached so that a person or thing can be held and drop slowly through the air.

parade people and vehicles moving along in a line, usually being watched by other people

paradise a word for heaven

paragraph a group of sentences in a story that are all about the same idea

parallel in the same direction: *parallel lines*

paralysis (par-AL-i-sis) loss of the ability to move parts of the body

paralyze, paralyse to have paralysis: *His legs have been paralyzed since the accident.*

paranoid always afraid that others are trying to harm you in some way

paraplegic (pair-a-PLEE-jik) paralysis of the lower part of the body

parasite an organism that lives off another living thing and gives nothing in return

parcel something wrapped and ready to be sent somewhere (see **package**)

pardon to forgive

parent 1 a person or animal who has a child
2 to raise a child or animal

park 1 a large space for enjoying nature and activities
2 to put something, such as a car, in a place and leave it there

parka a heavy winter coat, usually with a hood

parliament the group of people from all parts of a country who meet to pass laws and make decisions about running the country

Parliament in Canada, the House of Commons and the Senate

Parliament Buildings in Canada, the place where members of the government meet to work, to discuss things and to make decisions, etc.

parrot a large, brightly coloured, tropical bird. Some parrots learn to repeat words.

parsley a leafy, green vegetable

parsnip a pale yellow vegetable that grows underground

part 1 anything that is a smaller piece of something: *part of the puzzle*
2 to move things so that they are no longer together

partial (PAR-shal)
1 not complete
2 being very fond of: *Allie is partial to chocolate cake.*

particle a very tiny piece of something: *particles of dust*

Pp 173

particular (par-TIK-yew-lar)
  1 only this one and no other: *That* **particular** *story is my favourite.*
  2 very careful and fussy about things: *Cal is* **particular** *about what he eats.*

partner one of a pair of people who do things together

partridge a wild bird, brown and black in colour, somewhat smaller than a chicken

party 1 an event where a group of people gather to have fun
  2 a group of people who support the same ideas: *a political* **party**

pass 1 a narrow path through hills or mountains
  2 permission to enter or leave a place, or to be in a place: *a library* **pass**
  3 to go by: *We* **passed** *on the sidewalk.*

4 to hand something to someone: *Please* **pass** *the salt.*
  5 to be successful in a test: *Cassandra* **passed** *her driving test.*

passage 1 a way through
  2 a hall or corridor

passenger anyone travelling in a vehicle, such as a bus or an airplane, except the driver or crew

passport special papers provided by the government to show you are a citizen of that country

password a secret word or phrase that will let you go by guards or other security

past 1 any time before now
  2 beyond or farther than: *Our school is* **past** *the corner.*

pasta a mixture of flour, eggs and water made into things like spaghetti or noodles

paste 1 a liquid used to make things stick together
  2 the act of sticking things together, usually paper

pastime something pleasant you do in free time

pastor a minister or priest in charge of a church

pastry cakes, cookies and sweet buns

pasture (PASS-cher) grassland where animals can roam and eat

patch 1 a small piece of something: *patch of ground; a patch sewn on a piece of clothing*
2 to repair something

paternal behaving like a father (see **maternal**)

path a narrow trail

patience (PAY-shens) the ability to wait and be calm

patient 1 someone ill who is being looked after by others
2 able to bear pain or annoying things for a long time without getting angry

patio an area just outside a house where people sit, usually in fine weather

patrol to keep walking around a place to look after it

patter 1 the sound of a lot of talking
2 the sound of raindrops on a roof or window

pattern 1 anything that people copy and repeat over and over: *a pattern of behaviour*
2 a decoration on a piece of clothing

pause to stop what you are doing for a time

pavement a hard surface made of concrete

paw 1 an animal's foot
2 to scrape at something with the hand or foot

pay to give money for something: *Who paid for the ice cream?*

PC 1 an abbreviation for **personal computer**
2 see **Progressive Conservative 1** and **2**, and **Conservative**
3 an abbreviation for **politically correct**

pea a small, round, green vegetable that grows in pods

peace 1 a time without war
2 a time of quiet and rest

peaceful quiet

peach a round, soft, juicy fruit with a pit and yellow skin

Pp 175

peacock a large bird with bright tail feathers, which the male spreads out in the shape of a fan

peak 1 the very top: *a mountain peak* **2** a pointed part of something: *the peak of a cap* **3** to reach the end or the strongest point of something: *Our excitement peaked this morning.*

peanut a small, round nut that grows in a pod underground

pear a juicy fruit about the size and shape of a light bulb, with yellow or green skin

pearl a small, shiny, white ball found inside oysters and used in jewellery

pebble a small stone

peck to pick away at something with a pointed object: *Songbirds peck at food with their beaks.*

peculiar (pe-KEWL-yar) strange and unusual

pedal 1 a part that is pushed with the foot to make something work: *Bicycles have pedals.* **2** the act of pedalling: *to pedal your bike*

pedestrian (pe-DES-tree-an) someone who is walking

peek to look at something quickly and in secret

peel 1 the skin of some fruits and vegetables: *a banana peel* **2** to remove the skin: *to peel a banana*

peep 1 the short, high sound made by birds **2** see **peek**

pelican an ocean bird with a very large beak

pellet a tiny ball

pelt 1 a skin that has been removed from a fur-bearing animal **2** to throw a lot of things at someone

pen 1 a stick-like tool used for writing
2 a small, closed space for animals

penalty a kind of punishment

pencil a thin wooden stick used for writing and drawing

pendant a decoration that hangs from the neck on a string or chain

pendulum a rod with a weight hanging from one end so that it will swing back and forth

penetrate to make or find a way through something

penguin a black and white sea bird that does not fly but swims underwater

peninsula a large piece of land that sticks out into a body of water, such as a lake or an ocean. Part of the province of Nova Scotia is a peninsula.

penny a small coin, usually worth one cent

pentathlon in track and field, an event having five different things

people humans; men, women and children

pepper a strong, black spice

peppermint a candy with a strong mint flavour

perch 1 anything that a bird rests on when it is not flying
2 to sit on something, like a bird on a branch

percussion instrument any musical instrument that is hit or shaken, such as a drum or tambourine

perfect ① (PER-fekt) so good it cannot be better: *This is a* **perfect** *example of a fossil!*

perfect ② (per-FEKT) to improve or make better: *Sammy* **perfected** *his model for the science fair.*

perform to do something in front of an audience to entertain

performance an entertainment done in front of an audience

perfume (PER-fume) a liquid with a very sweet smell

Pp 177

perhaps possibly, maybe

peril danger

perimeter the outside edge of any defined area: *the perimeter of a field*

period 1 any specific length of time, such as a period in a hockey game
2 the dot at the end of a sentence

periscope a special tube with mirrors that allows you to see things that are above and away from you

perish to die

permanent lasting, or intended to last: *a permanent concrete cover*

permission the act of allowing: *Brenda gave us permission to use her basketball.*

permit to allow

perpendicular (per-pen-DIK-yew-lar) at a right angle to: *The walls are perpendicular to the floor.*

persecute to keep at someone with the intent of doing harm

persist to keep on doing something no matter what happens

person any child, woman or man

personal 1 belonging to one person: *Those are my personal notes.*
2 insulting to someone: *personal remarks*

personality the qualities in you that make you special

personally in person, with yourself present: *I spoke to the dentist personally.*

persuade to get someone to agree to something

pessimism (PES-i-mism) a gloomy outlook

pessimistic (pes-i-MIS-tik) to have a gloomy outlook

pest a person or animal that keeps causing trouble

pester to keep bothering

pesticide poison for killing insects or animals like rats

pet 1 an animal, such as a dog or cat, that is kept for pleasure
2 favourite: *someone's pet project*

petal one of the separate parts of a flower

petition (pe-TI-shun) a request for something signed by many people

petroleum crude oil from underground, used to make gasoline and other products

phantom something imagined, especially a ghost

phase one of the stages in a series of events: *Being "full" is one of the moon's **phases**.*

phobia a very strong fear of something

phone (informal) a word for **telephone**

phonics a method of teaching reading by connecting letters and sounds

photo, photograph a picture taken with a camera

photocopy to make a copy of a picture or piece of writing with a machine. The machine is called a **photocopier**.

phrase a group of words: *"In the green fields" is a **phrase**.*

physical (FIZ-i-kal) having to do with the body

piano a large musical instrument played by striking white and black keys with the fingers

pick 1 to choose: *You may **pick** only one of the three videos.*
2 to remove: ***Pick** apples only when they are ripe.*
3 to take something from where it rests: *Our garbage is **picked** up on Tuesdays.*

pickles cucumbers stored in vinegar

picnic a meal eaten in the open air for fun

picture a painting, drawing or photograph

pie fruit or meat baked in pastry

piece a part of something

pier a structure built from the land into a body of water for boats to be tied to

pierce to make a hole through: *A branch **pierced** the back part of the roof.*

pig 1 a mammal with a large body, flat nose and short legs, usually raised on farms for its meat
2 (informal and often impolite) a dirty or unpleasant person

pigeon a bird with a large body and small head

pile 1 a number of things on top of one another
2 (informal) a great amount: *Zach earned a **pile** of money last summer.*
3 to form or make into a pile

pilgrim someone who makes a journey to a place in the belief it is holy or special

pill a small, solid, round object containing medicine to be swallowed

pillar a post made of wood, concrete or stone

pillow a soft cushion on which to rest your head

pilot 1 a person who flies an airplane
2 a person who steers a ship through dangerous places

pimple a small swelling on the skin, usually red

pin 1 a pointed, metal object used to hold two things together

2 a piece of jewellery worn on clothing
3 one of the objects you try to knock over in the game of bowling
4 to fasten two things together with a pin (see **1**)

PIN abbreviation for **personal identification number**, a number used for security when using computer programs

pincers a device for holding two things together tightly while you work on them, or for pulling on small things

pinch 1 a small amount: *a **pinch** of salt*
2 to squeeze between two forces, often two fingers
3 in a pinch (informal) when you have no other choice and must do something quickly

pine a tall evergreen tree with cones for seeds and clusters of green needles for leaves

pineapple a large, tropical fruit with thick, scaly skin and stiff pointed leaves

ping-pong see **table tennis**

pink a pale, whitish-red colour

pioneer someone who is among the first to do something

pipe 1 a tube for carrying a liquid or gas from one place to another
2 a tube with a small bowl at one end for smoking tobacco

pirate someone on a ship who attacks and robs other ships

pistol a small handgun

pit 1 a hole dug in the ground
2 the stone inside some kinds of fruit like peaches and cherries

pitch 1 a black liquid made from tar
2 to throw
3 to put up a tent

pity the feeling you have when you are sorry that someone is in pain or in trouble

pixel a dot of light. Many pixels produce the images on a TV or computer screen.

pizza a large, round, flat piece of dough with tomato, cheese and other foods on it

place a space where something belongs

plague 1 a serious disease that spreads very quickly to many people
2 to bother very much

plaid (plad) a design made with crossing stripes: *Cecile wore a **plaid** skirt.*

plain 1 not decorated: *Jack's dad wore a very **plain** tie.*
2 easy to understand
3 a large area of flat ground

plan 1 an action worked out beforehand
2 a map of a building or town
3 to decide what is going to be done

plane 1 (informal) a word for **airplane**
2 a tool for making wood smooth

planet any of the large bodies in space that move around a sun. Earth and Mars are planets.

planetarium (pla-ne-TARE-ee-um) a special place like a museum where you learn all about things in outer space

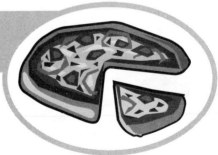

plank a type of lumber, like a board but thicker

Pp

plant 1 anything like trees, vegetables or flowers that grow in the ground **2** to put seeds and plants into the ground so they will grow

plaster a mixture of sand, lime and water applied to walls that hardens when it dries

plastic a light, strong material made from petroleum that can be made either stiff or pliable

Plasticine (plas-ti-SEEN) a soft, pliable material that you can make into many shapes with your hands

plate a flat dish

plateau (pla-TOE) a large piece of flat land that is high in the hills or mountains

platform an area that is built higher than the floor or ground

play 1 a story that is acted out **2** to be in a game **3** to make music with an instrument

player a person who takes part in a game, a play or an orchestra's performance

playground an area outside where children go to play

playwright a person who has written a play

plaza a shopping centre

plead to beg for something that you want very much

pleasant pleasing: *a pleasant holiday*

please 1 a polite word used when asking for something **2** to make someone happy: *Raj was pleased with the present I gave him.*

pleasure the feeling you have when you are pleased

pleat a flat fold: *a pleat in a skirt*

plenty 1 a lot of something: *plenty of seats in the room* **2** more than enough: *a land of plenty*

pliers a tool for holding something very tightly, or for cutting or bending wire

plod to walk very slowly and heavily

plot 1 a small piece of ground: *In the **plot** behind the house, he planted a garden.*
2 to make a secret plan: *The prisoners were **plotting** an escape.*

plow, plough (rhymes with cow) a machine used on farms for digging and turning over the soil (see **snowplow**)

pluck 1 to pull a feather, flower or fruit from the place where it is growing
2 to pull sharply at something and then let it go: ***pluck** guitar strings*

plucky brave

plug 1 in electricity, a device for connecting to the source of power

2 a device to fill a hole so liquid will not leak out
3 to fill a hole with something

plum a juicy fruit with a pit and yellow or purple skin

plumber (plummer) a person who installs and repairs water systems

plump somewhat rounded in appearance

plunder to rob a place and do much damage

plunge 1 to jump suddenly into something, usually water
2 to put something into water very suddenly

plural more than one (see **singular**): *The **plural** form of "city" is "cities."*

plus also, in addition to

plywood a large sheet of wood that is made by gluing many thin sheets together

PM (informal) in Canada, an abbreviation for **prime minister**

p.m. (also **P.M.**) an abbreviation for **post meridiem**, the time of day between noon and midnight

pneumonia (new-MO-nee-ah) a very serious disease of the lungs

poach 1 to hunt animals illegally
2 to cook food, usually an egg taken from its shell, in boiling water

Pp

pocket a part like a small bag sewn into some clothes, such as coats or pants

pod 1 a long seed case on some plants. Peas and some beans grow in pods.
2 a group of rooms arranged so that people can move from one to another easily

poem a piece of writing, usually with short lines, that presents an idea or feeling or both. Often, the words at the end of lines will rhyme. The plural is **poetry**.

poet a writer of poetry

poetic having a special feeling or sound, as in poetry

point 1 the sharp end of something: *the point of a pencil*
2 a score in a game: *Minnie is ahead by two points.*

3 intention, purpose: *What is the point of all this shouting?*
4 to direct your finger or other object at something to draw attention to it
5 to aim

pointed with a sharp end

poison any liquid or powder that can kill a living thing if it is taken into the body

poison ivy a plant with white berries and green leaves in groups of three. Poison ivy causes a serious rash in some people if they touch it.

poisonous likely to be harmful because it contains poison

poke to push hard with your finger or the sharp end of an object, such as a stick

poker 1 a game played with cards
2 a metal rod for poking at burning wood

polar bear a very large white bear that lives in the Arctic

pole 1 a long, round stick of wood or metal
2 either of two ends of a magnet

police people whose job is to enforce laws

polish to rub the surface of something to make it shine

polite behaving in a way that pleases other people

political having to do with politics

politically correct (also **PC**) carefully choosing words or actions so that you will not offend certain groups of people (see **PC 3**)

politics the different activities involved in governing a country, province or city

poll 1 a count of people to ask their opinion of something
2 a place where people vote

pollen the yellow powder inside a flower

pollute to cause harm to the environment by introducing things that are not natural to it, like chemicals, garbage, etc.

pollution the result of polluting

polygon a closed figure with five or more sides

poncho a large cloth worn like a coat. It has a hole in the centre that the head goes through.

pond a small lake

ponder to think about something very seriously

pony a small horse

poodle a kind of dog with very curly fur

pool a small body of water

poor 1 having very little money
2 unsatisfactory: *a poor crop of wheat*

popcorn dried kernels of corn that are heated until they explode

poplar a tall, straight tree that grows very quickly

poppy a bright red flower

popular liked by a lot of people

population 1 the exact number of people who live somewhere
2 all the people who live somewhere

porch a platform with a roof and open sides, added to the outside of a building

Pp 185

porcupine a wild, forest animal covered with hard, sharp, hair-like needles

pork the meat of a pig

porpoise a sea mammal, similar to a small whale

porridge a hot food made from oats boiled in water

port 1 an area on the shore of an ocean or lake where ships stop
2 the left side on a ship or airplane
3 an opening on a computer's main unit

portable light enough to be carried

portage on a river journey, to carry things by land in order to go around dangerous parts of the river

portal 1 a large, fancy gate or entrance
2 a web site that provides links to information or other web sites

porter a person whose job is to carry suitcases

portrait a painting of a person

pose 1 the way in which you hold your body
2 moving your body into a position: *posing for a picture*

position 1 the place where something is or should be
2 how something is arranged: *The body was in a sitting **position**.*

possess to own: ***Possessions** are things you own.*

possible can happen or be done: *It's **possible** that we may win today!*

post an upright pole in the ground

postal code a set of letters and numbers used to speed mail delivery

postcard a card that you can use to send a message by surface mail

poster a large picture or message, usually attached to a wall

postpone to put off until later: *Our game is **postponed** to tomorrow.*

potato a pale yellow- or red-skinned vegetable that grows underground

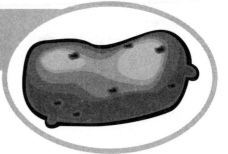

pottery cups, bowls and other things made with clay

pouch a small container

poultry (POLE-tree) birds raised on farms for their eggs or meat

pounce to suddenly jump on something

pound to beat on something very hard

pour 1 to hold a container so that the liquid in it will run out
2 to rain hard

pout to put an expression on your face to show that you are unhappy

poverty the state of being very poor

powder very tiny, very dry bits of material. Sugar is a powder.

power 1 the ability to do something
2 strength

powerful very strong or very important

practical likely to be useful: *a practical idea*

practice something you keep doing so that you will improve: *If you practice every day, it is likely you will soon play the piano very well. Tom! It's time for your piano practice!*

prairie a very large area of flat ground covered with grass

praise to say that someone or something is very good

prank mischief that is meant to be fun and not harmful

pray to perform an act of worship

prayer words that are used in worship

preach to speak to others, often in a church, suggesting how they might improve

precious very valuable

precipice (PRESS-i-pis) a very steep side of a mountain, hill or large rock

precipitation rain or snow

precise (pree-SICE) accurate and exact

predator an animal that hunts and kills living things for food: *Weasels are very efficient predators.*

Pp 187

preface notes at the beginning of something that are put there to explain

prefer to like one person or thing rather than another: *Randy prefers chocolate over vanilla.*

preference (PREF-rens) the act of preferring: *Randy says his preference is chocolate.*

prefix a letter, syllable or word put on the beginning of a word to change the meaning of it: *The prefix "un" turns happy into unhappy.*

pregnant expecting a baby

prehistoric belonging to a time very long ago

prejudice an unfavourable and usually unfair opinion about a person or group of people

premature too early; ahead of the expected time

premium 1 a special, extra gift that is sometimes offered if you buy a certain item
2 of very high quality: *This is the premium model, the salesperson told us.*

preparations things that are done to get ready

prepare to get something ready

prescription a written order for medicine

present ① (PREZ-ent)
1 something given to bring pleasure: *a birthday present*
2 the time right now: *Our teacher is away at present.*
3 here: *Our whole class is present today!*

present ② (pree-ZENT) to give someone a prize or gift in front of others

presently soon

preserve 1 to keep safe: *The shells are preserved in plastic covers.*
2 to do things to food so it will not spoil

president 1 someone who is head of a country
2 someone who is the leader of a company or club

press 1 the newspapers in a city or country

2 to push down hard against something

3 to make cloth appear smooth

pressure 1 how much one thing is pressing on another **2** the feeling some people get if there is too much to do

pretend to act as if something not true is true

pretty pleasant to look at

prevent to keep something from happening

previous (PREE-vee-us) coming before this one: *the **previous** week*

prey any animal that is hunted by another: *Rabbits are **prey** for foxes.*

price how much something costs

prick to make a tiny hole in something

pride the feeling that you are special for some reason

priest someone who leads people in their religion

primate any mammal of the group that includes monkeys, apes and humans

prime 1 of the highest quality: ***prime** grade beef* **2** most important: ***Prime** time on television is from seven to eleven p.m.*

prime minister the most important person in the government of some countries

primitive very simple: *That's a very **primitive** way of pumping water.*

prince the son of a king or queen

princess the daughter of a king or queen

principal 1 the most important: *The **principal** reason for making this rule is safety.* **2** the head person in a school

principle a way of thinking or believing that is important to you: *One of my **principles** is to tell the truth every time.*

print 1 a way of writing **2** to use a machine to produce newspapers, books, etc.

Pp

prison a place where criminals are kept as punishment

private 1 not open to everyone: *a private road* **2** not known by others: *your private thoughts*

prize an award that you win for being the best

probable likely to be true or to happen

probe to investigate

problem something that is difficult to understand or to answer

procedure (pro-SEED-yer) the special way to do something

proceed to go on

process 1 a series of actions that lead to something: *We learned about the process of making maple syrup.* **2** to treat or prepare something, especially to make it ready to sell: *processed food*

procession a group of people moving in a long line

processor the person or machine that processes

prod to push at someone or something

produce to make

producer the person or company that makes a product

production 1 the act of producing **2** the total amount produced

productive able to produce very well

profession an occupation that usually requires extra education

professor a teacher at a university

profile 1 a side view of someone's face **2** a short biography

profit money you get by selling something for more than it cost you

program, programme 1 a show on radio or television **2** a list for people in an audience telling them what is going to be presented

3 a list of instructions that tell a computer what to do

programmer a person whose job it is to write programs for computers

progress 1 improvement: *I've made real progress in math this year.*
2 under way: *The meeting is in progress already!*
3 to move forward: *From there, you will progress to the main building.*

progressive thinking and acting in an advanced, creative way

Progressive Conservative 1 a political party in Canada **2** in Canada, a member of this party

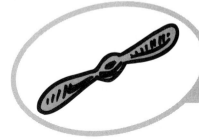

prohibit to say that something must not be done

project ① (PRAW-jekt) **1** a large amount of work **2** a plan

project ② (pro-JEKT) **1** to stick out **2** to say what will happen in the future

promise to say that you will definitely do or not do something

prompt done right away

pronounce 1 to say a word in a particular way **2** to make an important statement about something: *The Premier pronounced today a holiday!*

proof any evidence that shows something is true

prop 1 a long piece of wood or metal put under something as a support **2** to support one thing by leaning it against another: *to prop a ladder against a wall*

propel to make something go forward

propeller the set of blades that make an airplane or boat move

proper correct

property land that belongs to someone

properties the qualities of a person or thing

prophet someone who tells people what is going to happen in the future, usually as a warning

prose writing that is not poetry

Pp

prosecute in a court, to attempt to show that someone is guilty of something

prosper to become successful and rich

protect to keep safe from harm

protection something that protects

protein (PRO-teen) a natural substance in food necessary for good health

protest ① (PRO-test) an objection to something: *a protest march*

protest ② (pro-TEST) to make an objection: *Most of the citizens protested against the new law.*

proud very pleased

prove to show that an idea is true

proverb (PRAW-verb) a saying

provide to give something that is needed

provider a person, business, system or instrument that provides

province an area within a country: *Canada has ten provinces.*

prowl to move in a way so no one will notice

prune 1 a dried plum

2 to cut parts off a plant such as a tree

pry to loosen something or free it

psalm (salm) one of the hymns in the Bible

psychiatrist (sy-KY-a-trist) a doctor who treats people that have mental and emotional disorders

psychologist (sy-KOL-o-jist) someone who studies human behaviour

public 1 all the people **2** open to anyone

publish to prepare books, newspapers, etc. for printing and sale

puck a small, round, flat rubber disk used in playing ice hockey

pudding a soft, sweet food eaten as dessert

puddle a small pool of water

puff 1 a small amount of breath or air
2 to blow out small amounts of air

puffer see **inhaler**

puffin a seashore bird with a large orange and blue beak

pull 1 to get hold of something and make it come toward you
2 (informal) to have influence so that you can make something happen in the way you want it to

pulley a wheel with a groove in it

pulp anything from a plant, such as a tree, that has been ground up and made wet

pulpit a high wooden structure at the front of a church where someone stands to talk to the people

pulse the throbbing that can be felt at the wrist or other points as blood is pumped around the body

pump 1 a machine that pushes air or liquid to a place
2 to push air or liquid into something

pumpkin a large, round fruit with a thick, orange skin

punch 1 a tool for making holes
2 to hit with your fist

punctual (PUNK-chew-al) on time

punctuation marks, such as commas and periods, that help people to read and understand a piece of writing

puncture (PUNK-cher) to pierce a hole in something that is filled with air or liquid

punish to make someone suffer for a thing they have done

punishment something done to punish

pupil 1 someone who is being taught
2 the black spot at the centre of the eye

puppet a kind of doll that can be moved with the hand or with strings

puppy a very young dog

purchase to buy

Pp 193

pure with nothing else mixed in

purple a colour that is a mix of red and blue

purpose what someone intends to do

purr the sound a cat makes when it is content

purse a small bag for holding money

pursue to go after someone to try to catch her

push to use force to move something away from you

put to move something into a place: *Put the books away now, please.*

puzzle 1 a riddle or game that is difficult to solve or complete
2 to confuse: *a puzzling question*

pyjamas see **pajamas**

pylon 1 a metal tower that holds cables and power lines

2 a cone-shaped object placed on roads so that vehicles may avoid dangerous areas

pyramid a large, stone building with sloping sides that meet at one point at the top

python a large non-poisonous snake found in tropical countries

quack the sound a duck makes

quadruped (kwa-DREW-ped) any animal with four legs

quadruplet (kwa-DREW-plet) any of four babies in a single birth

Quaker a member of the Christian sect The Society of Friends

qualification a quality that makes you suitable for something

qualify 1 to have the necessary qualities or training: *Grandpa is old enough now to* **qualify** *as a senior.*
2 to show that you are able to be part of a competition: *Larkin* **qualified** *for the final race.*

quality 1 how good or bad something is
2 characteristic: *Dana will be a good president because he has leadership* **qualities**.

quantity an amount

quarantine (KWAR-an-teen) to keep someone or something apart because he may have a disease that will spread

quarrel an angry talk between people who disagree (see **argument**)

quarry 1 a place where stone and rock is taken from the ground
2 anything being hunted by a hunter

quarter one of the four equal parts something can be divided into

quartet any group of four people or things

queen a woman who is ruler of a country

quench to end your thirst by having a drink of something

quest a long and difficult search

question something you ask to get information

question mark a mark like this **?** used at the end of a written question

queue (kew) a line of people, vehicles, etc. waiting their turn

quiche (keesh) a pie made mostly of egg and cream

quick 1 done in less time than usual: *Now that was **quick**!* **2** fast: *a **quick** snack*

quicksand an area of wet sand in which objects may sink

quiet little or no sound or movement

quilt a bed cover, usually one that is sewn by hand

quit 1 to stop: *Please **quit** pushing!* **2** to leave something or exit a computer program

quite 1 very: ***quite** certain* **2** almost but not completely: *The show was **quite** funny.*

quiz 1 a test: *a spelling **quiz*** **2** a game with questions to answer

quotation the exact words someone has said

quotation marks punctuation marks like this **" "** used at both ends of a speaker's words in writing

rabbi a spiritual leader of Jewish people

rabies a serious disease that animals catch and may spread to humans

rabbit a furry animal with long hind legs and long ears

raccoon a wild animal with grey, brown and black fur, and a black face

race 1 a group of people having similar physical characteristics such as skin colour
2 a competition in which the first to finish is the winner

racism a belief that one race is better than another or not as good as another. A person who believes this is said to be a **racist**.

rack 1 a set of bars or a shelf where things can be placed
2 the antlers on a deer, elk or moose

racket 1 a kind of bat with crossed strings in a metal or wood frame: *tennis racket*
2 a lot of unpleasant noise

radar an electronic beam that can locate an object and tell the speed at which it is moving

radiant 1 bright: *radiant sunshine*
2 looking very happy: *a radiant smile*

radiate to give out heat or light

radiation a kind of energy given off by certain materials

radiator 1 the part of a car that helps control the temperature of the engine
2 an appliance used to heat rooms

Rr 197

radio a machine that receives and then plays electronic programs and messages

radioactive able to give off a certain kind of energy

radish a small, hard, round, red vegetable that grows underground

radius the distance from the centre of a circle to the edge

raffle a project to raise money. Tickets are sold to people who hope to win prizes.

raft a platform that floats on water like a boat

rafter one of the long pieces of lumber that hold up a roof

rag a torn piece of cloth

rage great anger

raid a sudden attack

rail 1 a bar or rod
2 part of a railroad track

railing 1 a fence made of metal bars
2 a fence that is built beside stairs

railroad 1 the tracks that trains run on
2 a company that owns and runs trains

rain drops of water that fall from the sky

rainbow a curved band of coloured light, seen in the sky when sun shines through rain

raincoat a coat that sheds water

raise 1 to lift something higher: *Raise that bar just a little, please.*
2 to gather together the money needed to do something: *Our class raised over a hundred dollars.*

raisin a dried grape

rake a long-handled garden tool

rally 1 a meeting of many people who come together to cheer for something
2 to begin to win again after losing for a while: *The Leafs rallied to win the game in overtime.*

ram 1 a male sheep
2 to run one thing very hard into another

RAM an abbreviation of **random access memory**, a term that describes the working memory of a computer

Ramadan the ninth month of the year in the Muslim religion, during which no food or liquid may pass the lips during daylight hours

rampage wild and senseless destruction

ran see **run**

ranch a large farm for raising animals such as cattle

random without any plan or organization

rang see **ring**

range 1 a large area with grass for animals to eat
2 the distance that a vehicle, animal, bullet or other object can travel
3 a large stove for cooking
4 a group of mountains

rank a title that shows the importance of someone: *Larkin's mother holds the rank of major.*

ransom money paid so that a prisoner will be set free

rap 1 to knock very loudly and quickly
2 a blow, usually on the head
3 a kind of music with rhyming speech and a loud electronic beat

rapid very quick

rare not often found

rash 1 red spots that suddenly appear on your skin
2 foolish: *Don't do anything rash that you may regret.*

raspberry a soft, red fruit in the shape of a small beehive

rat an animal that looks like a very big mouse

rate 1 a measured amount (see **rating**): *rate of speed; interest rate*
2 to regard or consider: *How do you rate Andar as a player?*

rather 1 fairly: *Rather cold, isn't it?*
2 prefer to: *I'd rather hike than play golf.*

Rr

rating a measure of how much something has been seen or used: *the* ***rating*** *of a television show*

rattle 1 a baby's toy that makes noise when shaken **2** to shake something so that it will make noises

rattlesnake a poisonous snake with hard rings on its tail that make noise when shaken

rave 1 a kind of very large dance party **2** to talk about something you like in a very loud and excited way

raven an entirely black bird, similar to a crow but larger

ravenous very hungry

ravine (ra-VEEN) a low area like a valley, often with a stream running through

raw uncooked

ray a thin beam of light

rayon a kind of synthetic cloth

razor a very thin, sharp blade, used mostly for shaving

reach 1 to stretch your hand out for something: *Excuse me while I* ***reach*** *for a glass.* **2** to arrive at: *We* ***reached*** *Cornwall on Tuesday.*

react to act in a certain way after something has happened: *When the lights came on, Simon* ***reacted*** *by jumping to his feet.*

read (reed) to be able to understand and say words that are written: *I can* ***read*** *this sentence. I* ***read*** *(red) it yesterday too!*

reader 1 a person who reads, either silently or out loud: *Sasha will be the* ***reader*** *of our story today.* **2** a book with stories and poems for children to read in school

ready 1 able to participate or be used right away: *Are you* ***ready*** *now? Is lunch* ***ready*** *yet?* **2** fit to be used: *Your car is* ***ready***, *Mrs. Smith.*

real not a copy

real estate any immovable property, like a house or land

real estate agent see **realtor**

realize to come to understand something completely: *I realize now that I was wrong yesterday.*

really 1 very: *Nick was really angry.*
2 truly: *Is it really starting to rain?*

realtor a person whose job is to sell real estate for the people who own it

rear 1 the back part of something: *the rear end*
2 to care for young children or animals: *The mother bear is rearing two cubs.*
3 to stand on the back legs and paw the air with the front legs

reason 1 a fact that explains why something happened: *The reason I stayed home is that I was sick.*
2 to think carefully in order to understand: *I will try to get Carrie to reason with me.*

reasonable 1 fair: *a reasonable price*
2 sensible: *Corinne behaved reasonably during all the excitement.*

rebel ① (REH-bl) someone who fights actively against the government or against people in authority

rebel ② (ree-BEL) to decide not to obey the people in charge

reboot to restart a computer

rebound to bounce back

rebus (REE-bus) writing in which some words are replaced by pictures

recall to remember

recede (re-SEED) to become smaller or move back to a different position: *The Red River floods are beginning to recede now; a receding hairline*

receive to get something that has been given to you

recent only a short time ago

recipe (REH-si-pee) instructions that tell you how to cook something

recital a performance given by one or a few musicians

recite (ree-SITE) to say out loud a poem or something else you have memorized

reckless likely to do foolish things without thinking, putting yourself in danger

recognize to correctly identify something or someone you have seen or met before: *Do you recognize me with this mask on?*

record ① (REH-cord)
1 the best that has been done in a sport, hobby or other achievement
2 the biggest or smallest that is known of something
3 facts that are written down about something

record ② (ree-CORD)
1 to write down
2 to make a musical reproduction on audio tape or compact disc

recorder a wooden or plastic wind musical instrument in the shape of a tube

recover 1 to get better after being ill
2 to get back something you have lost

recreation (reh-kree-AY-shun) activities that people do for pleasure in their spare time

recreational vehicle a vehicle that has living quarters inside and can be driven on roads

rectangle like a square, but with two parallel sides longer than the other two

recycle to gather used materials, such as glass or newspapers, and treat it so it can be used again rather than put into a landfill site

red a colour like strawberries when they are ripe

reduce to make smaller

reed a plant with a long stem that grows near water

reef a line of rocks or coral just below the surface of a lake or ocean

reek to have a strong, unpleasant smell

reel 1 a type of dance **2** a round piece of wood or metal that string, etc. is wound around: *a fishing reel* **3** to lose your balance because you feel dizzy

refer 1 to mention something while you are talking about another subject: *In his speech about trees, Pat referred to songbirds.* **2** to look in a book for information: *I suggest you refer to your dictionary.*

referee a person whose job is to enforce the rules in a game

reference the act of referring to something

reference book books like dictionaries, in which information is organized so that it can be looked up easily

referendum a vote to decide whether something should be done

reflect 1 to send back light from a shiny surface **2** to show a picture of something as a mirror does. The picture sent back is called a **reflection**. **3** to think about something for a time

refresh to make someone or something tired look and feel better again

refreshments drinks and snacks

refrigerator a machine for keeping things cold

refugee a person with no country to live in

refuse ① (ree-FEWZ) **1** to say you will not do something **2** to say you do not want something that is being offered to you

refuse ② (REH-fews) garbage

regard to think of someone or something in a certain way

region a part of a country or continent

register 1 a list of names: *a school register* **2** to sign up for something: *to register for soccer*

regret to be sorry you have said or done something

Rr

regular 1 usual: *our regular bus driver* **2** always happening at certain times: *eating regularly*

rehearsal a practice for a concert or play

rehearse to practice

reign (rain) **1** to rule as king or queen **2** the time when someone is king or queen: *during the reign of Queen Victoria*

reindeer see **caribou**

reins the straps used to guide a horse

reject to refuse to accept: *The union rejected an offer of $2 an hour.*

rejoice to be very happy about something

relate to tell

relation see **relative**

relations how two or more people or countries get along: *Canada and the U.S. have good relations.*

relationship a connection or association: *What is the relationship between these two clues?*

relative someone in the same family as you

relax to rest and become less tense

relay to pass information or an object to another person or persons

release to set free

relent to be less angry than you were

relentless to keep on and on at or about something

relevant connected to the matter being discussed: *Be sure you listen only to relevant questions after your speech.*

reliable able to be trusted

relic something very old, and usually very valuable

relief the feeling you have when you are no longer stressed about something: *Our family was relieved when Dad got home safely.*

religion what people believe and the way they show that belief through worship

reluctant not willing

rely to trust someone or something for help: *That blind lady relies on her dog to guide her.*

remain 1 to stay
2 to be left behind

remainder what is left over

remark 1 something that has been said: *Athar's remarks after the meeting got everyone upset.*
2 to say something: *Did you hear Athar remark on the meeting?*

remarkable something so unusual that it is easy to remember

remind to help yourself or someone else remember something

remote 1 far away
2 see **remote control**

remote control a hand-held instrument used to operate an appliance, such as a television set, from a distance

remove to take something away

rent an amount of money paid regularly for the use of something that belongs to another person

repair to mend

repeat to say or do the same thing again

repel to keep off: *This new coat should repel the rain and snow.*

repent to be very sorry for something you have said or done and say that you will not do it again

replace 1 to put something back
2 to take the place of another

reply to answer

report to tell or write news

represent (reh-pree-ZENT) to speak or do things on behalf of others: *Viola represented our class at the meeting.*

representation (reh-pree-zen-TAY-shun) something that is a copy, picture or model of something else: *This statue is a representation of the queen.*

representative a person who represents (see **represent**)

Rr 205

reproach to tell someone you are angry that he has done wrong

reproduce 1 to make an exact copy
2 to have children

reptile an air-breathing, cold-blooded animal that creeps or crawls. Snakes, turtles and lizards are reptiles.

reputation how everyone feels about a person

request to ask politely for something

require to need

rescue to save from danger

resemble to look like

reservation a special order that will hold something for you until you arrive: *to make reservations at a restaurant*

reserve to keep for later

reservoir an area where a large amount of water is stored

resist to fight against something and not give way

resolution 1 a promise to do something
2 how clear something is in a photograph or on a computer screen

resolve to decide very firmly: *I resolve to do exercises every day.*

resource (ree-ZORS)
1 a supply of natural things from the earth: *One of Canada's many resources is oil.*
2 a person whose job is to help: *a resource teacher*
3 a source of information: *This book and others like it are resources in our library.*

resourceful able to help yourself and get things done

respect a feeling of admiration

response an answer: *Did you get a response from Tammy yet?*

responsible in charge

rest 1 what is left over
2 the other people or things: *You can go, but the rest of the class must stay.*
3 to lie or sit without doing anything

restaurant a place to buy and eat a meal

restore to make something as good as it was before

restrict to keep from doing something or going somewhere: *Keep out! This is a restricted area.*

restriction a rule that says you may not do something

result 1 anything that happens because of other things: *The result of your carelessness is that the vase is now broken!*

2 the score at the end of a game, or marks at the end of a test

retire to stop working for pay

retreat to go back

retrieve 1 to bring back or recover: *Watch my dog **retrieve** this ball.*
2 to get data from a computer's memory

return 1 to come back to a place
2 to give something back

reuse to use something over again

reveal to let something be seen or known

revenge a wish to hurt someone because she has caused you a problem

Reverend (REV-rend) a title of respect for someone who is a church official

reverse the opposite side or direction

revolt see **rebel** ②

revolting so unpleasant that you feel sick

revolution a struggle, usually involving fighting, to change the government

revolver a handgun

reward a special present given to someone because of what she has done

rewind to wind back or wind again

rhinoceros a large, heavy quadruped found in Africa and Asia. Rhinoceroses have very thick skin and horns on their nose.

rhubarb (REW-barb) a sour-tasting plant with pink stalks and large green leaves

rhyme (rime) a similar or identical sound in two or more words: *"Snow" **rhymes** with "blow," and "cow" **rhymes** with "now."*

rhythm (RI-them) the beat or pattern in music and poetry made by strong and weak sounds

rib one of the curved bones around the chest

ribbon a strip of material, usually cloth, used for decoration

rice a grain grown in water in warm climates

Rr

rich having a lot of money

ridden see **ride**

riddle a question or puzzle in words

ride 1 to sit on a horse or bicycle and control it as it moves along: *Do you like riding? Yes, I have **ridden** many times. I **rode** twice yesterday.*
2 to travel in a vehicle like a car or train

ridge a long, narrow part, higher than what it is attached to, such as the top of a roof or a mountain

ridiculous so silly that people might laugh

rifle a long gun that is held to the shoulder when fired

right 1 on the side opposite the left
2 correct: *the **right** answer*
3 fair: *It is not **right** to cheat.*
4 completely: *Turn **right** around.*

right-handed preferring to use your right hand to do things such as write and throw

rigid (RI-jid) stiff, not able to bend

rim the edge of something

rind the skin or peel of some foods, such as oranges, cheese and bacon

ring 1 a circle
2 a circle, usually metal, worn on the finger
3 the sound a bell makes: *Hurry! The bell has **rung** twice now!*

ringleader a person who leads a group in an illegal or improper activity

rink an area of ice prepared for hockey and pleasure skating

rinse to wash something in clean water

riot a large group of people shouting and destroying things

rip to tear

ripe ready to be eaten: *ripe fruit*

ripen to become ripe

ripple a tiny movement on the surface of water

rise 1 to move upward: *Look! The sun is **rising**! Look again! It has already **risen**!* **2** to get up: *Everyone **rose** as the chief entered.*

risk possible harm or loss

ritual a ceremony performed on a regular basis or at special times

rival someone who is competing with you

river a large, fairly permanent flow of water in a natural channel

road a surface prepared for vehicles to move on

roam to wander

roar to make a loud, deep sound

roast 1 meat that is cooked in an oven **2** to cook meat or vegetables in an oven

robber someone who steals

robbery a time when a robber steals something

robin a popular, red-breasted bird that returns to southern Canada every spring

robot a machine that can move and do work like a human can

rock 1 a large mass of stone **2** to move gently back and forth

rocket a long, tube-shaped vehicle, with fuel that makes it fly into the air or into space

rod a long, thin piece of metal

rode see **ride**

role 1 a person's job or duty: *Shagreet's **role** is to thank the speaker.* **2** a character in a play, movie, etc.

roll 1 something rolled up in a round, tube-like form: *a **roll** of paper* **2** a list of names: *Tim, call the **roll**, please.* **3** a small piece of baked dough **4** to move by turning over and over

Rollerblade see **in-line skates**

roof the part that covers the top of a building

Rr

room 1 a separate space in a building, with walls around it
2 enough space

roost the perch where a bird rests for the night

root the part of a plant that is underground

rope a lot of strong threads twisted together

rose 1 a flower with a very pleasant smell and thorns on its stem

2 see **rise**

Rosh Hashanah in the Jewish religion, the beginning of the new year

rosy (informal) very satisfactory

rot to turn soft and smelly so that it cannot be used any more: *The apples have turned **rotten** because we forgot to pick them.*

rotate 1 to turn or spin
2 to take turns

rough 1 not smooth
2 not gentle: *He treated his dog very **roughly**.*
3 not exact: *a **rough** guess*

round in the shape of a circle or ball

rouse 1 to wake someone up
2 to make someone very excited

route (root *or* rowt) the way you have to go to get someplace

row ① (rhymes with toe)
1 a straight line
2 to use oars to make a boat move in the water

row ② (rhymes with how)
1 a quarrel
2 a lot of noise

royal belonging to a king or queen

Royal Commission in Canada, a special group of people set up by a government to investigate something

rubber 1 material that stretches, bends or bounces without breaking
2 see **eraser**

rubbish garbage

ruby a red gemstone

rudder a flat device fixed to the end of a boat or ship to help steer it

rude impolite

rugby a type of football in which an oval ball may be kicked, thrown or carried

rugged 1 rough, full of rocks: *rugged* countryside
2 very strong

ruin 1 a building that has fallen down
2 to destroy or spoil something

rule 1 a law or principle that everyone should obey
2 to be in charge of a country and the people who live there

ruler 1 someone, such as a king, who rules a country or empire
2 a strip of wood, metal or plastic with straight edges, used for measuring length and to assist in drawing straight lines

rumble a low, rolling sound like thunder

rumour, rumor an interesting story or fact that is being said but which may or may not be true

run 1 to move quickly on foot
2 to go or make go: *The car ran into a wall.*

3 to move or operate: *This engine runs very quietly.*
4 to extend: *The fence runs all the way around the field.*

rung 1 one of the short bars on a ladder
2 see **ring 3**

rural having to do with the country

rush to move quickly

rush hour a busy time in traffic, when many people are driving their cars at the same time

rust a rough, reddish-brown material that forms on iron and other metals

rustle a soft, gentle sound, like dried leaves in a breeze

rut a groove in the ground

RV an abbreviation for **recreational vehicle**

rye a grain grown in temperate climates

Rr 211

QqRr**Ss**TtUu

Sabbath a day of rest and religious worship in the Christian and Jewish religions

sack a large bag, usually made of strong material: *sack of potatoes*

sacrament a special ceremony in the Christian religion

sacred very holy

sacrifice to give up something very important

sad feeling unhappy

saddle a seat put on the back of an animal, like a horse, so that you can ride on it

safari (sa-FAR-ee) a journey taken in wild country to hunt or see animals like lions or elephants

safe 1 free from danger **2** a strong box with a special lock where money and important papers are kept

safety a situation or place free from danger: *The fire-fighter carried Esha to* ***safety***.

safety belt (also called **seat belt**) a special belt you wear in a vehicle to keep from being hurt in an accident

sag to go down in the middle because something heavy is pressing on it: *The couch* ***sagged*** *when our dog lay on it.*

said see **say**

sail 1 a large piece of cloth joined to a boat. Wind blows on the sail causing the boat to move. **2** to travel in a boat

sailor a member of the crew on a ship

saint 1 in the Christian religion, a very holy person who is declared to have a special place in heaven after death and therefore may be honoured and worshipped. The abbreviation is **St.** *St. Paul is a well-known Christian saint.*
2 (informal) a very kind, patient and unselfish person

sake benefit or good: *Jimmy turned down the CD player for the sake of others who wanted quiet.*

salad a mixture of vegetables or fruit eaten raw or cold

salamander a small animal similar to a lizard, but with skin instead of scales

salary money paid to someone on a regular basis for work done

sale 1 the selling of something: *Bernie made three big sales yesterday.*
2 a time when the price of things is reduced: *on sale*

salesperson (also called **sales representative**) a person whose job is to sell

sales pitch (informal) the reasons someone gives to get you to buy something or to agree to something

sales slip a paper that shows what you have bought and what you paid for it

sales tax an extra charge the government makes you pay each time you buy something

saliva (sa-LIVE-a) the liquid formed in your mouth

salmon a large ocean fish with pink flesh

salt a white, powdery substance that is often added to food for its strong taste

salute to raise your hand in a way that shows respect

same not different in any way: *My shirt is the same as yours!*

sample 1 a part of something that shows what the whole thing is like: *samples of fabric*
2 to try something to see what it is like: *Here, sample these cookies just out of the oven.*

sand the tiny bits that cover deserts, beaches and other ground

sandal a kind of light shoe with straps instead of laces

sandwich two slices of bread or a bun with other food between: *a roast beef sandwich*

sang see **sing**

sank see **sink 2**

sap the liquid inside a tree or plant

sapling a young tree

sarcasm a comment that is sarcastic

sarcastic using words that offend or insult because they are unpleasant or even rude

sardine a small ocean fish that swims in large schools

sat see **sit**

satellite 1 any machine or instrument that is put into orbit around the Earth

2 any natural body that is in orbit around another: *The moon is a satellite of the planet Earth.*

satin smooth cloth that is very shiny on one side

satisfactory good enough: *satisfactory work*

satisfy to be good enough to please someone

sauce a thick liquid put on food

saucepan a round metal pan for stove-top cooking

saucer a small plate made to hold a cup or bowl

sausage ground meat and spices stuffed into a tube-shaped skin

savage wild and fierce: *a savage animal*

save 1 to free someone from danger
2 to keep something so that it can be used at a later time

saw 1 a tool with a wide, thin blade that has teeth for cutting wood

2 to use a saw to cut wood by drawing it back and forth over the same place
3 see **see**

sawdust the powder that comes from wood when it is cut with a saw

saxophone a musical wind instrument made of metal in a curved shape, with keys for the fingers and a reed in the mouthpiece

say to speak words: *Baxter said he didn't say "Jump!" but I think he did.*

saying something wise that is often said, such as "The early bird gets the worm."

scab the hard, brown skin that forms over a cut when it heals

scald to burn yourself with very hot liquid

scale 1 an instrument for weighing
2 a thin piece of skin or bone that covers the outside of animals like fish and snakes
3 a set of measuring points on a device such as a thermometer: *the Celsius scale*
4 in music, a set of notes that begins at a particular note and then goes up or down
5 the size something is when compared to another: *On this map, the scale is 1 cm to 100 km.*
6 to climb up or down something: *scale a rock*

7 to change the size or amount: *We are going to scale down the amount of candy we give away.*

scalp the skin covering the top of your head where the hair grows

scalpel a very sharp knife used in surgery

scamper to run about very quickly

scan to look over something quickly: *Just a minute while I scan your story.*

scanner 1 a device for reading bar codes
2 a device for converting an image into digital form so that it can be used in a computer

scar a mark left on skin when some injuries heal

scarce not enough of something; not often found: *Water is scarce in the desert.*

scare 1 a sudden fright: *We gave them a big scare when we hid behind the door.* **2** to frighten someone: *Let's hide behind the door and scare them.*

scarecrow something that looks like a person that is put in fields to scare away birds, especially crows

scarf a piece of cloth worn around the neck or head (The plural is **scarves**.): *Mom said to put on your scarf.*

scarlet the colour of bright red

scatter to throw things so that they land in many different places

scene 1 the place where something happens: *the scene of a crime* **2** part of a play

scenery 1 a pleasant view of things in nature, such as rolling hills with trees

2 painted curtains and screens at the back of a stage in a play

scent a smell, usually a pleasant one

schedule (SKED-yewl or SHED-yewl) a timetable of events, duties, etc.

scheme (skeem) a plan

scholarship money or other prize given to a good student to help pay for studies

school 1 a place where people go to learn **2** a large group of fish swimming together

schooner a sailing ship with at least two masts

science knowledge about the world and everything in it, which we learn by observing different things, noting how they work and testing ideas about how they work

science fiction make-believe stories about space, life on other planets and the future

scientific having to do with science: *a scientific experiment*

scientist someone who studies science, develops ideas about things and does experiments to see if the ideas make sense

scissors a tool for cutting paper or cloth

scoff to make fun of something: *Elaine scoffed at my idea.*

scold to speak angrily to someone

scoop 1 a deep spoon for lifting out powdered material
2 to use your arms or a tool to gather something together and lift it

scooter 1 a two-wheeled vehicle with a wheel at both ends of a platform for your foot. At the front is a handle for balance and for steering.
2 a small motorcycle

scorch to heat something until it turns brown and leaves a burn mark

score 1 the number of points or goals a player or team has in a game: *The score is 3-1 for our team!*
2 to make a point in a game: *score a goal*
3 a word for twenty of something: *Two score rabbits is forty rabbits.*

scoreboard at a game, the board on which the scores are displayed

scorn to show that you think very little of a person, idea or thing

scout a person sent ahead to see what the rest of the group should expect

scowl to make your face look angry and disappointed

scramble to use your hands as well as your feet to climb somewhere

scrap 1 a small piece: *a scrap of paper*
2 garbage: *scrap heap*
3 to discard a thing or an idea

scrapbook a large book with blank pages for pasting in pictures, writing, etc.

scrape 1 to rub with something sharp
2 (informal) a disagreement or fight: *Our dog got into a scrape with another dog.*

Ss

scratch 1 a mark on the surface of something, such as your skin
2 to make such a mark
3 to rub the skin to make it stop itching

scrawl to write or print in a very untidy way

scream a very loud cry that shows pain or feelings of danger

screen 1 a thin wall or curtain used to conceal something
2 a web of thin wires placed over open windows to keep insects out
3 the front of a television set or a computer monitor, or the white panel in a theatre where images appear

screen saver in computers, a program that changes the images on a screen not in use so that the screen will not be damaged

screw 1 a kind of nail with grooves that is used to hold wooden things together

2 to turn or twist something, such as a screw

screwdriver a tool for turning screws

scribble to write or draw very quickly and untidily

script the printed version of a play or movie

scripture pieces of writing that are considered sacred in some religions

scroll a book written on a long sheet of paper that is rolled up

scrub to rub something very hard with a wet brush or cloth

sculptor an artist who makes shapes and patterns with materials like stone, wood, metal or clay

sea a very large body of salt water

seagull a common seabird with webbed feet and often with white and grey feathers

seahorse a small fish with a hooked tail and a head shaped like that of a horse

seal 1 a fur-covered, fish-eating, ocean mammal often found on the seashore

2 to close something by making two parts stick together: *seal an envelope*
3 to make something airtight

sea lion a type of large seal

seam the line where two pieces of cloth are sewn together

search to look very carefully

search engine a computer program that uses a set of keywords to return documents or other information

searchlight an electric light with a powerful beam that can be pointed in any direction

season 1 any one of spring, summer, fall or winter
2 to add spices to food to change the taste

seat a chair, stool or similar thing that people may sit on

seat belt see **safety belt**

seaweed a plant that grows in vine-like form in the sea

second 1 a very small measure of time: *Sixty seconds make one minute.*
2 the next after first: *second prize*

secondary 1 coming after something else
2 of lesser importance

secondary school a school that students attend after they have completed elementary school

second-hand owned and used by someone before

second-rate poor in quality

secret information hidden from others

secretary someone whose job is to assist others in matters like preparing letters and arranging things in an office

sect a group of persons sharing the same ideas or beliefs

section 1 a part of something
2 in western Canada, an area of land of a certain size

secure safe and strong

security 1 the feeling of being safe and protected from harm
2 in computer technology, a system for keeping files private and secret

Ss 219

sediment a solid left at the bottom of a container after liquid is poured out

see 1 to use your eyes to sense something: *Did you* **see** *the rainbow? Yes, I* **saw** *it. I've* **seen** *one twice today.* **2** to understand: *Do you* **see** *what I mean?* **3** to find out: **See** *who that is at the door, please.* **4** to visit: *We went to* **see** *my grandparents.* **5** to receive and talk to: *The doctor will* **see** *you now.* **6** to go with in order to lead: *Let me* **see** *you to the door.*

seed the tiny fruit of a plant that will grow another plant if it is put in the ground

seedling a very young plant that has just grown from a seed

seek to try to find: *The police* **sought** *(sot) everywhere for him.*

seem to appear as if something is so: *The old man* **seems** *to be asleep.*

seen see **see**

see-saw a long board balanced in the middle so that the two ends can be made to move up and down in turn

seize to take hold of something suddenly

seldom not often

select to choose

self everything in a person that makes her different from all others

selfish caring only about yourself and nothing else

self-service a system in stores, etc. in which you choose, take and sometimes pay for an item without any help

sell to give away for money: *I* **sold** *my bike yesterday!*

semi half of something: *a* **semi***-circle*

semi-detached partly, but not completely, attached to something. Usually refers to a pair of houses that share one wall.

semi-finals in sports, the set of games before the final ones that determine who is the champion

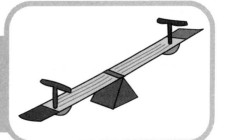

Ss

Senate in Canada, one of the two groups that make up Parliament. (The other is the House of Commons.) The Senate is sometimes called the **Upper House**.

send to make a thing or person go somewhere: *We sent Luis a letter yesterday.*

senior 1 older
2 having more power or authority: *a senior partner*
3 (informal) a senior citizen

sensation anything that you can feel happening to you: *Amanda had a sensation of falling.*

sensational (sens-SAY-shun-al) something very exciting

sensible wise

sensitive 1 very tender and easily hurt: *sensitive skin*
2 easily offended: *a sensitive person*

sent see **send**

sentence a group of words that begins with a capital letter and ends with one of these punctuation marks **. ? !**

sentry a soldier who is guarding something, usually the entrance to a building

separate apart, not joined to anything

sequin (SEE-kwin) one of many tiny, thin, round, shiny things used to decorate

sergeant a soldier or police officer in charge of others

serial a story or other information presented or sent in parts at regular intervals

series 1 a full set: *Clarence has the whole series of baseball cards.*
2 a number of things that are similar and come one after the other: *Over there you can see a series of oil wells.*

serious 1 careful and thoughtful: *a serious discussion; a serious student*
2 very bad: *a serious accident*

sermon a speech about how to improve ourselves

serpent a snake, usually a large one

servant someone whose job is to work in someone else's house

serve 1 to do things for someone or something: *to **serve** your country* **2** to sell things to a person in a store: *May I **serve** you?* **3** to give out food at a meal

server 1 someone who serves **2** in computer technology, the program that brings you pages from the Internet

service 1 the act of helping or serving: *Does this store give good **service**?* **2** providing something needed by people: *The city has a good bus **service**.* **3** a meeting for worship in a church: *a Christmas **service*** **4** repairing machinery, cars, etc. *a **service** station; repair **service***

serviette a piece of paper or cloth used to wipe your mouth and fingers at a meal

session a meeting for a special purpose: *The band had two practice **sessions**.*

set 1 a group of people or things that belong together: *a **set** of golf clubs; a chess **set*** **2** a device or instrument: *a television **set***
3 the surroundings where a movie is being made or a play is being presented: *Quiet on the **set**!* **4** to become solid or hard: *Has the jelly **set**?* **5** to put or place: ***Set** the table in the corner.* **6** to adjust: *Our alarm was **set** for 6 a.m.* **7** to start or begin: *We **set** out at 7 a.m.*

setting 1 the place where an event happens: *Our picnic was held in a beautiful **setting**.* **2** the way the controls on an instrument or appliance are arranged: *The **settings** on our television satellite can be changed easily.*

settle 1 to decide: ***settle** the argument* **2** to become comfortable: *We're **settling** into our new home.*

settlement a new town or village

settler one of the first to arrive at a place and live there (see **pioneer**)

several more than a few, but not many

severe 1 very bad or intense: *a **severe** storm* **2** unkind and difficult: *a **severe** master*

sew (so) to use a needle and thread to join pieces of cloth together

sewage waste matter carried in sewers

sewer a pipe, usually underground, for carrying human waste to a place for treatment

sex see **gender**

sexist something, usually a comment, that is thought to be insulting to one of the sexes

shabby looking worn and faded

shack a rough hut

shade 1 an area that is darker and cooler because sunlight does not touch it
2 how light or dark a colour is: *a light shade of blue*
3 to make part of a drawing darker: *I think you should shade in the leaves.*

shadow a dark shape that you see on a surface when there is something between it and a source of light

shaft 1 a long, deep hole: *a mine shaft*
2 a long, thin pole or handle

shaggy having long, untidy hair or fur

shake to move quickly from side to side or up and down:

When the trees were being shaken by the wind, I shook with fear.

shall a word that shows something must happen in the future: *You shall write the test tomorrow whether you want to or not!*

shallow not deep

shame the feeling you have when you have done something wrong or foolish

shameful so bad that it brings shame

shampoo liquid soap for washing hair, fur or fibres

shape the pattern made by drawing a line around the outside of something. A basketball has a round shape.

share 1 to divide something into parts and give one to each person: *Bettina shared her cake with all of us.*
2 to use something along with someone else: *May I share your book?*

Ss

223

shark a large ocean fish with sharp teeth

sharp 1 with an edge or point that can cut or make holes: *a sharp knife*
2 sudden: *a sharp bend in the road*
3 quick to notice things or learn: *sharp eyes; a sharp student*
4 in music, a note one halftone higher (see **flat**)

shatter to break suddenly into tiny pieces

shave 1 to cut hair from the skin and leave it smooth
2 (informal) a frightening experience: *That was a close shave!*

shawl a piece of cloth worn like a cloak

she a word used instead of the name of a ship or a female person or animal

sheaf a bundle of grain tied together at harvest time (The plural is **sheaves**.): *several sheaves*

shears large scissors used for cutting plants, hair or wool and fur from animals

shed 1 a small hut
2 to lose leaves or hair: *Trees shed leaves; cats shed hair; snakes shed skin.*

sheep an animal kept for its wool and meat

sheer very steep

sheet 1 one of the large pieces of cloth put on a bed
2 a whole piece of paper, glass or metal

sheik, sheikh (shake) a leader or important person in an Arab community

shelf a long piece of wood or metal fastened to a wall: *Sally built a shelf above her desk.*

shell 1 the thin, hard part around an egg or nut, and around some kinds of animals like oysters
2 part of a bullet

shelter a place that protects you from wind and rain, etc.

shelves more than one shelf

shepherd someone whose job is to look after sheep

sherbet a fruit-flavoured frozen dessert

sheriff a type of police officer

shield a large piece of metal or wood put in front of someone or something for protection

shift 1 a period of time for working at a job: *the day shift*
2 to move something sideways

shimmer to shine with a wavy light

shin the front of the leg between the knee and the ankle

shine 1 to give out light
2 to rub something until it gives off light

shingle one of many flat, rectangular pieces of material put on a roof to keep out rain and snow

shiny with a surface that shines

ship a large boat that makes long journeys on the ocean

shirt a piece of clothing for the top half of the body

shiver to shake because you are cold or frightened

shock a big surprise that is usually not pleasant

shock wave 1 a sudden and great rise in temperature and air movement because of an explosion or earthquake
2 a sudden and widespread feeling of fear because of something bad that has happened

shoe a strong covering for the foot: *a pair of shoes*

shone see **shine**

shook see **shake**

shoot 1 to use a weapon like a gun or bow and arrow
2 to hurt or kill by shooting
3 to move something quickly like a hockey puck

shop 1 a store
2 to go into a store to buy or to look at the items for sale

shoplift to steal things from a store when it is open for business

shore the land along the edge of oceans, lakes, rivers and streams

short 1 brief: *a short movie*
2 not tall: *a short person*

shortcut a quick way of doing something or going somewhere

Ss

shorthand a method of writing things down in a quick way

shorts a pair of pants that end above the knees

shot 1 see **shoot**
2 the firing of a gun
3 (informal) attempt: *Take your best* **shot***!*

should ought to: *I* **should** *be reading instead of watching TV.*

shoulder the part of the body between the neck and the arm

shout to call or speak very loudly

shove to push hard

shovel a wide, curved scoop with a handle

show 1 singing, dancing and other entertainment arranged for an audience
2 things that have been put together and arranged so that people can come to look at them: *a home* **show**
3 to let something be seen: **Show** *me the new car.*
4 to teach or make something clear: *Stephen has* **shown** *everyone how to tie that knot.*

shower 1 a brief, light rainfall
2 a lot of things falling like rain: *a* **shower** *of stones*

3 the part of a bathroom where you stand under a spray of water
4 to stand under the spray in **3** and clean yourself

shown see **show**

shrank see **shrink**

shred 1 a tiny strip or piece of something
2 to cut paper or cloth into very small pieces

shriek a short, high scream

shrill sounding very loud and with a high tone: *a* **shrill** *whistle*

shrimp a small ocean creature with a shell

shrink to become smaller: *Did your jeans* **shrink***? Yes, I* **shrank** *them! My sweater* **shrunk** *too.*

shrivel to curl up like a dead leaf because of dryness

shrub a bush

shrunk see **shrink**

shudder to shake suddenly because you are cold or frightened

shuffle to drag your feet along as you walk

shut 1 to cover an opening: *Shut the door.*
2 to turn off or stop something: *Shut off the engine!*

shutdown to close down something, such as a computer

shutter 1 a wooden cover fitted to the edge of a window

2 the part inside a camera that opens and closes to let in light

shy 1 not comfortable when meeting other people
2 easily frightened: *Rabbits are shy.*
3 just short of: *Your answer is shy of the correct one by only two.*

sick ill

sickening very annoying

side 1 a flat surface: *A cube has six sides.*
2 an edge: *A triangle has three sides.*
3 one of the outer parts between the front and back of an animal, thing or person
4 a group or team that is playing or fighting against one another: *to take sides*

sideshow something that is going on near another event that is more important

sidewalk a pathway, usually concrete, for people to walk on

sideways with one side ahead: *Is he walking sideways?*

siege (seej) a time when an army surrounds a town or castle so that no one can get in or out

sigh to breathe out in a way that shows you are feeling sad

sight 1 the ability to see
2 something that is seen: *What a sight!*

sign 1 anything written or drawn to tell people things: *road signs*
2 to write your name on something (see **signature**)

signal a sound or movement to catch people's attention

signature your name in writing

Sikhism a religion founded by Guru Nanak in India

silence a time when there is no sound at all

silent without any sound

silk very fine, shiny cloth made from threads spun by silkworms

sill a ledge underneath a window

silly foolish

silver a valuable, shiny metal

similar very much like another person or thing

simple 1 easy: *a simple question*
2 plain: *a simple dress*
3 not complicated

since 1 from that time: *Ever since the storm, our dog has been afraid.*
2 because

sincere truly meant: *a sincere thank you*

sing to make a tune with your voice: *Sing the carol you sang yesterday. No, we've sung it too often!*

single 1 only one of something
2 not married

singular only one person, place or thing (see **plural**): *"Book" is singular; it means one book and one only.*

sink 1 a device with a basin and taps for water

2 to go under water: *Oh no! The ship has sunk! It sank in deep water too!*

sip to drink a very small amount at one time

sir 1 a polite word used instead of a man's name: *Excuse me, sir.*
2 a title given to certain men: *Sir Robert Borden was a Canadian prime minister.*

siren a machine that makes a loud, wailing noise to warn people

sister a girl or woman who has the same parents as another person

sit to rest on a chair: *Karl was told to sit down. The chair broke after he sat on it.*

site an area of land set aside for something: *a building site*

situation the things that are happening to you: *With one bear in front and another behind, Fanny was in a difficult* **situation**.

size 1 how big or small something is: *I'll take the large* **size**.
2 the measurement of something: **size** *five shoes*

sizzle a crackling noise some foods make when heated

skate 1 a boot with a steel blade fixed to the bottom for gliding on ice (see **in-line skates**)
2 to glide on ice with skates

skateboard a platform on wheels. Skateboarders balance on it as it moves over the ground.

skeleton the framework of bones in a body

sketch to draw quickly and not always with accuracy

ski a long, flat, slender piece of wood, fibreglass or other material used to glide across snow after it is strapped to a boot: *We put on our* **skis** *before we left to go* **skiing**.

skid to slide without meaning to

skill the ability to do something well

skim 1 to deal with something very quickly, while not paying much attention
2 to take something off the top

skin 1 the outer covering of the body
2 the outer covering of some fruits and vegetables (see **peel**)

skip 1 to move lightly and quickly by hopping
2 to jump over a rope that is turning
3 to miss on purpose: *I* **skipped** *questions two and four.*

skipper a person in charge of a ship or team

skirt a piece of clothing that hangs down from the waist

skull the bony framework of the head

skunk a black animal about the size of a large cat. It has a white stripe on its tail and can give off a very bad smell.

sky the space above the earth where the stars and planets are seen

skyscraper a very tall, modern building

slab a thick piece: *a slab of marble*

slack 1 not pulled tight: *a slack rope*
2 careless: *a slack piece of work*
3 not busy: *a slack day*

slain see **slay**

slam to close something or put something down hard and quickly

slang words in a language that are not used formally

slant to slope or lean at an angle: *a slanting line*

slap to hit with the flat part of your hand

slapshot in hockey, a fast and not always accurate shot made with a swinging stroke at the puck

slash to make violent cuts in something

slaughter (SLOT-er) to kill animals

slave a person who belongs to someone else, who must work without wages, and who is not allowed to move about at will

slay to kill: *The dragon was slain by the knight.*

sled see **sleigh**

sleep to close your eyes and allow your body to rest

sleet a mix of rain and snow

sleeve the part of a coat or shirt where the arm goes

sleigh (rhymes with play) a vehicle for travelling over snow

slender thin

slept see **sleep**

slice 1 a thin, flat piece of something, such as bread
2 to cut

slide 1 to move quickly and smoothly over something **2** a long piece of metal raised up at one end, usually found on a playground and used for gliding down **3** a small photograph that can be shown on a screen

slight 1 small: *a **slight** cold* **2** thin: *a **slight** person*

slim thin

slime wet, slippery stuff that is not pleasant

slink to move in a secret way because you feel guilty about something

slip 1 a mistake **2** a piece of paper **3** a kind of underwear **4** to slide suddenly **5** to go away quietly and quickly

slipper a soft, comfortable shoe worn indoors

slippery with a very smooth surface that is easy to glide on

slit a long, narrow cut or opening

slope a rising or falling line like a hill

slot a narrow opening to put in something, such as a coin or piece of paper

slouch to move, sit or stand with the head and shoulders hanging forward

slow 1 taking more time than usual: *a **slow** train* **2** showing a time that is later than what is correct: *My watch is **slow**.* **3** not quick to figure out things

sludge any thick, sticky, oily liquid

slumber sleep

slush melting snow and ice

sly clever at tricking people

small little

small talk any unimportant conversation

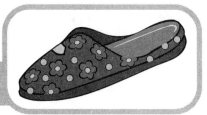

smart 1 dressed well and in a neat and tidy way **2** clever and quick to learn **3** to feel a sudden, stinging pain

smash to break something into pieces

smear 1 to make rude and insulting comments **2** to rub something over a surface, leaving it marked and dirty

Ss 231

smell 1 any odour that you become aware of through your nose
2 to use your nose to find out about something: *Michel bent over and smelled the rose.*

smile to make your face show you are pleased

smog fog mixed with air pollution

smoke 1 a blue and grey cloud that is given off by things that are burning
2 to take smoke from a cigarette, etc. into your lungs

smoke detector a device that sets off an alarm when smoke is near it

smokescreen anything used to hide the truth

smooth free from rough parts

smother 1 to cover something thickly: *a cake smothered in cream*

2 to cover someone's nose and mouth so that he cannot breathe

smuggle to bring a thing or a person into a place illegally

snack a small meal, usually eaten informally

snack bar a small, informal restaurant

snail a small, slow-moving creature somewhat like a short, thick, brown worm. Snails have shells and live on land or in water.

snake a reptile with a long body and no legs. Some snakes are poisonous.

snap 1 to break something by bending it too much or by stretching it too far
2 to make a biting motion with the teeth
3 (informal) to say something angrily and very quickly at someone

snapshot a photograph

snare 1 a trap
2 to catch something in a trap

snarl the sound a dog makes when it is warning people or other dogs to stay away

snatch to take something quickly

sneak to move in a way so that you are not seen or heard

sneer an insulting look that shows disrespect

sneeze a sudden rushing of air out of your nose

sniff to take air into the nose in short, quick breaths

snip to cut a little bit off

snob a person who behaves as if others are not as clever or important

snore to make very noisy breaths through the nose and mouth while you sleep

snorkel a tube to breathe through when you are under water

snout an animal's nose and mouth that sticks out from the rest of the face

snow small, white pieces of frozen moisture

snowball snow packed into the shape of a ball for throwing

snowbird (informal) a person, especially a Canadian, who goes to warmer climates in wintertime

snowblower a machine that blows snow from roads and sidewalks

snowdrop a very small, white flower that blooms in early spring

snowfall the amount of snow that falls in a particular time and place: *The **snowfall** was light in Winnipeg but heavy in Flin Flon.*

snow fence a fence with small slats, or in a web form, that can prevent snow from drifting onto roads, etc.

snowflake a single little bit of snow

snowman a statue of snow that is made to look like a person

Ss 233

snowmobile a powered vehicle that travels over snow on skis and a wide rubber belt

snowplow, snowplough a powered vehicle that pushes snow from roads and sidewalks, etc.

snowshoe a platform made of webbing attached to an oval frame. Snowshoes are worn on the feet to help people walk over deep snow.

snowsuit a warm, one-piece set of outer clothing

snow tire a tire with deep grooves that makes it easier for vehicles to drive on roads that are covered with snow

snub to ignore someone in a rude way, especially if she is trying to be friendly

snug cozy

snuggle to curl up in a warm and comfortable place

so 1 to such a degree: *Jennifer was **so** tired she fell asleep at dinner.*
2 therefore: *It was raining, **so** Julie went inside.*
3 also: *Peggy came, and **so** did Mark.*
4 about, more or less: *I'll be finished in a minute or **so**.*
5 true: *Ernie says that's not **so**!*
6 in the same way: *Dolores says we should go, and I think **so** too.*

soak to make something very wet

soap something used with water for washing

soar to fly very high in the air

soccer a game that two teams play with a round ball that they try to kick into each other's net

soccerball the ball that is used in soccer

social 1 living and spending time with others rather than being alone: *Bees are* **social** *insects.*
2 organized so that people can be together for pleasure rather than business: *The prime minister attended a* **social** *function.*

socialism the belief that wealth should be spread among everyone in a community and that everyone should have equal access to a community's services

socialist a person who believes in the ideas of socialism

socialize 1 to spend time with others, usually in a pleasant activity
2 to organize something according to the ideas of socialism: **socialized** *medicine*
3 to be able to be together with people easily: *Our dog is* **socialized** *now.*

society (so-SY-e-tee) **1** all the people in a community or a country: *Canadian* **society** *believes in things like taking turns.*
2 a group of people that meet and do things together because they believe in and enjoy the same things: *the Music* ***Society***

sock a piece of clothing for the foot

socket the part that an electric light bulb, plug or computer, etc. attaches to

sofa a long, comfortable seat, like a chair for more than one person

soft 1 not firm. Things like cotton and wet clay are soft.
2 quiet: **soft** *music*

softly gently

software programs that can be run on a computer

soggy wet all the way through

soil 1 the top layer of the ground, where plants have their roots
2 to make dirty in some way: *Try not to* **soil** *your shoes this time.*

solar having to do with the sun: *the* **solar** *system*

solar cell a type of battery that uses radiation from the sun to make power

solar panel a large platform containing solar cells

solar system a sun with all its planets, asteroids and satellites

sold see **sell**

Ss

soldier a member of the army

sole 1 the flat platform at the bottom of a shoe **2** an ocean fish

solemn quiet and serious: *a* **solemn** *ceremony*

solid 1 not hollow: *Golf balls are* **solid***; tennis balls are not.* **2** very likely: *Justin has a* **solid** *chance of winning today.* **3** firm: *The tower was built on* **solid** *rock.*

solitary alone or lonely

solo something performed or done by one person: *a* **solo** *piano piece*

soluble able to be dissolved in a liquid, such as water

solution answer

solve to work out an answer

some 1 a few: **some** *candy* **2** a certain number or amount: **Some** *of the students stayed inside.* **3** remarkable, interesting: *That was* **some** *jump shot!*

somebody a person

somehow in some way

someone a person

somersault (SUM-er-salt) a body rolling head over heels along the ground or in the air

something a thing

sometimes at some times but not others

somewhere in or to a place

son a boy or man who is someone's child

song words that are sung to music

soon in a very short time from now

soothe to make someone who is upset feel calm

soprano the highest singing voice in people, or the highest range for musical instruments

sorcerer (SOR-ser-er) a character in stories who can do magic things

sore painful when it is touched: *a* **sore** *arm*

sorrow a feeling of sadness

sorry 1 to feel sad and wish you had not done something: *Sheena was* **sorry** *she yelled at her sister.*

Ss

2 to feel sad because of what has happened to another person: *I'm so **sorry** you broke your arm.*

sort 1 a kind: *I like this **sort** best.*
2 to arrange things in groups or rows

sought see **seek**

soul 1 the quality and character of a person
2 in some religions, a person's spirit that continues after the body dies
3 a kind of music or food, usually associated with people whose ancestors are from Africa

sound 1 anything that can be heard: *What's that strange **sound**?*
2 to make a sound: *Quick! **Sound** the alarm!*

sound effects (sometimes written **FX**) a recording or imitation of a sound used in movies or other performances

soundtrack the recorded music, voices and sounds used in a movie or other video production

soup a liquid food, usually served hot

sour 1 a dry, bitter taste, as a lemon has
2 not fresh, spoiled: ***sour** milk*

source the place something comes from

south 1 a compass point
2 the direction to your right when you face east (see **east**)
3 a region of a country or continent: *They moved down **south**.*

southern from the south or in the south

souvenir (SOO-ven-eer) an item you keep because it is special to you

sow ① (rhymes with toe) to plant seed in the ground

sow ② (rhymes with how) a mother pig

soy, soya a food in solid or liquid form that we get from the soybean plant

soybean, soya bean a plant that produces beans very high in protein

soyamilk a substitute for animal milk, made from the soybean

space 1 the distance between things: *I don't like having a big **space** between the chairs.*
2 a place with nothing in it
3 all the area beyond the Earth's atmosphere, also called **outer space**

spaceship a vehicle that travels in space

Ss 237

spade 1 a tool for digging (see **shovel**)
2 one of the four suits in a deck of playing cards

spaghetti a kind of pasta in the shape of a string

spam unwanted email that you receive (see **junk mail**)

span the full distance or extent: *a span of sixty metres; a span of sixty years*

spaniel a kind of dog with a wide nose, silky fur and long ears

spare 1 not in use, but kept if needed: *a spare tire*
2 to give up to someone else: *Can you spare some of that bread?*

spark 1 a tiny piece of glowing material thrown out by a fire
2 to give off sparks
3 liveliness: *Manuel's spark will help this group to win.*

sparkle to shine with a lot of tiny flashes of bright light

sparkler a stick of material that gives off sparks when flame is touched to it

sparrow a small, brown bird with white, grey and black markings

spawn to give birth to, usually used to refer to eggs laid by fish

speak to say words: *Did you speak to Les? Yes, I spoke to her, but I haven't spoken to Juan.*

spear a long pole with a sharp point, used as a weapon

special different from any other kind

species (SPEE-sees) a separate group or sort: *species of plant*

specific (spe-SI-fik) particular and exact

specimen 1 an example of one kind of plant or animal
2 a small amount of something that shows what the rest is like

speck a tiny mark

speckled covered with tiny marks

spectator a person watching a game or show

speech 1 a talk given to a group of people
2 the power to be able to talk

speed how quickly something moves or happens

spell 1 to write a word using the right letters in the right order
2 a period of time: *It rained for a **spell** and then stopped.*
3 in stories, magic words that make a character do something: *cast a **spell***

spend 1 to use money to pay for things
2 to pass time: *Cassie **spent** Tuesday at home.*

sphere (sfeer) a round figure like a ball or the moon

spice a special food, often in powdered form like salt, that adds special flavour

spider a small creature with eight legs. Many spiders weave webs to catch flies.

spike a larger version of a nail (see **nail 1**)

spill to cause something to fall out of a container: *Oh, oh! Lannie **spilled** the juice!*

spin 1 to turn around and around quickly
2 to make thread by twisting long pieces of wool or cotton

spinach (SPIN-ich) a green, leafy vegetable

spine 1 the long bone down the centre of the back
2 the part of a book cover that holds the pages together

spinoff a new product, material or idea that comes from something else

spiral the shape of a line that keeps going round and round in smaller or larger circles

spiral staircase a staircase that goes round and round instead of straight up and down on a slant

spire the tall, pointed top of a church tower

spirit 1 a ghost
2 a quality that makes a person lively and brave
3 see **soul 2**

spiteful full of a wish that harm will come to someone

splash to jump into water in a way that makes a noise and causes water to fly about

splendid excellent, very pleasing

splint a straight piece of wood or metal tied to a broken bone to make it stable

splinter a small piece of wood, glass or metal that has broken off a larger one

split 1 to break into parts: Manny **split** wood for the fire.
2 to divide up: We **split** the chips three ways.

spoil 1 to become too ripe or too old and no longer useful
2 to be too kind to a child so that she believes she can always have what she wants

spoke, spoken ① see **speak**

spoke ② one of the wire rods in the wheel of a bicycle, etc.

spool a round piece of wood or metal that thread or wire is wound on

spoon a device used to scoop up food

sport any game that exercises the mind and body

sportsmanship behaviour that shows a belief in fair play

spot 1 a mark, often round in shape
2 a place: This is a warm **spot**.
3 to notice: Elaine was the first to **spot** the train.

spotlight a strong light that can shine on one small area

spouse a person one is married to

spout the part of a container where liquid pours out

sprain to twist a part of the body, such as an ankle, and injure it

sprang see **spring**

sprawl 1 anything spread widely over an area: urban **sprawl**
2 to sit or lie with your arms and legs spread wide

spray to make tiny drops of liquid fall all over something

spread 1 to stretch something out to its full size: *The bird spread its wings.*
2 to make something cover a surface: *Spread the blanket over the grass.*

spreadsheet a computer program that shows numbers in boxes called **cells**

spring 1 the season when the weather turns warm and plants begin to grow
2 a place where water comes out of the ground
3 a piece of metal wound in a spiral shape that returns to this shape after being pressed upon
4 to move suddenly upward: *Willie tried to spring up to catch the ball, but he sprang too late. If only he had sprung a second sooner.*

sprinkle to make a few tiny pieces or drops fall on something

sprint to run very quickly for a short distance

sprout 1 the first growth of a plant
2 to start to grow

spruce a common evergreen tree with leaves in the shape of needles

sprung see **spring**

spun see **spin**

spurt 1 a sudden upward movement of water
2 a sudden increase in speed

spy 1 a person who secretly gathers information from an enemy or competitor
2 to notice: *Who spied the first robin?*

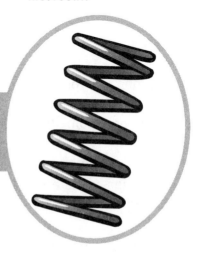

squabble to argue about something that is not very important

squad 1 any small group organized for a special purpose: *a cleanup squad*
2 in sports, a word sometimes used instead of team

square 1 a shape with four sides that are equal in length
2 a public area in a community: *the town square*

squash 1 an oval or round vegetable, usually green, with a hard skin and soft inside
2 an indoor game for two people played with rackets and a ball hit against a wall
3 to press something so hard it goes out of shape

squat to sit close to the ground with your knees bent

squeak a short, soft, high sound

squeal a long, loud, high sound

squeeze to press something between two other things, such as your hands

squid an ocean creature with eight short arms and two very long ones

squirm to twist and turn your body about in the same spot

squirrel a small, furry animal with a long tail. Squirrels are excellent tree climbers.

squirt to make a thin stream of water come out of something

St. 1 an abbreviation for **Street**
2 see **saint**

stab to push at with the sharp, pointed end of something, often a knife

stability (sta-BILL-i-tee) being very dependable and solid

stable 1 a building where animals are kept
2 steady, not likely to fail: *a **stable** person; a **stable** ladder*

staccato (sta-CA-toe) continuing sounds that are short and very quick

stack 1 a pile
2 to make a pile

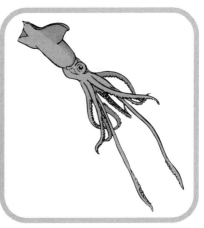

stadium a large building where people can watch sports and other events

staff the people who work in a place

stage 1 a raised floor in a theatre or other place where people stand to perform
2 the point someone has reached in an activity or project

stagger to walk crookedly as if you may fall over

stagnant not flowing or fresh: *a stagnant pool of water*

stain a dirty mark made on something

stair one of a set of steps that lead from lower to higher or vice versa

staircase a set of stairs with railings on it

stake a thick, pointed stick

stale not fresh: *stale bread*

stalk (stok) **1** the stem of a plant
2 to secretly follow a person or animal

stall 1 one of a set of small shops all in a row, where people sell things: *Markets have stalls.*
2 a place for one animal in a stable

stallion a male horse

stammer to keep repeating certain words or sounds because it is difficult to say them

stamp 1 a special paper you stick on pieces of mail to pay the post office to deliver it
2 to bang a foot on the ground

stand 1 something made to place things on: *a cake stand*
2 a stage: *Our band will play on the stand over there.*
3 to be on your feet without moving: *Keep standing while the band plays.*
4 to be in a position for a long time: *The statue stood at the corner.*
5 to tolerate: *I won't stand for that!*
6 to set something in place: *Stand the lamp in the corner.*

standard how good something is: *a high standard of work*

standby something available to be used: *standby seats*

stand-in a replacement

standing reputation

stank see **stink**

star 1 one of the tiny, bright objects seen in the sky at night
2 a famous person, usually an actor, singer or sports person

Ss 243

stare to look at someone or something for a long time without moving your eyes or blinking

starling a brownish-black bird with gold flecks about the size of a robin

start 1 to take the first steps in something: *Jannie started taking violin lessons.* **2** to make something happen: *Eduardo will start the car.*

startle frighten

starvation illness or death caused by great hunger

starve to be very ill or die from lack of food

state 1 how someone or something is: *in a state of good health*
2 a country or part of a country
3 to say something, usually important: *State your reasons for doing this!*

statement words that say something, usually important

station 1 a place where people get on or off trains or buses
2 an office or centre for police and fire departments

stationary not moving

stationery paper, envelopes, etc., used to write and send letters

statue (STA-chew) a model of someone or something made from wood, metal, stone or other material

status a person's or group's importance compared to others

status quo the state or condition of things at present

statute a law passed by a government

stay 1 to continue to be in a place: *Stay in bed for a few days.*
2 to visit for a while: *We stayed in St. John's for the holidays.*

steady 1 not likely to shake or fall over: *Is this ladder steady?*
2 regular and dependable: *a steady breeze; a steady worker*

steak (rhymes with rake) a thick slice of meat

steal to take something that does not belong to you and keep it: *Did she really **steal** it? Yes, she **stole** it. And it's not the first thing she's **stolen** either.*

steam a very hot vapour that rises from boiling water

steel a strong metal made from iron ore

steep a very sharp rise or slant

steeple a tall, pointed tower on a building, usually a church

steer 1 a male cow
2 to make a vehicle go in a particular direction

steering wheel a device for steering as in **steer 2**

stem see **stalk 1**

step 1 the movement you make with your foot when you walk
2 the flat place you put your foot when you climb stairs

3 a move or action to accomplish something: *A first **step** in writing is to pick up your pen!*
4 **step down** resign or retire so that someone else may lead
5 **step in** to intervene or interfere

stepbrother a boy or man who has brothers or sisters because one of his parents has married someone with children

stepdaughter a spouse's daughter from a previous marriage

stepfather a man who is married to your mother but who is not your birth father

stepladder a short ladder that folds in two and stands like a triangle

stepmother a woman who is married to your father but who is not your birth mother

stepsister girl or woman who has brothers or sisters because one of her parents has married someone with children

stepson a spouse's son from a previous marriage

stern 1 the back end of a boat
2 serious and strict

Ss 245

stethoscope a device for listening to a person's heart

stew a mixture of meat and vegetables cooked in liquid

stick 1 a long, thin piece of wood
2 a long, thin piece of anything: *a **stick** of gum*
3 to fasten together: *I'll **stick** them together with glue, and they'll be **stuck** that way for good!*
4 to press into something: ***Stick** the candles into the cake.*

stickhandle to use a hockey stick to move a hockey puck back and forth in a way that helps you move it around other players

sticky able to become fastened to other things

stiff 1 not easily bent: ***stiff** cardboard*
2 hard to move: *My legs are **stiff**.*
3 (informal) completely: *bored **stiff***

still 1 not moving: ***still** waters*
2 silent: *Be **still** so we can hear!*
3 the same now as before: *Is he **still** sick?*

stilts a pair of poles you can use to walk high above the ground

sting to hurt with a sharp point: *A bee **stung** me!*

stink to have a very strong smell: *The stable was filthy and **stank**.*

stir 1 a fuss: *Sanja caused a **stir** when she picked up a snake.*
2 to move a liquid around with a spoon
3 to start to move: *The lions began to **stir** at sunset.*

Ss

stitch 1 an action with a needle in sewing or knitting **2** a pain in a muscle, usually your side

stock 1 the things a business has for sale **2** belief or trust: *I don't put much* **stock** *in what she says.*

stockbroker someone whose job is to buy and sell shares in businesses

stock exchange a place where stockbrokers conduct business

stocking an item of clothing to cover the foot and leg

stole, stolen see **steal**

stomach 1 the part in the middle of the body where food goes when it is eaten **2** (informal) tolerate: *I can't* **stomach** *that kind of music.*

stone 1 a small piece of rock **2** see **pit 2**

stood see **stand**

stool a small seat without a back

stoop to bend the body forward

stop 1 to put an end to: **Stop** *all this noise!* **2** a place where things pause: *a bus* **stop** **3** the act of stopping: *We must put a* **stop** *to this.*

4 something that causes things to quit moving: *a door* **stop** **5** to stay briefly: *We* **stopped** *at Red Deer.*

store 1 a business where you can buy things **2** to keep things until they are needed

storey any of the levels of a building: *a four-***storey** *apartment*

story words that tell about something that has really happened or that has been made up

stout large in size

stove an appliance that gives out heat for cooking or warmth

stowaway someone who hides or is hidden on a vehicle that is travelling a long distance, often to another country

Ss 247

straight 1 level, not curved, bent or crooked
2 accurate and truthful: *a straight answer*
3 ordinary and usual, especially in lifestyle

straighten to make or become straight

strain 1 to stretch or push too hard
2 to hurt yourself by stretching or pushing too hard
3 to separate a liquid from solids

strange 1 unusual, not known or seen before: *a strange place*
2 unusual and very surprising: *a strange story*

stranger someone who is not known by others in a place

strap a flat strip of strong material

strategy (STRA-te-jee) a plan for doing something

strategic (stra-TEE-jik) important

straw 1 the dry stalks of grain after it has been harvested
2 a thin tube for drinking liquid

strawberry a sweet berry that is red when ripe

stray 1 an animal that is without a home: *a stray cat*
2 to wander from the proper path

streak 1 a long, narrow mark
2 to move very quickly

stream a flow of water that is moving across an area of land

streamer a long strip of paper or ribbon, usually used to decorate

street a road with buildings along the sides

streetcar (sometimes called **trolley**) a type of bus that runs on rails like a train

strength how strong someone or something is

stretch to pull something to make it longer, wider or tighter

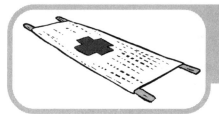

stretcher a pair of poles with material stretched between them so that a person can be carried

strict keen on always being obeyed

stratosphere the upper layer of the Earth's atmosphere

strike 1 an event where employees stop working to get something from the employer
2 to hit: *Lightning **strikes** very tall trees.*

string a thin kind of rope, similar to thread

strip 1 a long, narrow piece: *a **strip** of cloth*
2 to take off clothes or covering

stripe a coloured band across or down something

stroke 1 a hitting movement: *golf **stroke***
2 a sudden, serious illness
3 to move your hand slowly and gently along a surface: *to **stroke** the back of a pet*

stroll to walk slowly and easily just for the sake of walking

strong 1 healthy and able to do things that need a lot of energy: *a **strong** horse*
2 not easily broken: *a **strong** rope*
3 with a lot of flavour: ***strong** tea*

struck see **strike**

structure anything that has been built, such as a house or a bridge

struggle 1 a difficult time doing something: *It was a **struggle** for her to climb the tree.*

2 to try very hard to do something

stubborn not willing to change your idea even though it may be wrong

stuck 1 see **stick**
2 to be in a situation or place longer than you want to be: *We were **stuck** in traffic.*

student someone who studies and learns, usually in a school (see **pupil 1**)

studio a place where an artist works and displays her work

study 1 to spend time learning something
2 to examine something very carefully

stuff 1 any kind of material: *Give me some **stuff** to put on this cut, please.*
2 to push some material into something: ***Stuff** these clothes into the laundry bag.*

stuffing 1 the material used in some furniture, especially chairs and sofas
2 a mixture of food put inside chickens, etc. before cooking them

stuffy 1 in need of fresh air: *a **stuffy** room*
2 not very much fun

stumble to fall over something

Ss

stump the part of a tree, pencil or tooth that is left when the top breaks off

stun 1 to hit someone or something so hard that it cannot think or act normally **2** to surprise

stung see **sting**

stunk see **stink**

stunt 1 a trick or clever action that entertains people: *circus stunts*
2 an action meant to attract attention (see **gimmick**): *an advertising stunt*

stupid 1 very silly
2 slow to learn and understand

sturdy strong and healthy

stutter see **stammer**

sty 1 a very sore swelling on the eyelid
2 a pen for pigs

style 1 the way something is done or made
2 the way someone behaves

subject 1 the topic that you write or speak about
2 a citizen in a country that is ruled by a king or queen

submarine a ship that can travel under water

submerge to put under water

submit to give in to

substance any kind of material

subtitle a second, different title written underneath the main title

subtract to take away from, usually involving numbers: *Two subtracted from six leaves four.*

subtraction the act of subtracting

suburb a community on the border of a city

suburban having to do with the suburbs

subway an underground tunnel for travelling in vehicles or on foot

subway train a train that travels in a subway

succeed to do or get what you wanted to do or get

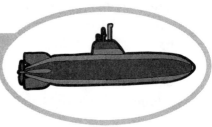

successful able to do or get what you want

such 1 of a similar kind: *toys such as these*
2 so great: *It was such a surprise.*

suck 1 to take in air or liquid from something
2 to keep moving something, such as candy, in your mouth until it dissolves

sudden quickly and without much warning

sue to use a lawyer and the courts to take action against someone

suede (swayd) a kind of soft leather that is not shiny or smooth

suet (SOO-it) a kind of hard fat that comes from animals

suffer to have to put up with something unpleasant, such as pain

sufficient (suh-FISH-ent) enough

sugar a sweet food that is added to other foods

suggest (su-JEST) to present an idea that you think is useful

suicide the act of ending one's own life

suit 1 a jacket and pants or a skirt that are meant to be worn together
2 one of the four different types of cards in a deck of playing cards
3 to fit in well with someone's plans: *I'd come today but it doesn't suit me to do so.*
4 to look good on someone: *The new uniform suits everyone on the team.*

suitable just right for something: *suitable shoes for hiking*

suitcase a container used for keeping your things when you travel

suite 1 a set of rooms in a building: *We rented a suite at the hotel.*
2 a set of furniture: *a kitchen suite*

sulk to stop speaking or co-operating because you are angry

sultan the ruler of a Muslim city or country

sum the amount you end up with when adding things together

sumac, sumach (SOO- or SHOO-mak) a shrub that grows widely in Canada. Its leaves turn very bright red in fall.

summer the season of the year when the weather is warmest

summit 1 the top of a mountain
2 a meeting of the most important people: *a summit conference*

sun the main star in our solar system

sunburn a painful reddening of the skin caused by sunlight

sunflower a very tall flower with a large, usually yellow, bloom

sung see **sing**

sunglasses a pair of glasses with dark lenses

sunk see **sink 2**

sunny with the sun shining

sunrise the time when the sun comes up

sunscreen a liquid mixture worn on the skin to prevent sunburn

sunset the time when the sun goes down

sunshine the light and heat that comes from the sun

sunstroke fainting and dizziness that may occur to someone exposed to too much sunlight

suntan see **tan 1**

superhuman something that is more than normally expected from a person: *During the storm, Dee made a superhuman effort to close the door.*

supermarket a very large store where people serve themselves groceries and then pay at a checkout counter

supersonic faster than sound travels

superstar a famous person who is even more famous than others in her field (see **star 2**)

superstition (soo-per-STI-shun) a fear of or a belief in things that are not natural: *An old superstition is that walking under a ladder will bring bad luck.*

superstitious accepting and believing in superstitions

supervise to be in charge and make sure that things are done correctly

supper a meal you eat in the evening

supply 1 things kept ready to be used when needed: *a supply of paper*
2 to give what is needed: *The army will supply trucks for the parade.*

support 1 to hold up something so that it does not fall
2 to help someone who is having trouble

suppose to accept that something is true or possible

supreme the most important or very best

sure (shoor) knowing that something is true or right

surf 1 the line of foamy waves on a seashore

2 to ride on top of these foamy waves on a board called a **surfboard**

3 to open a number of Internet sites one after the other without being really certain what you are looking for

surface 1 the outside of something: *A cardboard box has six surfaces.*
2 the top of something: *the surface of my desk*
3 how something looks at first: *On the surface, it appears to be safe.*

surfboard a board for riding on surf (see **surf 2**)

surgeon a doctor whose job it is to perform operations in hospitals

surgery treating the body by removing or repairing a diseased part

surname your last name

surprise 1 something that happens which is not expected
2 to do something that is not expected

surrender to stop resisting and give up

surround to be all around someone or something

survival the act of surviving (see **survive**)

survive to continue to live after something terrible has happened: *Everyone in the village **survived** the earthquake.*

suspect ① (SUS-pekt) a person that is believed to be guilty of doing something: *The police have arrested a **suspect**.*

suspect ② (sus-PEKT) to believe that a certain thing is true or that a certain person has done something: *I **suspect** that someone has hidden our coats.*

suspicious (sus-PISH-us) the feeling that something is not right

swallow 1 a small bird with a long tail, pointed wings and a dark blue body

2 to make something go down your throat

swam see **swim**

swamp an area of very wet ground with plants in it (see **bog** and **marsh**)

swan a large water bird with a long, curved neck

swap (rhymes with hop) to trade

swarm a large number of things close together, usually insects

sway 1 to move from side to side
2 to make someone change her mind: *Amnon's opinion was **swayed** by the newspaper story.*

swear 1 to make a very serious promise: *He has **sworn** to tell the truth.*
2 to use rude and offensive words

sweat to lose moisture from the body as it comes through your skin

sweep to use a brush or broom to clear away things: *Liam **swept** this floor just yesterday!*

sweet very pleasant, usually in taste

swell to get bigger: *His ankle is really **swollen** now.*

swelling a swollen place on the body

swelter to be very hot and uncomfortable

swept see **sweep**

swerve to move suddenly to one side so that you will not run into something

swift quick

swim to move the body on or in deep water without touching the bottom: *I swam across yesterday; I'll swim it today; by Sunday, I'll have swum it six times.*

swindle to cheat

swing 1 to move back and forth: *The door swung open and closed in the wind.* **2** a seat hung by ropes or chains so that it can move back and forth

swipe to hit at

swirl to move around quickly in circles

switch 1 anything that is turned or pressed to make something begin or stop working: *a light switch; a switch for a machine* **2** to change from one thing to another: *to switch seats*

swollen see **swell**

swoop to fly downward suddenly

sword (sord) a weapon like a knife with a very long blade

swore, sworn see **swear**

swum see **swim**

swung see **swing**

syllable (SILL-a-bul) any word or part of a word that has a separate sound: *The word syllable has three syllables: sill, a and bul.*

symbol something that people realize stands for something else: *A dove is a bird, but it's also a symbol for peace.*

symmetrical (si-MET-ri-kal) having two parts that are exactly alike but turned in the opposite way: *A butterfly's wings are symmetrical.*

sympathy the feeling you have when you fe͡͡ ͡͡ someone ͡͡ ͡͡

sympathet. sympathy

symphony a long, serious piece of music played by an orchestra

symptom a sign that something is happening: *A fever and a runny nose are often symptoms of a cold.*

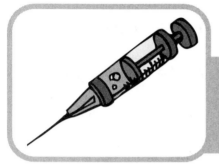

synagogue (SIN-a-gog) a house of worship in the Jewish religion

synchronize (SIN-kron-ize) to make adjustments and arrangements so that two or more events will happen together

synthetic manufactured rather than natural

syringe (srinj) a device for holding and pushing liquid, usually medicine, into a hollow needle, which then goes into the body

syrup a thick, sweet and sticky liquid

system a set of parts, things or ideas that are designed to work together

's

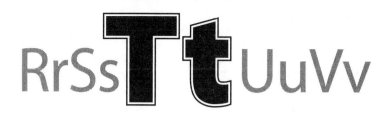

RrSs**Tt**UuVv

tab 1 a small flap or loop on the edge of a piece of cardboard or on clothing **2** (informal) the bill in a restaurant or store **3 keep tabs on** (informal) to supervise

table 1 a piece of furniture with a flat surface supported by legs **2** a list of facts, such as numbers, arranged in a special order

tablecloth a piece of material spread on the surface of a table

tablespoon a spoon for serving food

tablet a pill

table tennis a game between two people who use small round rackets to hit a hollow plastic ball over a net strung across a table (see **tennis**)

tack 1 a small nail with a flat head **2** the equipment used for riding or driving a horse

tackle 1 the equipment needed for doing something: *fishing tackle* **2** (informal) to try to do a job that needs doing: *tackle the leaky pipes* **3** to try to knock someone over in a game such as football

tadpole a water creature that hatches from an egg and will develop into a frog or toad

tag 1 a thin piece of material fastened to another item to tell something about it: *price tag; dog tag* **2** to put on such a tag: *Tag every item for sale.*

Tt 257

3 a game in which one person chases and then touches another. The person touched must then chase and touch another. *Tag, you're it!*
4 to follow: *My kid brother always tags along.*

tail the part at the end. Animals have tails; so do airplanes and kites.

tailor someone whose job is to make clothes

take 1 to get into possession and control: *Who took the hammer?*
2 requires: *It takes courage to do that.*
3 to adopt: *She took another name when she married.*
4 to do an action: *Who wants to take a walk?*
5 to help get somewhere: *Who took you to the movie?*

tale a story, usually one that is made up

talent the ability to do something very well: *a talent for singing*

talk 1 a conversation or discussion: *There has been a lot of talk about this.*
2 to communicate in words that you speak

talkative fond of talking a lot

tall measuring above average from top to bottom

Talmud in the Jewish religion, the books of laws and ceremonies

tambourine a percussion instrument that you shake or hit with your hand

tame not wild or dangerous

tamper to make changes in something so that it is different and may not work properly

tan 1 skin that has turned brown after being exposed to sunlight
2 a light brown colour

tangerine (tan-jer-EEN) a type of small orange

tank 1 a large container for liquid
2 a large, heavy vehicle used in war. It runs on tracks and contains several guns of different sizes.

tanker 1 a large ship for carrying liquid
2 a large truck for carrying liquid

tap 1 see **faucet**
  2 a light touch or knock: *tap* on the door
  3 to drill a hole into something: to *tap* maple trees in spring

tap dance a type of dancing in which the performer makes sounds with the feet in addition to movements

tape 1 a narrow strip of material
  2 to record sound

tape measure a ruler made of thin material that will bend easily

tape recorder a machine that will both record and play back sound

tar a thick, black, sticky oil

tarantula a type of large, hairy spider. Only a few species of tarantulas are poisonous.

tardy lagging behind and always late

target 1 something that you try to hit with a thing you throw or shoot
  2 a goal that you want to achieve: My personal *target* is to win a medal.

tart 1 a small, round pastry filled with fruit
  2 very sour

tartan a type of woollen cloth woven into different checked patterns. Tartan has a special association with Scotland.

task a piece of work to be done

taste 1 the flavour that a food or drink has
  2 to sample a food or drink to see what it is like

tasty with a strong taste that you like

tattered badly torn

tattoo a mark or design put into the skin with needles

taught see **teach**

tax money that people have to give to a government

taxi a vehicle that you hire with a driver to take you somewhere

TB see **tuberculosis**

tea a hot drink made with boiling water and the leaves of a tea plant

teach to make someone else able to understand or do something: *Maggie taught me how to swim.*

teacher someone whose job is to teach

team a group of people who play or work together in a co-operative way

tear ① (rhymes with ear) a drop that comes from your eye when you cry

tear ② (rhymes with air) to pull something apart, usually cloth, so that it is damaged: *Not only did he tear his coat, he tore his shirt. His pants were torn too.*

tease to bother or annoy, usually in fun

teaspoon a small spoon for stirring liquid

techie, tekkie (There are several ways to spell this word.) a person who is very clever with computer technology and seems to prefer this work to anything else

technical something based on special knowledge: *It takes technical skill to repair a computer.*

technician (tek-NISH-an) a person very skilled in something

technique (tek-NEEK) a special style or manner for doing something: *The skater's technique was amazing to watch.*

techno a prefix used before a word to tell you that the word will be about some kind of technology

technology the use of special knowledge along with special machines, especially in industry and the computer field

tedious boring and uninteresting

teem 1 to rain very hard **2** to be very full of moving things: *The river is teeming with fish.*

teenager someone between twelve and twenty years of age

teeter-totter see **see-saw**

teeth more than one tooth

telecast a television program

Tt

telecommunication the science of sending information through wires or by satellite

teleconference a discussion on the telephone by more than two people at once

telephone 1 an instrument that enables you to talk to someone who is far away **2** to use a telephone to speak to someone

telephoto lens a camera lens that makes distant objects appear very close

telescope a tube with lenses at both ends that make far away things appear closer and larger

television a machine that receives pictures and sound through the air

tell to speak to someone in order to pass on information, etc.: *Didn't I tell you? Yes, you told me.*

temper 1 the mood someone is in: *in a good or bad temper* **2 to lose your temper** to become very angry

temperature how hot or cold something is

temple a building in which some people worship

temporary for a short time only: *Be patient. The problem is temporary.*

tempt to try to make someone do something that may be wrong to do

temptation something that makes you want to do a thing even though you know it may be wrong

tend 1 to be likely to do something: *Grandpa tends to fall asleep after lunch.* **2** to look after and care for: *Who is tending the sheep?*

tender 1 loving: *a tender smile* **2** soft: *tender meat* **3** sore: *tender skin*

tennis a game played by two or four people, using rackets to hit a ball back and forth over a net

tense very nervous because you are worried about something

tension the feeling of being tense

tent a kind of shelter, made of material such as nylon, stretched over poles

tentative (TEN-ta-tiv) uncertain, just being tried out

tepee, tipi a kind of tent in the shape of a cone, once used by native peoples in North America

term a certain length of time: *The school* ***term*** *is 190 days this year.*

terminal 1 part of a computer system where you can input information or receive output
2 a station where ships, buses, trains and other transport vehicles take on and unload passengers and freight
3 causing death: *a* ***terminal*** *illness*

termination end point: *This is the* ***termination*** *of the tour.*

terrace a raised, flat piece of ground next to a house or in a garden

terrarium a small tank made of glass for keeping plants and small reptiles in dry conditions (see **aquarium**)

terrible very bad

terrier a kind of small dog

terrific 1 very good: *a* ***terrific*** *idea*
2 very noticeable for some reason: *a* ***terrific*** *noise*

terrify to make a person or animal very frightened

territory land that belongs to one country or person

terror great fear

test 1 a set of questions to find out how much you know or understand about something
2 to try out: ***test*** *the brakes*

test ban an agreement between countries not to test weapons

test tube a hollow, narrow, glass cylinder, closed at one end

text 1 the words of something written or printed in a book, newspaper, etc.
2 an abbreviation for **textbook**
3 the words seen on a computer screen

textbook a book used for study in school

texture (TEXT-jer) how something, usually cloth, feels when you touch it: *a rough* **texture**; *a smooth* **texture**

than compared to another person or thing: *younger* **than** *Juan*

thank to tell someone that you are pleased and grateful

thankful wanting to thank someone for what he has done

that the one there. The plural is **those**. *That one is mine. This is yours.* **Those** *are ours.*

thaw the melting of snow and ice

the a word used to mean a certain person, animal or thing: **The** *book I want is not here.*

theatre, theater a place where plays, movies and other shows are put on

theft the act of stealing: *The* **theft** *of May's diamond shocked everybody.*

their belonging to them: **their** *house*

them see **they**

theme the main idea or subject of a story or project

theme park an outdoor entertainment centre with rides, etc. that are all designed around one idea

themselves they and no one else

then 1 at that time: *We didn't know* **then** *that the car was gone.*
2 next, after that: *We played soccer;* **then** *we played tag.*

theory (THEE-o-ree) an idea that has not been proven by science and may or may not be true

there in that place or to that place: *Take the flag* **there** *and stand* **there** *until I call you.*

therefore and so

thermometer an instrument that measures the temperature of the atmosphere or a body

these see **this**

they the people or things you are talking about: *They like cake so I gave **them** some.*

thick measuring a lot from one side to the other: *a **thick** slice of bread*

thicken to make or get thicker

thief one who steals

thigh the top part of the leg down to the knee

thin not fat or thick

thing anything that can be seen or touched

think to use your mind to figure things out and to have ideas: *Did you **think** about this carefully? Yes, I have **thought** about it a lot.*

think-tank (informal) an organization of people whose job is to give advice about many things that they believe will happen

third 1 one of three equal parts that something can be divided into. A third can also be written like this: $\frac{1}{3}$.
2 coming after the second: *third prize*

thirst the need for a drink

thirsty wanting a drink

this the one here. The plural is **these**. *This is mine. That is yours. These are ours.*

thistle a plant with prickly leaves and purple flowers

thorn 1 a sharp, pointed part on the stem of a plant
2 (informal) very annoying: *She's a **thorn** in my side.*

thorough (THER-o) **1** done properly and carefully: *a **thorough** job*
2 complete: *a **thorough** mess*

those see **that**

though and yet, although: *It was cold **though** it didn't snow.*

thought 1 see **think**
2 an idea, something that you think

thoughtful sensitive and kind to others

thread 1 a long, thin piece of material, used for sewing or weaving
2 to put thread through a hole in a needle or other object

threat a promise that you will do something bad if what you want does not happen

threaten to make threats

thresh to separate the seeds of grain from the rest of the plant

threw see **throw**

thrill a sudden, excited feeling

thrilling very exciting

throat the tube that goes down from the inside of your mouth

throb to beat heavily: *My heart **throbbed** when I saw the movie star!*

throne a special chair for a king or queen

throng a large number of people

throttle on a machine, the instrument that controls the amount of power

through from one end to the other: *right **through** the tunnel*

throughout all through: *There was a hush **throughout** the church.*

throw to make something move through the air: *Sadie **threw** a stone. It was **thrown** through the window too.*

thrust to push hard

thud the sound when something large and heavy hits the ground

thumb the short, thick finger at the side of your hand

thump to hit hard with your fist

thunder the loud noise that occurs after a flash of lightning

tick 1 a small mark like this ✓ **2** the sound that some clocks make

ticket a piece of paper or a card you buy so that you can ride on something or enter a place to see a show, etc.

tickle to touch someone in a way that makes them laugh

tide the regular movement of the ocean toward and away from the shore

tidy neatly arranged with nothing out of place

tie 1 see **necktie 2** to fasten something with a knot: *He's **tying** rope around the box.*

tiger a large wildcat with yellow and black stripes found in Asia

Tt

tight fitting very closely: *tight* shoes; a *tight* lid

tighten to make or get tighter

tile 1 a hard, flat piece of material, usually square, that is put on the floors and walls of buildings **2** a hard clay tube like a pipe that is put underground to drain water away

till 1 until **2** the box or drawer where money is kept in a store

timber trees that will be cut down or logs from trees already cut

time 1 seconds, minutes, hours, days, months, years and centuries **2** a certain point in the day: *What* **time** *is it? Is it* **time** *for recess?* **3** the particular rhythm and speed of a piece of music

timeline see **timetable**

timetable a list that shows when things are supposed to happen: *Our* **timetable** *says we have lunch at 1 p.m.*

timid not brave, easily frightened

tinkle the light sound that small bells make

tinsel thin, shiny, silver ribbon, usually used to decorate Christmas trees

tinted with a small amount of colour added

tiny very small

tip 1 the part right at the very end of something **2** an amount of money given to a server or other person for his help **3** to make something fall over

tiptoe to walk on your toes without making a sound

tire the circle of rubber around a wheel on vehicles such as cars

tired 1 needing to rest or sleep: *I'm* **tired,** *so I'm going to bed now.* **2** to be weary of something or bored with it: *I am* **tired** *of playing baseball.*

tissue (TISH-yew) very thin, soft paper

Tt

title 1 the name of a book, movie, etc.
2 a word or phrase like Right Honourable that goes in front of the name of a person who has a special job or status

titter to laugh in a silly way

to 1 in the direction of: *Move to one side please.*
2 for the purpose of: *Let's go home to eat.*
3 as far as: *Move the chair to the wall.*
4 until: *The show went on to four o'clock.*
5 along with: *We danced to really great music.*
6 before: *It's five to six already!*
7 rather than: *I prefer apples to oranges.*

toad a land amphibian with rough, dry skin

toadstool a poisonous, soft, brown and white fungus with a thick stem and a large, round top

toast 1 bread that has been cooked until it turns brown
2 to heat bread until it turns brown

toboggan a kind of sleigh, used for sliding down hills covered with snow

today this day

toddler a young child who is just beginning to walk by herself

toe one of the separate parts at the end of a foot. Humans have five.

together 1 with another: *joined together*
2 at the same time as another: *We ran together.*

toil hard work

toilet a large bowl with a seat. Toilets are used to get rid of human waste.

token a round item like a coin, used instead of a ticket: *bus or subway token*

told see **tell**

tolerance the ability to put up with difficulty

tolerate to accept without resisting or arguing: *I will not tolerate rudeness.*

toll money paid for the use of a road, tunnel or bridge

Tt

tomato a soft, red, round, very juicy vegetable that grows on vines

tomb (rhymes with room) a place where a dead person's body is buried

tomorrow the day after today

tone 1 a musical sound **2** the kind of sound someone's voice has

tongue the long, soft, movable, pink flesh in the mouth

tonight this evening or this night

tonne a unit of weight: *two tonnes of corn*

tonsils a pair of growths in the throat

too 1 as well: *May I come too?* **2** more than is needed or wanted: *too much; too hot*

took see **take**

tool any instrument such as a hammer, etc. that you use to do a job

toonie in Canada, a two-dollar coin

tooth one of the hard, white objects in your mouth. The plural is **teeth**.

toothache a pain in a tooth

toothbrush a small brush with a long handle, for cleaning teeth

toothpaste a thick paste put on a toothbrush, used for cleaning teeth

top 1 the upper limit of something: *top of the hill* **2** the upper surface of something: *top of the table* **3** a toy that is spun on a pointed end

topic the subject you are writing or speaking about

topsoil the upper layer of earth

Torah in the Jewish religion, a book of laws

tore see **tear** ②

torment to annoy someone a great deal

torn see **tear** ②

tornado a big storm with very powerful winds

torpedo a long, round bomb that travels underwater, shot from submarines: *two torpedoes*

Tt

torrent a very fast stream of water

tortilla (tor-TEE-ya) a type of thin pancake, used to wrap around other foods

tortoise a creature with four legs and a hard, mounded shell covering its whole body

torture1 great pain that seems as if it will never end **2** to make someone suffer great pain for a long time

toss to throw into the air

total the amount you have when everything is added up

totally completely: *The barn was **totally** destroyed by the tornado.*

totem a symbol with special meaning, especially for native peoples

totem pole a tall pole with images carved into it. In Canada, most totem poles are found on the coast of British Columbia.

touch 1 to feel something with part of your body: *I **touched** the camel's skin!* **2** to be so close that there is no space between: *Do you see where the branch **touches** the roof?*

tough 1 strong: *Denim is a **tough** cloth.* **2** (informal) able to endure physical pain and able to cause it too: *a **tough** guy* **3** hard to chew

tour 1 (tewer) a journey you make to different places **2** to walk around somewhere, with or without a guide, looking at things

tourist a person who goes to a place to enjoy a vacation there

tow (rhymes with toe) to pull along behind: *The truck **towed** our car home.*

toward, towards in the direction of something

towel a piece of cloth to wipe away moisture

tower a tall, narrow building or part of a building

town a community with houses, schools, stores, factories, etc., usually smaller than a city

Tt 269

townhouse one of several houses in a row, all connected, but with its own entrance and small backyard

township an area, usually rural, set aside for local government

toy anything entertaining that you can enjoy playing with

trace 1 a mark left by something **2** to copy a picture or other image by drawing its outline on a transparent sheet of paper that you have placed over the picture or image

track 1 a kind of path **2** a railway line **3** a line of footprints **4** to follow a trail left by an animal or person **5** the belt that goes over the wheels of certain vehicles and enables the vehicles to travel where there is no road

track and field sporting events, such as foot races and the high jump, that can be done on a track or in a field

track meet a gathering where many track and field events are held

tracksuit a warm, comfortable suit worn by athletes and others

tractor a powerful machine on wheels, used to pull other machines

trade 1 to exchange something you have for something someone else has **2** the business of buying and selling: *the fur* **trade**

tradition a custom that people are used to doing: *Giving gifts on a birthday is a* **tradition**.

traffic cars, buses, trucks and other vehicles moving on the roads

tragedy a play with a serious theme in which someone usually dies

tragic so sad it makes people very upset

trail 1 a path: *a hiking* **trail**; *a bike* **trail** **2** smells and marks on the ground that tell where an animal has gone **3** to drag along the ground

trailer 1 a kind of cart towed behind a car or truck

2 a large towed vehicle that people can live in (see **recreational vehicle**)

trailer park a kind of campground for recreational vehicles

train 1 a set of railway cars pulled by a locomotive
2 to teach a person or animal how to do something: *to **train** a dog to come when you call*
3 to prepare yourself for competition, usually an athletic event

traitor a person who gives away secrets about his country

tramp to walk very heavily

trample to spoil something by walking on it too much or too heavily

trampoline a large piece of material joined to a metal frame with springs

trance a kind of sleep in which your eyes are open but your mind does not work properly

transaction a piece of business, such as the sale of something

transfer to move someone or something to another place

transform to change into: *That caterpillar will **transform** into a butterfly one day.*

transit 1 in motion, going from one place to another: *in **transit** from Vancouver to Toronto*
2 a public transportation system

translate to say in one language what someone is saying in another language

transparency a sheet of thin plastic on which writing or images can be produced

transparent something that can be seen through

transport 1 a truck used to carry things
2 to carry people or things from place to place

trap 1 something made to catch an animal
2 to catch a person or animal by using a trap or a clever trick

trap door a small, flat door in the floor or ceiling

Tt 271

trapeze a bar hanging from ropes, used by acrobats to do stunts in the air

trash 1 garbage
2 to destroy or ruin something

travel to go from one place to another

trawler a fishing boat that pulls a large net along in the water

tray a flat piece of metal or other material, used for carrying a number of cups, glasses, etc.

treacherous (TRECH-er-us) not to be trusted: *A **treacherous** guard killed the general.*

treason giving away your country's secrets to an enemy

treasure gold, silver and other valuable things

treasurer a person who looks after a group's or a company's money

treat 1 a special gift or favour that is very pleasing: *a birthday **treat***
2 to pay for someone else's food or drink: *Let me **treat** you to an ice cream bar.*
3 to behave toward someone or something in a certain way: *This horse has been poorly **treated**.*

tree any tall plant with leaves, branches and a thick wooden stem

trek 1 a long and challenging hike or journey on foot
2 to make such a journey

tremble to shake because you are frightened

tremendous very large or great: *a **tremendous** noise*

trench see **ditch**

trespass to go on someone else's land without asking if you may do so

trial 1 trying something out to see how well it works: *The **trial** of the new software showed how well it works.*
2 the time when a prisoner is in court and a decision is made about whether she is guilty and what should be done

triangle a flat shape with three sides joined together

tribe a group of people living together, usually in simple conditions

trick 1 something clever that a person or animal has learned to do
2 to make someone believe something that is not really true

trickle a very thin, weak stream of water

tricky 1 clever in a way that may fool you
2 something very difficult: *a tricky puzzle to solve*

tricycle a vehicle with three wheels, handlebars, two pedals and a seat

tried see **try**

trigger the part of a gun that is pulled to make it fire

trim 1 decoration
2 to cut away parts of something to make it more attractive

trio a set of three

trip 1 a journey
2 to fall over something

triumph (TRI-umf) **1** a victory: *The Oilers' triumph means they're in first place.*
2 to win a victory: *The Oilers triumphed in that game!*

triumphant (tri-UMF-ant) to enjoy the feeling of being the winner

trolley a small table on wheels

troop an organized group of people with a leader

tropical belonging to very hot areas in Africa, Asia and South America: *tropical climate; tropical plants*

trot one of the ways a horse can move. A trot is faster than a walk but not running.

trouble 1 anything that upsets, worries, bothers or causes danger: *Kevin is in trouble! Let's go help him!*
2 to bother or make a fuss: *Don't trouble yourself. I'll do this myself.*

trough (trawff) a long, narrow container that holds food or water for animals

Tt 273

trousers see **pants**

trout a fish found in rivers and lakes

trowel a small shovel with a very short handle, meant to be used with one hand

truck a vehicle with a container or platform for carrying things

true correct, real, dependable: *a true story; a true friend*

truly in an honest way

trumpet a brass musical wind instrument

trunk 1 a tree's thick stem
2 an elephant's long nose
3 a large box for storing things or carrying them on a journey

trust to believe that someone or something can be depended on

trustee a person who is either appointed or elected to supervise

truth that which is true

try 1 to work at something you want to be able to do: *Abe is trying to learn how to dance.*
2 to test something: *I tried it out before I bought it.*

tub a round container

tube 1 a long, round, thin container that is open at one end and closed at the other: *a tube of toothpaste; a test tube*
2 a long, thin, hollow piece of material that is open at both ends: *A water pipe is a kind of tube.*

tuberculosis (too-BER-cu-LOH-sis) (also **TB**) a serious disease that affects the lungs

tuck to tidy away the loose ends of something: *Tuck your shirt in, please.*

tuft a small patch of feathers, grass, hair, etc.

tug 1 a small, very powerful boat used for moving other boats around
2 to pull hard

tulip a spring flower that is shaped like a cup and appears in many colours

tumble to fall

tumbler a drinking glass

tumour, tumor a growth in the body that is not normal

tuna a large ocean fish

tune 1 a series of notes that make a piece of music: *That's a happy tune! What's the title of the song?*
2 (also called **fine-tune**) to make adjustments in order to work with or be in harmony with others

tunnel a long hole that has been made underground

turban a head covering made of cloth that must be worn in a certain way

turbine a kind of engine with a wheel inside that turns to produce power

turf 1 short grass and the soil it grows on
2 (informal) someone's neighbourhood

turkey a large bird raised for its meat

turn 1 the time when you are doing something that some have already done and others are waiting to do: *It's Melanie's turn now.*
2 a change in direction or condition: *a turn in the road; a turn for the worse*
3 to become or change into: *Cynthia turned pale.*

4 to rotate while in the same place; spin: *Pak turned to see a bear behind him! The wheel is turning.*
5 to move to a new position or direction: *Turn to page six.*

turnout the number of people who show up for something

turning point the time when something changes

turpentine a kind of oil that can clean paint or dirt from a surface

turtle a reptile with a hard, oval shell that can live on land or in water (see **tortoise**)

tusk one of two long, pointed teeth on elephants and some kinds of pigs

tuxedo a very fancy suit, usually worn by a man

Tt 275

tweed thick cloth that is woven from wool

tweezers a small tool used for getting hold of very thin things

twice two times

twig a tiny, thin branch

twilight the dim light at the end of the day just after the sun goes down

twin one of two children born to the same mother at the same time

twine thick, strong string

twinkle to shine with small dots of light that blink on and off

twirl to spin around several times quickly

twist to turn or bend: *a twisted ankle*

twitch to keep making sudden movements with various parts of the body

twitter the short, light sounds that birds make

type 1 one kind or sort: *a type of music*

2 to press the letter or number keys on a keyboard

tyrant a cruel ruler

Tt

UFO an abbreviation for **unidentified flying object**

ugly not pleasant in appearance

ultimate 1 at the very last: *Our **ultimate** destination is St. John's.* **2** (informal) the greatest or very best: ***ultimate** performance; **ultimate** Frisbee*

umbrella a round piece of cloth stretched over a metal frame, with a handle for holding the cloth part above your head, used for protection from the rain or sun

umpire a supervisor whose job is to make sure that rules are followed, usually in a game

un 1 a prefix meaning **not,** as in **unable** (not able) **2** a prefix meaning **the opposite of,** as in **undo** (the opposite of do). **Un** is not always a prefix, as in under or uncle.

unanimous (yew-NAN-im-us) agreed upon by everyone

unassuming mild and quiet in the way you behave with others

unattended not being looked after

unauthorized (un-AH-thor-izd) without permission; without the right to do something: *My employee's comment yesterday was **unauthorized**.*

uncharted 1 no map available: *an **uncharted** mountain area* **2** new and not yet tried out: *His suggestion would take us into **uncharted** places.*

uncle the brother of one of your parents, or your aunt's husband

uncomfortable 1 causing discomfort: *The heat in this room makes me uncomfortable.*
2 being in a state of discomfort: *Meisha was very uncomfortable whenever our dog was near.*

unconscious (un-KON-shuss) to be in a very deep sleep from which no one can wake you

under below

undercurrent
1 see **undertow**
2 slightly hidden: *There was an undercurrent of rudeness in his speech.*

underdog a person or team that is expected to lose

underground 1 under the ground
2 hidden from the government or from other people in charge

undergrowth bushes and other plants growing under trees

underline 1 to draw a straight line under a word, <u>like this</u>

2 to draw special attention to something: *Let me underline what I just said. I am not fooling!*

understand to know what something means or how it works

undertaker a person who prepares a dead person for burial or cremation

undertow a separate flow of water that moves in a different direction from the water on the surface. Undertows can be very dangerous to swimmers.

underwear clothes made to be worn next to the skin and under other clothes

undo to open something that is fastened: *Did you undo the knot? Yes, I undid it. Just look; it's undone.*

undress to take off clothes

uneven bumpy, not level or smooth

unfair not right; favouring one side

unfortunate not lucky

unhappy sad

unhealthy 1 ill or at risk of becoming ill
2 not good for you: *Too much junk food can be unhealthy.*

unicorn a make-believe animal, usually white, that looks like a horse with a long, straight horn growing from its forehead

uniform 1 the special clothes that people in a specific job or group wear: *school, band or military* **uniform**
2 the same as others around it: *Pick only apples of a* **uniform** *colour.*

union a group of people who have joined together for a reason

unique (yew-NEEK) one of a kind: *a* **unique** *painting*

unison exactly together: *sing in* **unison**

unit an amount used in measuring or counting. Centimetres are units of length; dollars are units of money.

unite to join together

universal having to do with everyone and everything: *In Canada, we believe that freedom of religion should be* **universal***.*

universe all solar systems and everything in them

university a place where people learn and study after high school

unkind somewhat cruel and unpleasant

unless if not

unlimited without restrictions

unnecessary not needed

unruly badly behaved and hard to control: *an* **unruly** *horse*

untidy messy

until up to a certain time: *I was in the store* **until** *noon.*

unusual not happening very often, out of the ordinary

unwell sick

up 1 to or in a higher place: **up** *the hill;* **up** *the tree*
2 to a place farther along: *You can find it* **up** *the road.*
3 over, at an end: *Time's* **up**!
4 out of the ground or from a surface: *Pull* **up** *weeds. Take* **up** *the old rug.*
5 out of bed, to rise: *I got* **up** *early.*

Uu

6 apart: *Tear it **up**.*
7 completely: *The log has almost burned **up**.*
8 next: *Who is **up** to bat after Herbie?*

upbringing how someone was taught to behave by the adults in her home and community

update to change by adding the most recent information

uplifting making a person's spirit and general mood happier: *an **uplifting** news story*

upon on or on top of

upper higher

upright 1 standing straight up: *an **upright** post*
2 honest: *an **upright** person*

uprising an act of revolt against those in charge

uproar a loud noise or a fuss made by people who are upset

upset 1 to make someone unhappy
2 being unhappy
3 to knock over something

upside down turned over so that the bottom is on the top

upstairs the part of a building reached by going up a set of stairs

uptight (informal) very nervous and easily upset

up-to-date having the most recent information, style, behaviour, etc.

upward, upwards 1 to a higher point: *The hikers climbed **upward** for hours.*
2 nearly or about: *They climbed for **upwards** of two hours.*

urban having to do with the city: *Traffic is only one of the **urban** problems.*

urge 1 a sudden, strong wish to do something: *an **urge** to shout out loud*
2 to try to get someone to do something: *Everyone was **urging** Dale to jump.*

urgent so important it must be acted on at once

us a word that refers to the person speaking as well as others there

use 1 the purpose or value of something: *This broken pole is of no **use** to us.*
2 to do a job with something: *Denise **used** glue to fix the cup.*

user someone who uses something

user-friendly able to be used easily

useful 1 able to be used a lot: *a **useful** tool*
2 helpful: ***useful** information*

usual happening most often: ***Usually,** we eat lunch at noon.*

utensil any tool, pot or pan used in a kitchen

U-turn to turn a vehicle around on a road and go in the opposite direction

Uu

TtUu**Vv**Ww

v. , vs. an abbreviation for **versus**

vacant with no one or nothing inside: *a vacant room*

vacation a time away from what you normally do, often spent resting or travelling

vaccination (VAK-sin-AY-shun) an injection that helps to prevent disease

vacuum 1 a complete emptiness
2 to clean with a vacuum cleaner

vacuum cleaner a machine that sucks up dust and dirt

vague not clear, uncertain: *a vague idea*

vain 1 too proud of how you appear

2 in vain without success: *They tried in vain to move the log.*

valid official: *This ticket is valid for one more day.*

valley the low land between hills

valuable worth a lot of money: *a valuable watch*

valuables a collection of things that are worth a lot of money: *They stole jewellery, silver dishes and other valuables.*

value 1 the amount of money something is worth: *What's the value of this land?*
2 how important or useful something is: *Horses were of great value to the pioneers.*

valve a part in a machine that controls the amount of air or liquid going in or out

van a kind of truck with closed sides and a roof

vandalize to destroy or mar property for no good reason

vanilla a flavouring added to other food

vanish to disappear suddenly and not be seen any more

vanity being vain

vapour, vapor many tiny droplets that rise in the air

variety 1 a lot of different kinds of things: *a **variety** of colours*
2 a certain kind or type: *This is an unusual **variety** of tomato.*

various different, several: *We tried **various** ways of making him smile.*

varnish a clear liquid painted on wood to protect it and make it look good

vary to be different: *Their answers did not **vary** by much.*

vase (vawz or vayz) a jar for holding flowers

vast very large

VCR an abbreviation for **videocassette recorder**

veal meat from a calf

vegan someone who does not eat meat, fish, dairy products or eggs

vegetable part of a plant used as food

vegetarian someone who does not eat meat

vehicle anything that can carry people from place to place

veil (rhymes with mail) a piece of thin material worn over all or part of the face

veiled 1 wearing a veil: *Two of the girls were **veiled**; one was not.*
2 not clear but easy to understand anyway: *to make a **veiled** threat*

vein a narrow tube that has liquid or ore in it: ***veins** in your arm; a **vein** of coal in the ground*

velvet thick material that is very soft on one side

venom the poison of snakes and other poisonous animals

ventilator (VEN-til-ay-tor) a device for bringing air into a building or vehicle

Vv

veranda, verandah a long, open platform with a roof, built onto the outside of a house

verify to prove

verse part of a poem or song

version someone's own way of telling what has happened: *That's Bandar's **version** of the accident; what's yours?*

versus against, opposed: *the Leafs **versus** the Senators*

vertical upright

very most

vessel 1 any container for liquid
2 a boat or ship

vest a type of jacket without sleeves

vet an abbreviation for **veterinarian,** someone whose job is to look after the health of animals

viaduct a long bridge with a railway or road on top of it

vice 1 a prefix meaning second in command: ***vice**-chairperson; **vice**-president*
2 a bad habit: *Most people think smoking is a **vice**.*

vice versa the other way around also

vicious (VISH-uss) mean and cruel

victim someone who has had an accident or other harm done to them

victory the winning of a struggle, game, contest, etc.

video 1 (informal) a movie available for rent or sale on videocassette
2 the visual part of a television broadcast or other program seen on a monitor

videocassette a flat, plastic box containing videotape and two reels

video game an electronic game in which players move controls and watch the result on a monitor

videotape 1 a long, thin ribbon on which you can record both images and sound
2 to record images and sound

view 1 what can be seen from a place
2 what a person thinks of something

vigour, vigor strength and energy

vile very unpleasant: *a vile taste; a vile smell*

village a community of houses, stores, etc., usually smaller than a town

villain a bad person

vine a plant with a very long stem that grows along the ground or along other things that will support it. Fruit such as grapes or vegetables such as cucumbers grow on vines.

vinegar (VIN-ig-er) a sour liquid used in preparing foods

vinyl a kind of plastic

violate to break a law, promise or agreement

violence rough behaviour that may hurt or destroy things

violent very strong and rough: *a violent storm; violent behaviour*

violet 1 a purple colour
2 a small plant with purple or white flowers

violin a stringed musical instrument played with a bow

violinist a person who plays a violin

VIP an abbreviation for **very important person**

virtual something that seems to be real but is not

virtuoso (ver-chew-O-so) a musical performer who is believed to be much better than others

virus 1 a type of contagious germ that causes disease
2 a computer program that may attach itself to other programs and cause damage to stored data

Vv

visibility how clearly something can be seen

visible able to be seen

vision the ability to see

visitor someone who goes to see a person or place

visual involving the sense of sight: *Maps are one kind of visual aid.*

visualize to imagine the sight of something in your mind

vital important to life: *Smoking damages vital organs, such as your lungs.*

vitamin a compound in food that is necessary for good health

vivid 1 bright: *vivid colours* **2** lively: *a vivid imagination* **3** so clear it seems real: *a vivid dream*

vixen a female fox

VJ an abbreviation for **video jockey,** someone whose job is to be the host of a musical program on television

vocabulary the words someone understands and uses

voice the sound you make with your mouth when you sing or speak

voice mail a system that records your voice on someone's telephone system

volcano a cone-shaped mountain, which can contain hot liquid and gas that may come bursting out: *two volcanoes*

volleyball a game with two teams on either side of a net. The teams hit a ball filled with air back and forth, each trying to make the other team miss.

volume 1 quantity or amount: *The volume of business at that store is bigger this year.* **2** how much space something takes: *Because of the volume, we had to use two trucks.* **3** the loudness of sound: *Turn up the volume.* **4** one of a set of books: *the first of three volumes*

volunteer someone who offers to do something he does not have to do

vote to say which person or idea you think should be chosen. Sometimes you vote by putting a mark on a piece of paper; other times you raise your hand.

vow to make a serious promise (see **oath**)

vowel any one of the letters a, e, i, o, or u, and sometimes y

voyage a long journey by boat

voyageur in early Canada, a person who worked for a fur company carrying furs and supplies for long distances by canoe (see **coureur de bois**)

vulture a large bird that lives on the flesh of dead animals

wad a thick piece of folded cloth or paper

wade 1 to walk through water: *Lennie* **waded** *across the stream.*
2 (informal) to do some work that is long and dull: *Last week I had to* **wade** *through a really boring book.*

wag to move from side to side quickly

wage, wages the money paid to someone for work she does

wagon a cart with four wheels and a handle for pulling

wail to make a long, sad cry

waist the part at the centre of the body

wait to stay for something that you expect

waiter a man whose job is to bring food to customers in a restaurant

waitress a woman whose job is to bring food to customers in a restaurant

wake to stop sleeping: *Wake up, Dan! Nina* **woke** *up hours ago!*

walk to move along on foot

walkie-talkie a hand-held, wireless communication system

wall 1 a barrier made of bricks or stone around a piece of property
2 one of the sides of a building or room

wallet a small, flat, leather case for money and papers that you carry in a pocket or purse

walnut a round nut with a hard shell

walrus a large sea animal with flippers and tusks

waltz a kind of dance

wand a thin stick

wander to move about with no real sense of where you are going

want 1 to feel that you would like to have something: *What I want right now, please, is a drink of water.* **2** to be in need

war a fight between two or more countries or two or more areas within one country

ward in a hospital, a room with several beds

wardrobe the clothes that a person has and may choose to wear: *Mae-Ling has quite a large wardrobe.*

warehouse a large building where things are stored

warm not cool but not quite hot

warn to tell someone he is in danger

warrior someone fighting in a battle

wart a hard, dry growth on the skin

was see **be**

wash 1 (also **washing**) a pile of clothes being cleaned with soap and water **2** to clean with soap and water

washer 1 a machine that washes clothes **2** a round, flat piece of metal with a round hole in the centre

washing see **wash 1**

wasp a flying insect that can sting

waste 1 things that you do not need or want any more: *waste paper* **2** to use more of something than is necessary

watch 1 a small clock, often worn on the wrist **2** to look at: *We watched the seals playing.* **3** to await the appearance or arrival of something: *Everyone was watching for the ship.*

water a clear, natural liquid that falls as rain or is in rivers, lakes, etc.

watercolour material for painting that is mixed with water rather than oil

waterfall a stream of water falling from a high place

water lily a kind of plant with a bloom and large green leaves, called pads, which floats on the surface of still water

watermelon a large, oval fruit with a thick, green skin over red, juicy flesh

waterproof made of material that will not let water through: *a **waterproof** coat*

water ski a wide ski on which someone can stand and be pulled over the surface of water by a motorboat

watertight made so that water cannot get in

waterworks a system for supplying fresh water to a community

watt a small unit of electrical power

wave 1 one of the lines you can see on the surface of a large body of water
2 an electronic signal
3 to move your hand to say hello or goodbye

wavy with curves in it

wax a soft material that is used to make things like crayons, etc.

way 1 a road or path: *the **way** to school*
2 how something is done: *a right **way** and a wrong **way***

we a word used to refer to the speaker or writer along with other people: *Jeff and I are leaving. **We** are going home.*

weak not strong

weaken to get or make weaker

wealth a lot of money

wealthy rich

weapon an instrument, such as a gun or knife, used to hurt or kill

wear 1 clothing: *children's **wear***
2 to have clothing on: *I **wore** my Raptors sweater yesterday.*
3 to use something so much it can no longer be used: *You are going to **wear** that brush down to nothing!*
4 to make someone very weary: *I think we played too long; Mom is **worn** out.*

weary very tired

weasel a small, furry animal with a long body. Weasels are predators.

weather rain, snow, ice, fog, wind, sun, etc.

weave to make clothing, rugs, etc. by crossing threads under and over other threads

web 1 a thin, sticky net spun by a spider to trap insects **2** (informal) see **WWW**

webbed having a foot with toes joined together by skin

web browser a software program used for displaying and viewing pages on the Internet

web page one of the parts of a web site

web site a group of web pages all connected to the same topic or idea

wedding the ceremony at which two people get married to each other

wedge 1 a piece that is thick at one end and thin at the other, like a triangle or the letter "V": *a **wedge** of pie* **2** to separate two things by pushing something between them

weed any wild plant that grows where it is not wanted

week seven days

weekend a time at the end of a week, usually from Friday evening to Sunday evening

weep to cry tears: *He **wept** when his dog ran away.*

weigh (rhymes with way) **1** to measure how heavy something is **2** to have a certain weight

weight how heavy something is

weird (rhymes with beard) very strange and odd

welcome to show that you are pleased when someone arrives

Ww 291

welfare 1 the health and happiness of people: *Our council was elected to look after our welfare.*
2 money given by the government to people in need

well 1 a hole dug in the ground for water or oil
2 healthy
3 in a good way: *Manuel swims well.*

went see **go**

wept see **weep**

were see **be**

west 1 a compass point
2 the direction where the sun sets
3 (often **the West**) the part of the world that includes North America and most of Europe

western 1 from the west or in the west
2 a movie set in the west

wet covered with water or moisture

whack (informal) to hit hard with a stick

whale the largest of all ocean animals, somewhat in the shape of a fish

wharf a place where ships are loaded and unloaded

what 1 which thing: *What is that?*
2 that which: *Tell me what you think.*

whatever no matter what: *I'll be there whatever happens.*

wheat a grain plant from which the seed is used to make flour for baking

wheel a circle of wood or metal, fixed in the middle so that it can turn on an axle

wheelbarrow a small cart with one wheel at the front and handles for pushing

wheeze to make hissing sounds in the chest when breathing, usually because of asthma or another disease or illness

when 1 at what time: *When did the train arrive?* **2** at the time that: *When it moved, we jumped.*

whenever at any time

where in what place

wherever no matter where: *Wherever you are, I'll find you.*

whether if

which what person or thing: *Which one do you want?*

wildlife the birds, animals and insects that exist in nature without the interference of people

while in the time that something else is happening: *While she was sleeping, we cleaned the house.*

whimper a soft, crying sound, such as a kitten makes

whine the long, sad sound an animal or person makes when they are unhappy

whip 1 a long, thin piece of material used for hitting, usually used on animals **2** to stir cream hard enough to make it thick: *whipped cream*

whirl to turn around very quickly

whisker a strong hair that grows on the face of most men and most cats

whisky a strong drink, usually made from grains

whisper to speak very softly

whistle 1 a small instrument that makes a very high, shrill sound when air is pushed through it

2 to make a shrill sound by blowing through the lips

who what person: *Who did this?*

whoever no matter what person: *Whoever did it will be caught!*

whole 1 the entire: *He ate the whole egg in one swallow!* **2** not broken: *He swallowed the egg whole.*

whoop a loud, swooping call or cry

whooping cough an illness during which you make long, loud coughs over and over

whose belonging to what person: *Whose pen is this?*

why for what reason: *Why did you do this?*

wick the string that goes through a candle

wicked very bad

wide 1 measuring a lot from one side to the other: *a wide street*
2 completely: *wide awake; wide open*

widow a woman whose husband has died

widower a man whose wife has died

width how wide something is

wiener a long, thin sausage

wife a woman married to someone: *King Henry had six wives.*

wig a head covering of artificial hair

wild 1 natural, not looked after by people: *a wild flower*
2 uncontrolled: *That horse is pretty wild. Don't try to ride it.*

wilderness an area of a country where no one lives

wilful always wanting to do something even when you are told not to

will 1 a kind of letter left by someone who has died. It tells what to do with the things left behind.
2 the power to choose what you want to do
3 is going to: *Savia will be here this afternoon. I know because she said she would.* (**Will** is often written as **'ll** *I'll be here tomorrow.* **Would** is often written as **'d** *I'd like to stay home.*)

willing ready and happy to do what is wanted

willow a kind of tree that grows near water, has yellowish bark and thin, long branches

wily very clever in a sneaky way

win 1 to get a prize: *I won some new software as a door prize.*
2 to beat someone else or another team in a game

wince to show with your face that you are feeling pain

wind ① (rhymes with grinned) air moving quickly: *Let the wind blow. I'm warm and cozy.*

wind ② (rhymes with find) to wrap string or other material around something: *Pak wound tape around the broken stick.*

window 1 a glass-covered opening in the wall of a building, used to let light in **2** a kind of frame with information in it that appears on a computer screen

wine a strong drink, usually made from grapes

wing 1 one of the parts of a bird, insect or airplane used in flying **2** a section of a building that leads off from the main part: *the west wing*

wink to close and open one eye quickly, usually meant as a signal

winter the season of the year when the weather is coldest

wipe to rub something with a cloth to dry or clean it

wire a long, thin strip of metal that can be bent into different shapes

wisdom the ability to understand many things and therefore to act with good sense

wise able to understand and act in a sensible way

wish to say or think what you would like to happen

witch in stories, a woman who uses magic to do bad things

with 1 having: *a man with a red coat* **2** in the company of: *I came with a friend.* **3** using: *It was written with a pen.* **4** against: *Harry fought with Jacques.*

wither to dry up and get smaller: *withered leaves*

without not having: *without any money*

witness 1 someone who sees something important happen: *Sol was a witness to the accident.* **2** to see something important: *Sol witnessed the accident.*

witty clever and funny

wives more than one wife

wizard in stories, a person, usually a man, who can do magic things

wobble to shake

woke, woken see **wake**

wolf a wild animal like a large, fierce dog

woman a grown female person: *One **woman** sat outside and three **women** were inside.*

won see **win**

wonder 1 a feeling of surprise because of something strange and marvellous **2** to ask yourself about something: *I **wonder** who did it.*

wonderful so good that it surprises you: *a **wonderful** vacation*

won't an abbreviation for **will not**

wood the branches and trunks of trees cut into pieces for burning or building

wooded filled with trees: *a **wooded** area*

woodchuck see **groundhog**

wooden made of wood

woodpecker a bird that pecks through the bark of trees to get insects to eat

woods a lot of trees growing together: *The fox ran into the **woods** and disappeared.*

woodwork making things out of wood

wool the hair that grows on sheep, which people can cut off and spin into yarn for knitting or to make cloth

woollen made of wool

word a sound, or a group of sounds, that means something when you say it, write it or read it

word processor a machine with a keyboard and a video display that you can use to put in and retrieve text

wore see **wear**

work 1 a job or something else you have to do: *Helen can't play; she has* **work** *to finish.*
2 to do a job: *Helen is* **working** *at the variety store.*
3 to be functioning: *We fixed the computer and it* **works** *now.*

worker a person paid to do things on a job

workshop 1 a place where things are made or mended
2 a special meeting where people learn how to do something

workstation a small area with a computer where a person can work

world Earth, or anything else in space that is like it (see **planet**)

worm see **earthworm**

worn see **wear**

worry to be upset because you are thinking something bad may happen

worse more serious: *The damage is* **worse** *over here.*

worship to love, praise and do honour to

worst most serious: *The damage at the back is the* **worst***.*

worth with a certain value: *That old stamp is* **worth** *a thousand dollars!*

worthless not worth anything

would see **will**

would-be a person who hopes to do or become something: *a* **would-be** *poet*

wound ① (woond) an injury from a knife or bullet

wound ② (rhymes with sound) see **wind** ②

wove, woven see **weave**

wrap to put cloth or paper around something

wreath flowers, leaves and other decorations wound together into a ring

wreck 1 a ship, car or building that is too badly damaged to be used any more
2 to damage badly

wren a small, brown songbird

wrench a tool for turning bolts

wrestle 1 to struggle with someone or something using your body **2** to think a lot about a problem while you try to solve it

wretched (RECH-id) poor, ill and unhappy

wriggle to twist and turn about in the same spot

wring to squeeze and twist at the same time

wrinkle 1 a small crease in skin or cloth: *Oh, look at the **wrinkles** in my shirt!* **2** (informal) small problems that need to be solved: *There are still a few **wrinkles** in his plan.*

wrist the thin part of the arm where it is joined to the hand

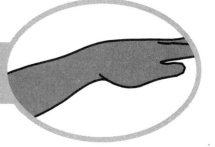

write to put words or signs on paper so that people can read them: *Did you **write** this? Yes, I **wrote** it. It was **written** yesterday.*

writing something that has been written: *untidy **writing**; a long piece of **writing***

written see **write**

wrong not right: *the **wrong** answer*

wrote see **write**

wrung see **wring**

WWW an abbreviation for **world wide web,** an international network where computers can communicate with one another and can retrieve information

xeno a prefix: very strange, different from what people understand

xerox (informal) to photocopy a piece of writing or a picture

X-rated (informal) containing scenes that people in authority think young people should not see

X-ray, x-ray a special kind of photograph that shows some of the inside parts of the body

xylophone (ZY-low-fone) a musical instrument with a row of bars that are hit with small hammers

yacht (yot) **1** a light sailboat, used for racing
2 a large motorboat, used for pleasure cruising

yak an animal from Tibet that looks like a cow and has long horns and long hair

yard 1 an area of ground next to a house or other building, often with a fence around it
2 a special area for some kinds of work: *a railway* **yard**

yarmulke, yarmelke (YAR-mul-ka) a small, round cap worn by some Jewish men

yarn 1 a long, continuous thread made of wool or cotton
2 (informal) a story that is not true, but amusing and harmless

yashmak a veil worn over the face in public by some Muslim women

yawn to open your mouth wide when you are tired and take in and then let out a deep breath

year a measure of time. A year is twelve months long or 365 days. (see **leap year**)

yearbook a special book put together by a group, such as a class in a school, which tells of what happened over the past year

yeast a kind of spreading fungus that produces many tiny bubbles of gas

yell to shout

yellow the colour of ripe lemons or butter

yelp a short, quick cry, like a dog in pain would make

yen an urge

yesterday the day before today

yet 1 up to now: *The rain has not* **yet** *started.*
2 by now: *Are you finished* **yet**?

Yiddish a language written and spoken by some Jews

yield 1 the amount of grain or fruit produced: *Last year the* **yield** *from that farm was smaller.*
2 to give in and let someone win or go first: *The driver* **yielded** *to the other car, just as she should.*

yodel a kind of singing and calling with sounds that rapidly go low, then high, then low again

yoga a kind of exercise that some people do to help both their body and spirit

yogurt, yoghurt (YO-gert) a thick liquid made from sour milk

yolk the yellow centre of an egg

Yom Kippur a very holy day in the Jewish religion

you the person or people you are speaking to: **You** *own this dictionary.*

young born not long ago

youngster someone who is young

your belonging to you

yourself, yourselves
1 you and no one else
2 by yourself, by yourselves on your own

youth 1 a boy or young man: *I saw an old man and three* **youths** *in the car.*
2 the time in your life when you are young

yo-yo a toy made of a pair of solid wheels joined with a peg that has string wound around it

yule, yuletide referring to Christmastime

XxYy**Zz**

zany (informal) silly, clownish

zebra an African animal that looks like a horse with black and white stripes

Zen a short term for **Zen Buddhism** (see **Buddhism**)

zenith (ZEE-nith) the very top or very best of something

zero the number "nothing." Zero is also written **0**.

zigzag a line like this

~~~ with sudden turns in it

zinc a bluish-white metal that does not rust easily

zinnia a large flower that has blooms in many colours

zipper a fastener that joins two pieces of material together using metal teeth

zodiac a chart that uses the stars in the sky to do things like tell the future and tell people about themselves

zone a special area that has been set aside for some reason: *a no parking zone*

zoo a park where wild animals from around the world are on display and studied

zoom to move toward or away from something very quickly

zucchini (zoo-KEE-nee) a vegetable with dark green skin that grows on a vine

Canada's Provinces and Territories

Province/ Territory	Became Province/ Territory on	Capital	Provincial Flower	Provincial Bird	Provincial Tree
British Columbia	July 20, 1871	Victoria	Dogwood	Stellar's Jay	Western Red Cedar
Alberta	Sept. 1, 1905	Edmonton	Wild Rose	Great Horned Owl	Lodgepole Pine
Saskatchewan	Sept. 1, 1905	Regina	Western Red Lily	Sharp-tailed Grouse	White Birch
Manitoba	July 15, 1870	Winnipeg	Prairie Crocus	Great Grey Owl	White Spruce
Ontario	July 1, 1867	Toronto	White Trillium	Common Loon	Eastern White Pine
Quebec	July 1, 1867	Quebec City	Blue Flag	Snowy Owl	Yellow Birch
New Brunswick	July 1, 1867	Fredericton	Purple Violet	Chickadee	Balsam Fir
Nova Scotia	July 1, 1867	Halifax	Mayflower	Osprey	Red Spruce
Prince Edward Island	July 1, 1873	Charlottetown	Lady's Slipper	Blue Jay	Red Oak
Newfoundland & Labrador	Mar. 31, 1949	St. John's	Pitcher Plant	Puffin	Black Spruce
Yukon Territory	June 13, 1898	Whitehorse	Fireweed	Common Raven	—
Northwest Territories	July 15, 1870	Yellowknife	Mountain Avens	Gyrfalcon	Tamarack
Nunavut	April 1, 1999	Iqaluit	Purple Saxifrage	Rock Ptarmigan	—

Appendix 303

Website Provincial/Territorial [http://www.

British Columbia	gov.bc.ca (English)
Alberta	gov.ab.ca (English)
Saskatchewan	gov.sk.ca (English)
Manitoba	gov.mb.ca (English/French)
Ontario	gov.on.ca (English/French)
Quebec	gouv.qc.ca (French/English/Spanish)
New Brunswick	gov.nb.ca (English/French)
Nova Scotia	gov.ns.ca (English)
Newfoundland & Labrador	gov.nf.ca (English)
Prince Edward Island	gov.pe.ca (English/French)
Yukon Territory	gov.yk.ca (English/French)
Northwest Territories	gov.nt.ca (English) (with telephone service in French and eight native languages)
Nunavut	gov.nu.ca (English/Inuktitut)

From Largest to Smallest in Area	From Largest to Smallest in Population
Nunavut	Ontario
Quebec	Quebec
Northwest Territories	British Columbia
British Columbia	Alberta
Ontario	Manitoba
Alberta	Saskatchewan
Saskatchewan	Nova Scotia
Manitoba	New Brunswick
Yukon Territory	Newfoundland & Labrador
Newfoundland & Labrador	Prince Edward Island
New Brunswick	Northwest Territories
Nova Scotia	Yukon Territory
Prince Edward Island	Nunavut

From Largest to Smallest in Number of People per Square km

Prince Edward Island
Nova Scotia
Ontario
New Brunswick
Quebec
Alberta
British Columbia
Manitoba
Saskatchewan
Newfoundland
Yukon Territory
Northwest Territories
Nunavut

The Ten Largest Lakes in Canada

[Lake Superior,
    shared with US]
[Lake Huron,
    shared with US]
1   Great Bear Lake (NT)
2   Great Slave Lake (NT)
    [Lake Erie, shared with US]
3   Lake Winnipeg (MB)
    [Lake Ontario,
    shared with US]
4   Lake Athabasca (SK)
5   Reindeer Lake (SK/MB)
6   Smallwood Reservoir (NF)
7   Nettilling Lake (NU)
8   Lake Winnipegosis (MB)
9   Lake Nipigon (ON)
10 Lake Manitoba (MB)

The Ten Longest Rivers in Canada

1   Mackenzie (flows into
        Arctic Ocean)
2   Yukon (flows into
        Bering Sea)
3   St. Lawrence (flows into
        Gulf of St. Lawrence)
4   Nelson (flows into
        Hudson Bay)
5   Columbia (flows into
        Pacific Ocean)
6   Saskatchewan River (flows
        into Lake Winnipeg)
7   Peace (flows into
        Lake Athabasca)
8   Churchill (flows into
        Hudson Bay)
9   South Saskatchewan
        (flows into
        Saskatchewan River)
10 Fraser (flows into
        Pacific Ocean)

The Ten Highest Waterfalls in Canada

1   Della Falls (BC)
2   Takakkaw Falls (BC)
3   Hunlen Falls (BC)
4   Panther Falls (AB)
5   Helmcken Falls (BC)
6   Bridal Veil Falls (BC)
7   Virginia Falls (NT)
8   Chute Montmorency (QC)
9   Ouiatchouan Falls (QC)
10 Churchill Falls (NF)

Niagara Falls has a 54 m
drop. Churchill's drop is 75 m
and Della Falls is 440 m.

Appendix

Cool Canadian Facts

The geographic centre of Canada is at Arviat, NU.

The middle (from west to east) is just outside Winnipeg, MB.

The middle (from north to south) is just outside Yellowknife, NT.

The longest distance from west to east is 5,514 km, from the Yukon/Alaska border to Cape Spear, NF.

The longest distance from north to south is 4,634 km, from Cape Spear, NF to Middle Island, ON (in Lake Erie).

Canada has the longest ocean coastline in the world (243,798 km).

Eight of the ten largest islands in Canada are in Nunavut, including the largest, Baffin Island. (Vancouver Island is number 11!) Nine of the ten highest mountains in Canada are in Yukon Territory.

The largest city in population is Toronto, ON.

The largest city in area is Timmins, ON.

Canada's First Olympic Gold Medal Winners

(Summer/Men)
1904: Étienne Desmarteau (weight throw)
George Lyon (golf)
Galt Football Club (soccer)
Winnipeg Shamrocks (lacrosse)

(Summer/Women)
1928: Ethel Catherwood (high jump)
Fanny Rosenfeld, Ethel Smith, Florence Bell, Myrtle Cook (relay)

(Winter/Men)
1920: Winnipeg Falcons (ice hockey)
The Winter Olympics started in 1924, but hockey was an event in 1920. The Toronto Granites won gold in 1924.

(Winter/Women)
1948: Barbara Ann Scott (figure skating)

Appendix

Canada's Prime Ministers

Sir John A. Macdonald (b. Scotland)	1867 – 1873	Conservative
Alexander Mackenzie (b. Scotland)	1873 – 1878	Liberal
Sir John A. Macdonald	1878 – 1891	Conservative
Sir John Joseph Caldwell Abbott (b. Quebec)	1891 – 1892	Conservative
Sir John Sparrow David Thompson (b. Nova Scotia)	1892 – 1894	Conservative
Sir Mackenzie Bowell (b. England)	1894 – 1896	Conservative
Sir Charles Tupper (b. Nova Scotia)	1896	Conservative
Sir Wilfrid Laurier (b. Quebec)	1896 – 1911	Liberal
Sir Robert Laird Borden (b. Nova Scotia)	1911 – 1920	Conservative/Unionist
Arthur Meighen (b. Ontario)	1920 – 1921	Conservative/Unionist
William Lyon Mackenzie King (b. Ontario)	1921 – 1926	Liberal
Arthur Meighen	1926	Conservative/Unionist
William Lyon Mackenzie King	1926 –1930	Liberal
Richard Bedford Bennett (b. New Brunswick)	1930 – 1935	Conservative
William Lyon Mackenzie King	1935 – 1948	Liberal
Louis Stephen St. Laurent (b. Quebec)	1948 – 1957	Liberal
John George Diefenbaker (b. Ontario)	1957 – 1963	Progressive Conservative
Lester Bowles Pearson (b. Ontario)	1963 – 1968	Liberal
Pierre Elliott Trudeau (b. Quebec)	1968 – 1979	Liberal
Charles Joseph Clark (b. Alberta)	1979 – 1980	Progressive Conservative
Pierre Elliott Trudeau	1980 – 1984	Liberal
John Napier Turner (b. England)	1984	Liberal
Martin Brian Mulroney (b. Quebec)	1984 – 1993	Progressive Conservative
Avril Phaedra (Kim) Campbell (b. British Columbia)	1993	Progressive Conservative
Joseph-Jacques Jean Chrétien (b. Quebec)	1993 –	Liberal

Our National Anthem

Music by Calixa Lavallée, written 1880
French lyrics by Adolphe-Basile Routhier, 1880
English lyrics by Robert Stanley Weir, 1908; altered 1968

O Canada

O Canada! Our home and native land!
True patriot love in all thy sons command.
With glowing hearts we see thee rise,
The True North strong and free!
From far and wide, O Canada,
We stand on guard for thee.
God keep our land glorious and free!
O Canada, we stand on guard for thee.
O Canada, we stand on guard for thee!

Ô Canada

Ô Canada! Terre de nos aïeux,
Ton front est ceint de fleurons glorieux!
Car ton bras sait porter l'épée,
Il sait porter la croix!
Ton histoire est une épopée
Des plus brillants exploits.
Et ta valeur, de foi trempée,
Protégera nos foyers et nos droits,
Protegéra nos foyers et nos droits.